Engraved by Wm Barnard.

LIEUTENANT GENERAL HUGH MACKAY, of SCOWRY,

*Commander in Chief of the Forces in Scotland during 1689 & 1690.
Colonel Commandant of the Scotch Brigade in the Service of
Holland, and a Privy Counsellor in Scotland.*

From an Original Picture in the Possession of Lord Reay.

LIFE

OF

LIEUT. GENERAL HUGH MACKAY

OF SCOURY,

COMMANDER IN CHIEF OF THE FORCES IN SCOTLAND, 1689 AND 1690,
COLONEL COMMANDANT OF THE SCOTTISH BRIGADE, IN THE
SERVICE OF THE STATES GENERAL, AND A PRIVY-
COUNSELLOR IN SCOTLAND.

BY

JOHN MACKAY, Esq. OF ROCKFIELD.

" NE QUID FALSI DICERE AUDEAT NE QUID VERI NON AUDEAT."—TACITUS.

The Naval & Military Press Ltd

in association with

The National Army Museum, London

Published jointly by

The Naval & Military Press Ltd
Unit 10 Ridgewood Industrial Park,
Uckfield, East Sussex,
TN22 5QE England

Tel: +44 (0) 1825 749494
Fax: +44 (0) 1825 765701

www.naval-military-press.com
www.military-genealogy.com
www.militarymaproom.com

and

The National Army Museum, London
www.national-army-museum.ac.uk

In reprinting in facsimile from the original, any imperfections are inevitably reproduced and the quality may fall short of modern type and cartographic standards.

TO THE

RIGHT HONOURABLE ERICK LORD REAY,

THE FOLLOWING WORK IS RESPECTFULLY INSCRIBED

BY

THE AUTHOR.

PREFACE.

The first sketch of the following work was drawn up with the view of its being prefixed to an edition of General Mackay's Memoirs, then in course of preparation for the press, from a manuscript copy in the Library of the Faculty of Advocates. The Editors were three members of that learned body, viz. Patrick Fraser Tytler, Adam Urquhart, and James Hogg, Esquires, who, as members of the Bannatyne and Maitland Clubs, were about to enrich their historical collections, by presenting, according to custom, each member with a copy of that valuable work.

It may be proper to state, for the information of some readers, that these clubs are composed of noblemen and gentlemen, associated for the laudable purpose of drawing from the obscurity of public and private repositories, and printing for distribution among the members, original manuscripts and works out of print, calculated to elucidate the history and antiquities of Scotland, not otherwise easily accessible. As the clubs consist of nearly two hundred members, considerable publicity is given to works put into their hands, and thus comparatively ready access is afforded to future historians.

General Mackay's Memoirs found their way into the Advocates' Library about a century ago, but they do not appear to have attracted much notice, till about the year 1776, when the first edition of Sir John Dalrymple's Memoirs of Great Britain and Ireland, was published. That ingenious and imaginative historian, frequently refers to them, in which his example has been followed, with more or less care and impartiality, by all subsequent writers concerning that period. It is General Mackay's public conduct, however, with which they are chiefly concerned. Of his family and private history, they appear to have known no more than what they were able to collect from the few incidental notices, communicated either by himself or by Bishop Burnet, from whom they have copied, and transmitted to posterity, at least one material error.

To supply this want of correct information, the learned Editors, understanding that I was the General's representative in the male line, requested of me to furnish them with some particulars of his life, to be prefixed to the proposed volume. I accordingly drew up for their use, a brief sketch of the parentage, life, and character, of my distinguished relative, of which the Editors inserted an abstract in their "Preliminary Notice," considering the whole too long for their purpose, but recommended the enlargement and publication of the sketch submitted to them, which would thus diffuse more widely a just impression of the peculiar merits of the General.

To appear before the public in the character of an author, was to me an idea, which, though not altogether new, I had not till then seriously contemplated, and could not easily venture to adopt. Though not unacquainted with letters, I had never before written a line for the press; and at the age of threescore and twelve, it seemed too late to begin. To these were to be added the still more formidable difficulties, arising out of my having spent the last forty-three years of my life excluded from the light of heaven, with "wisdom at one entrance quite shut out." Keenly alive to the obstacles thus presented to my performing the duty of biographer of my venerated kinsman, in a manner that should prove worthy of the subject, or satisfactory to myself, I applied to two eminent literary friends in succession, to undertake the office, namely, to the late reverend and deeply lamented Dr. M'Crie, so advantageously known to the public, by his learned, historical, and biographical researches, and to Thomas Thomson, Esq. whose acknowledged learning and taste, as well as the facilities afforded him by his official situation, as Deputy-keeper of the Records, pointed him out as peculiarly fitted for such an undertaking. Both these gentlemen admitted the strong claims of the subject, but declined engaging in it, on account of the multiplicity of their other vocations. They were pleased however, to approve of the sketch put into their hands, and advised me to proceed with it myself, kindly promising me every assistance in their power.

Disappointed, on the one hand, in my endeavours to engage a more practised pen, and thus encouraged, on the other, by two such high authorities, to undertake the work myself, I re-commenced it about three years ago, but made slow progress with it, owing to the necessity I was under, of employing the eyes of other men, and to impediments proceeding from ill health, and other unavoidable causes. Having now at length brought it to a conclusion, I am forcibly reminded of the saying of a young Italian painter, who, when first introduced to the works of the great masters, felt abashed at the inferiority of his own performances, and exclaimed, in a tone of deep humility, "*ed io anche son pittore.*" I in like manner, might exclaim, and I too am a biographer; but alas, at what an immeasurable distance have I followed those eminent men who have preceded me in the same walk. It is however some consolation for me to reflect, that my ill success, (if such should be the result) will in some measure be attributable to the scantiness of my materials.

For the General's public history during the two short periods of his service in Scotland and Ireland, he has himself left ample materials in his memoirs, and official correspondence, French and English, from which a limited selection will be found in the Appendix to the following work, extracted from a larger, in that presented to the Bannatyne and Maitland clubs. With respect, however, to what constitutes the great charm of biography, the interior of the man, his social and domestic habits, there is not a single letter, or even line, bearing on these points, to be found in the repositories of Lord Reay, descended from the General's eldest sister, of the Hon. Mrs. Fullarton, descended from his eldest daughter, or of his relatives, the Hon. Cornelius, and John Louis Mackay, both Barons of the kingdom of the Netherlands, with all of whom I have been in communication on the subject. This is the more to be lamented, as it makes it impossible to give, in the present sketch, that prominence to the General's religious character, which formed so essential a part of the man, and will disappoint the pious reader of a view of the Christian experience, and the devout meditations and reflections of this eminent Christian soldier.

General Mackay was a man of high station as well as character, who had stood before kings and princes, assisted at their

PREFACE.

deliberations in council, and commanded their armies in the field, so that even at the present day, the circumstances of his life and death form a part of the history of Europe.

It is therefore not a little singular that, of such a man, the only written memorials extant should be confined to a small quarto manuscript volume, comprehending a history of military transactions in Scotland, from the period of his arrival at Edinburgh to assume the chief command, the middle of March 1689, to that of his final departure from Scotland, the end of November 1690; and the history of his Irish campaign of 1691, commencing in May and ending in October of the same year, when he returned for the last time to Holland. The Memoirs may be divided into the three following parts, *first*, a narrative of military transactions during his command in Scotland, to which are added fragments containing additional facts, and observations on the foregoing; *second*, a narrative of the Irish campaign of 1691, in which he served under the Baron de Ghinkel; the *third* consists of letters to the King and the Earl of Portland, from 14th January to 4th November 1690. Both the second and third parts are in French, evidently drawn up with greater care and attention to style; the second especially, as being probably more intended for the public eye. Of these I should have inserted extracts, as specimens of the General's manner, had I not been dissuaded by a military friend better acquainted with the French language, on account of their numerous inaccuracies, which appear to have proceeded from the transcriber's imperfect knowledge of the language. The first part is in the first person, after the manner of Cæsar's Commentaries, and is written in a homely and rather antiquated style, such however, as was in general use among the educated classes of that age in Scotland. The sentences are long, involved, and often obscure, from their length and the little attention paid to punctuation; all which faults have been multiplied and aggravated by the negligence, or ignorance of those through whose hands they appear to have passed.* The whole was written, or transcribed at Bommel in Guelderland, where the General resided with his family; the first part written during the winter of 1690-91, the second during that of 1691-92, and the third at the dates which the letters respectively bear.

The reader is requested to take notice, that what has been usually termed "General Mackay's Memoirs," is limited to the small quarto volume already mentioned, and that it is now swelled to a larger, by the addition of the selections from his English letters in the edition presented to the clubs. These bear evident marks of having been written in haste, on the spur of the moment; such of them as are addressed to the privy council frequently concluding with a request that their Lordships would be pleased to order copies to be taken, and forwarded to Court, as he had no time to get them transcribed.

The Scottish campaign, though in it General Mackay was Commander-in-Chief, while only fourth in command of the Irish, was, of the two, by much the more irksome and trying to his patience. In the former, it is true, he had the sole responsibility, but he was harassed, sometimes by injudicious interferences with his peculiar department, sometimes by a factious op-

* These faults, when glaring, I have taken the liberty of correcting, by modernizing to a certain degree, the orthography, shortening the sentences, and amending the punctuation, I trust without injury to the character of the composition.

position to his measures on the part of his colleagues in the council, and what was still more mortifying, he received not that support from his sovereign, which his character deserved, and the interest of the service required. In Ireland he had no such annoyances to endure. A large army was there assembled, regularly organized, and well disciplined, under general officers of great experience, and knowledge of their profession. The Commander-in-Chief, the Baron de Ghinkel, though his military talents were not of the first order, yet possessed such urbanity of manners, that the service went on smoothly under him, and though differences occasionally took place among the general officers at their councils of war, in which Mackay sometimes stood alone, that circumstance never interrupted the harmony of their meetings. Responsibility was so divided, that it was only a small part fell to his share, and the specific duties assigned to him he performed in a manner so masterly, that to him, more than to any other individual, was by general consent, ascribed the successful issue of the war. Of the general officers present, four-fifths were foreigners, and these, on returning to their respective countries, spread throughout all Europe the fame of General Mackay's exploits in the Irish campaign. To this circumstance, together with another co-incident in point of time, that of Marlborough's falling into disgrace with King William, in consequence of his alleged clandestine correspondence with the court of St. Germains, was probably owing the distinguished honour conferred on Mackay, of commanding the British division of the grand allied army in the following campaign.

The circumstances stated in the preceding pages, will, I trust, plead my excuse for thus obtruding myself on the public notice. It cannot be expected, that in the present turmoil of public affairs, this, or indeed any other work of a nameless author, not affecting private interests, or stirring up private passions or prejudices, will excite much public attention. I feel however a secret satisfaction in the consciousness of having collected, as it were, into a focus, from various quarters, scattered rays of information, relating to the life, death, and character of General Mackay, whom I have ever held in the highest veneration, and the contemplation of whose character, I conceive, may be beneficial to private Christians, as well as to men of the profession of arms. In particular, I indulge the hope that it may refute the erroneous notion of Bishop Burnet, respecting the supposed tendency of piety to unfit men for military command; and prove useful to young soldiers and sailors, by shewing them that ardent piety, so far from being incompatible with the character of a hero, gives it a brighter lustre; and by proving to them that no man is so fit for any daring enterprise—a forlorn hope, for instance, mounting a breach, or storming a battery, as he who to the military requisites, adds habitual piety towards God, a firm reliance on his Providence, and in regard to himself, a well grounded assurance that, let death come when it may, it will be to him an immediate entrance to a happier and more glorious state of existence.

JOHN MACKAY.

EDINBURGH, STAFFORD STREET,
    22d *February* 1836.

LIFE

OF

LIEUTENANT GENERAL HUGH MACKAY

OF SCOURY, &c.

LIEUTENANT GENERAL HUGH MACKAY OF SCOURY was descended from Mackay of Strathnaver, chief of the clan Mackay, in the county of Sutherland. From what country the Mackays originally migrated, and at what precise period they settled on the west and north-west coasts of Sutherland, are questions foreign to the present undertaking. Suffice it to say, that, at the beginning of the fourteenth century, they had attained to such a degree of power and importance, that Donald Mackay of Strathnaver is mentioned among the chiefs who, at the head of their respective clans, fought under the banners of Robert Bruce, at Bannockburn, A. D. 1314. Angus Mackay of Strathnaver (sometimes denominated Dow, or Dhu, that is, black, or swarthy, from his dark complexion) supposed to have been the great-grandson of Donald, is the same who is described by the continuator of Fordun, as the leader of 4000 Strathnavermen. He fought a bloody battle near Dingwall, with Donald Lord of the Isles, A. D. 1411, and soon afterwards married Elizabeth of the Isles, as she was styled, eldest sister of Donald, and daughter of John Lord of the Isles, by Margaret, daughter of King Robert II.* The fifth in descent from Angus,

---

* By some genealogists, a different husband is assigned to this lady; but that the above-mentioned Angus Dow Mackay was her *real* husband, is proved by a charter, dated 8th October 1415, and registered among the Acta Dominorum Concilii, 15th February 1506, Book 18,

was Hugh, or Iye Dow Mackay of Strathnaver, who succeeded his father Donald, A. D. 1550, and after surmounting such a series of difficulties as would have paralyzed the efforts of ordinary men, died in 1572, in quiet possession of his family estate.

He was twice married, first to his cousin Eupheme, daughter of Hugh Macleod, laird of Assynt in Sutherland, and by her had Donald of Scoury. His second wife was a daughter of Sinclair, laird of Dun in Caithness, by whom he had two sons, Hugh of Strathnaver, father of the first Lord Reay, and William of Bighouse, from whom are descended the modern Bighouse family. Hugh, though the younger brother, was preferred to Donald in the division of the paternal property, for reasons which the curious reader will find detailed in Robert Mackay's History of the Clan Mackay. Donald, the first of Scoury, married a daughter of Munro of Assynt in Ross-shire, brother of Sir Hector Munro, the first bart. of Foulis, and by her had three sons, Hugh, Donald, and William. First, Hugh carried on the line of the family; second, Donald of Borley,* so designed from having the lands of Borley in wadset, a species of tenure, now obsolete, but frequently resorted to in those days, to make provision for younger sons; and, third, William, a lieutenant-colonel in the service of Gustavus Adolphus, was killed at Lutzen, 1632, at the same time with that renowned Protestant hero.

---

part ii. fol. 200. This charter is from Donald Lord of the Isles, and grants the lands of Strathalyadil (or Haladale, afterwards Bighouse) to his brother-in-law Angus Mackay of Strathnaver, and his son Neil, by his (Donald's) sister Elizabeth, and to their heirs; in whose possession these lands have continued from that period down to 1830, when they were sold by Mrs. Louisa Mackay and her son Major Colin Campbell Mackay of Bighouse, to the late Marquis of Stafford, afterwards created Duke of Sutherland.

* Donald of Scoury having been born about 1555, and his son Donald of Borley 25 or 30 years later, it is somewhat remarkable, that the author is no more than fifth in descent from the former, and fourth from the latter, whose son, Captain William Mackay of Borley, was the author's great-grandfather. See Appendix, No. II. This is a degree of longevity far exceeding the usual calculation of 30 or 33 years to a generation.

Hugh of Scoury, Donald's eldest son, was, in 1643, appointed by parliament, a commissioner for raising supplies, and in 1648, a member of the committee of war for the sheriffdom of Sutherland; in 1649, being with the royal army at Balveny castle, he was surprised, and taken prisoner, together with his son-in-law, John Lord Reay; but owing to some unexplained cause, was permitted to return home peaceably, with the Strathnavermen, while his Lordship was sent, in custody, to Edinburgh castle. By the act of 1650, for calling out all fencible men between the ages of sixteen and sixty, he was appointed a colonel of foot, which rank Charles the Second confirmed to him at the Restoration. In 1661, Hugh, now Colonel Hugh Mackay of Scoury, was reappointed a commissioner for raising supplies; and died in 1662, universally lamented, as a man of great probity and worth. He married Ann, daughter of John Corbet of Arkboll or Arboll, in the county of Ross, and had issue, four sons and several daughters; of whom Barbara, the eldest, married her cousin, John second Lord Reay; and from this marriage, all the subsequent lords of Reay have descended. William, and Hector, the eldest sons, were waylaid, and barbarously murdered in Caithness, at the instigation, it was supposed, of persons of distinction in that county; against whom criminal letters were in consequence issued, yet, so wretched was the administration of justice, and so impotent the arm of the law, that, though all the preliminary forms were gone through, the criminals were never brought to trial. The third son was Hugh, on whose life we are now to enter, usually known among his countrymen by the appellation of Sheneral More Mackuye, *i.e.* the Great General Mackay, to distinguish him from his grandson and other general officers of the same name. The fourth son, James, was lieutenant-colonel of his brother's regiment in the Scottish Dutch Brigade, and was killed at Killiecrankie, as will be seen in its proper place. Of Hugh's early history it is to be regretted that little more is known, than that he was born about the year 1640, at Scoury, a romantic and beautiful spot, in the parish of Eddrachillis, on the west coast of Sutherland, the property of his father, and grandfather, and from which the former took his designation.

Our countrymen, the Scots, had from the earliest ages, been distinguished as a warlike nation, and never, perhaps, was the passion for arms more prevalent, than at the period of which we are now treating. Towards the conclusion of the 16th century, they furnished essential aid to the infant Dutch republic, then struggling for their religion and liberties. In the early part of the 17th century, they sent powerful succours to Gustavus Adolphus, and the protestant Princes of Germany, who were engaged in the same glorious cause. Of these succours a considerable portion consisted of Mackays, and Monroes, and their followers, under the command of Donald first Lord Reay, and the Laird of Foulis. The Mackays of Scoury, being connected by blood with both these chiefs, several individuals of the family held commissions in one or other of the two regiments. Such of them as lived to return, delighted to recount their exploits under the Lion of the North, as Gustavus was termed, and thus diffused more widely a martial spirit among their countrymen. Young Hugh of Scoury was from his childhood in the habit of daily hearing those narratives, and they kindled in his mind a military flame, which was extinguished only with his last breath.

Very early in life he wished to enter into the army, but it was not till 1660, when he had attained the age of manhood, that he had it in his power to gratify his favourite passion: having, at the Restoration, been appointed an ensign in Douglass' or Dumbarton's, now the Royal regiment, or First Foot of the British line.* The regiment was, soon after,

* This is perhaps the oldest, and certainly one of the most celebrated regiments in Europe. It was formed from the Scots Guards, employed more than three centuries in the service of France, in which they acquired great renown and unprecedented distinctions, on account of their valour and fidelity. In 1633 they were sent back to Scotland by Louis XIII, in order to be present at the coronation of Charles the First, and Henrietta, sister of Louis; and from that period they have formed part of the military establishment of their native sovereigns, under the title of Scots Royals, or Royal Scots, or 1st Foot of the British line. On the breaking out of the civil wars in 1641, they preserved their loyalty, and adhered to King Charles; and in 1645, when his fortunes underwent a reverse, they returned to France, and continued to serve in that country with little interruption, till 1678, when they finally re-entered the British

lent by Charles the Second to the French king, in virtue of a treaty of alliance between the two sovereigns; and young Mackay accompanied it to France. In 1664, it would appear that he came over to England, and was presented at court, when he received from his Majesty a patent, as it is called, or open letter of introduction, dated at Whitehall, 26th August of that year. It was written in Latin, and addressed " *Ad omnes populos,*" recommending the bearer, Lieutenant Hugh Mackay, to the favour of all into whose hands these presents might come. With this document in his possession, he returned to France, and by means of it, obtained an easy introduction to those great masters in the art of war, the Prince of Condé, and the Viscount of Turenne, under one or other of whom he continued to serve, and study his profession, for some years.

Among his brother subalterns was young Churchhill, afterwards the great Duke of Marlborough, with whom he kept up a friendly correspondence to the day of his death. In 1669, he was employed in the service of the Venetian republic, on the following occasion. The Venetians, after having enjoyed quiet possession of the Island of Candia for five centuries and a half, were, A. D. 1645, suddenly attacked by the Turks, in the midst of profound peace, and after a long and sanguinary contest, were finally expelled from the island. Louis the XIV. sent a powerful armament to their assistance, under the command of the Duke of Beaufort, Admiral of France. Several young men, the flower of the French nobility, volunteered their services on the expedition, and were accompanied by a corps of 100 reduced officers, all eager to gain military experience, and share the glory of humbling the Ottoman power. They arrived at Candia, the capital of the island, on the 19th June, and on the 25th, made a desperate sally against the besiegers, but were repulsed with

---

service. Lord George Douglas, fourth son of the first Marquis of Douglas, was appointed colonel in 1645, and was removed by King William in 1690. He was created Earl of Dumbarton in 1675, followed King James to France, and died in 1692.—*See Major Weatherall's Historical Account of the Royal Regiment,* printed by order of His Grace the Duke of Gordon, and presented by him as their colonel to the regiment.

loss, the admiral, their leader, being slain. One of the reduced officers was Mackay, who so greatly distinguished himself in this, and other bloody engagements, during the two months the French remained upon the island, that he received from the republic, a medal of great value, as a due acknowledgment of his services.* The death of his father, as already mentioned, followed, in 1668, by that of his two elder brothers, opened to our young soldier the succession to the family estate, which, however, he was not destined to revisit, after it became his own property. In 1672, we find him a captain in Dumbarton's regiment, which was still in the service of France, and employed in the unprincipled expedition of Louis, against the United Provinces.

The horrors of this short but desolating campaign, of which Mackay was thus a reluctant spectator, if not an actor, made such a deep impression on his mind, as led him to entertain serious thoughts of retiring from the service of both sovereigns, and returning to his native country. While deliberating on this measure, Providence so ordered events, as to remove from his mind all doubts with respect to the course he ought to follow. His regiment, forming part of that division of the army, which, under the orders of Turenne, took the town of Bommel, in Guelderland, it was his lot to be billeted on the house of a respectable widow lady, whose husband, the chevalier Arnold de Bie, had been burgomaster of the town. Here the grave and serious deportment of Captain Mackay, so different from that of most of his brother officers, whether French or English, attracted the notice of Madame de Bie, and her family, and gained their esteem. She had several daughters, of whom the three youngest, being unmarried, were sent, on the first rumour of the invasion, to Dort as a place of safety, and out of the way of the French cavaliers. Louis having, however, issued a proclamation, ordering all who had fled from their habitations, to return forth-

* The medal is mentioned by Sir James Dalrymple, a contemporary writer. *Second edition of Camden's Description of Scotland*, page 195. And in 1792, it was in the possession of Mrs. Prevost, great-grand daughter of General Mackay.

with, under severe penalties, Madame de Bie recalled her daughters from Dort, as her family now enjoyed the protection of a respectable Scottish officer, their inmate. Mackay had by this time become so domesticated in the family, as to participate in all their recreations : with Madame de Bie, he played her favourite game of chess, and read with her daughters. Under such circumstances, it was not likely that the young ladies and their protector could long remain indifferent to each other ; and in fact, Clara, the eldest unmarried daughter, soon made an impression on his heart. After some further acquaintance, he made his proposals in form. Madame de Bie, unwilling to give her daughter to a man who served the enemy of her country, at first opposed his addresses, but yielded when she found he was inclined to resign his present service, and enter that of the republic. Such a change, from the one service to the other, was at this time unusual, and attended with difficulties ; but these being at length overcome, Mackay was transferred, with his rank of captain, from Dumbarton's regiment to the Scottish brigade, in the service of the States General. The only obstacle in the way of his marriage being thus happily removed, he was speedily united to Clara de Bie, the object of his affection, whose country he appears, from this date, to have adopted as his own.

Thirteen years had now elapsed since he entered the army, and during this time various causes had been in progressive operation, to weaken the ties which connected him with his native country. Among these may be enumerated, the tyrannical government of Charles the Second in Scotland, which, year after year, was driving many of his best subjects from the southern and western counties, into exile in Holland ; and the lawless state of the Highlands, in which bloody family feuds, and even private wars among the clans, were not yet extinguished ; and above all, the atrocious murder of his two elder brothers, still unavenged by public justice. These and other causes of the like nature, gave Mackay a gradual distaste for his native country, while, on the other hand, his gracious reception by the Prince Stadtholder, and the kindness with which he had, though a stranger, been admitted into the bosom of the pious family of De Bie, strongly inclined him to fix his residence among them. He had the advantage of an early religious education, under the eye of an excellent father; and the good seed thus sown, though checked, perhaps in its growth, by the pernicious example of his associates, in the service of two of the most licentious sovereigns in Europe; yet, when transplanted into the more genial soil of Holland, sprang up and brought forth fruit an hundred-fold, as will appear in the sequel. It is not improbable that about this time, or soon after, a thought first occurred to Mackay's mind, which was acted on, thirty years afterwards, by his son, who sold his paternal estate to his brother-in-law George third Lord Reay, thus re-uniting the two family estates, and investing the proceeds of the sale in an estate of equal value in Holland. Mackay may have been the more inclined to this measure, as his sister Lady Reay, who had been married but a few years, had already presented her lord with three boys of uncommon promise,—concerning whom hereafter.

Having thus endeavoured to sketch the outline of General Mackay's life, from his earliest days to the period of his marriage, and his entering into the service of the States General, it may not be improper to suspend his personal narrative, while we endeavour to trace the origin of the Scottish Brigade, with which his future name and character are so intimately connected.

The glorious stand, in defence of their religion and liberty, made by the United Provinces against the tyrannical government of Philip the Second of Spain, excited admiration and sympathy throughout all Europe; and nowhere more intensely than in England and Scotland. The more abundant resources of the former kingdom, administered by the skilful hand of Elizabeth, enabled her to send the insurgents immediate supplies of men and money. The latter, with an empty treasury, and a distracted government, could give no pecuniary aid, but permitted, nay encouraged her subjects to assist with their personal services. Balfour of Burley, Halket of Pitfirran, Preston of Gorton, Scott of Buccleugh, and other public-spirited individuals, raised men at their own expense, and proceeded at their head to the scene of action in the low countries. The troops thus levied, were at first formed into independent companies, and these into regiments, which, in process of time, were incorporated into a brigade, consisting of three regiments. Such was the origin of the Scottish Dutch Brigade. They had from their very first appearance on the continent, distinguished themselves by their native valour, and, when to this was added, the discipline which they learned from the great captains opposed to them, as well as from those under whom they served,—they soon became a match for the finest troops of Spain, and were enabled to baffle the best concerted schemes of the Prince of Parma, and Don John of Austria. In the famous battle of Reminant, near Mechlin, in 1578, where those two great commanders were defeated by the army of the States, the success of the day is ascribed by De Thou,* chiefly to the Scots and English, who, from the heat of the weather and their ardour in the combat, stript off their doublets and armour, fighting in their shirts and under clothes. The leader of the English was Sir John Norris, and Sir Robert Stewart of the Scots.† The three first, and most illustrious Princes of the House of Orange, viz. William, the founder of the Republic, and his two distinguished sons, Maurice, and Frederick Henry, fully acknowledged the value of the services of the Scots, and denominated them the bulwark of the Republic. The States, too, grateful for the aid which they had received, sent an embassy in 1595, to congratulate King James on the birth of his eldest son, with a present of two massive golden cups, and an obligation to pay the young prince 4000 florins yearly, until he should arrive at the age of majority. They also instructed their ambassadors to solicit a further supply of men, which was granted, notwithstanding the conscientious scruples at first entertained by the king, against countenancing rebellious subjects. The Scots therefore, as well as the English, may be said to have rocked

* De Thou, book xvi. cap. 12. Bulkley's edition, vol. iii. page 608.

† There is an allusion to the same spirited conduct on the part of the Scots and English at Reminant in the discourse on war by Lord Bacon, who also ascribes to it the victory of the day.

the cradle of the infant Dutch republic, and to have supported their first tottering steps towards independence. In this manner commenced a connection between Scotland and the Dutch republic, which, with the exception of about thirty years, from the usurpation of Cromwell to the death of Charles the Second, had lasted above 200 years, when, in 1781, it was terminated by commercial and political jealousies between the two countries. The recognition of the independence of the Dutch republic, by the other powers of Europe at the peace of Westphalia, in 1648, held out to that state, humanly speaking, a prospect of long repose, which, however, was not realized. In 1650, the second Prince of Orange, of the name of William, died, leaving an infant son, afterwards the illustrious King William, an event which proved the signal for civil commotions in the state. The ruling party taking advantage of the young prince's minority, abolished the office of Stadtholder, and by withdrawing public attention from military to maritime affairs, brought on a ruinous naval war with England. The army henceforth, was neglected, and the discipline of the Scottish brigade in particular, gradually relaxed. Hitherto the brigade had been recruited both with officers, and men, exclusively from Scotland, but the troubles of that country, and the wars between England and the Republic, cut off that source of supply. The oldest officers gradually died out; others resigned in disgust, and the vacancies thus occasioned, were filled up by adventurers of the lowest description from all parts of the world, while private men were enlisted from the refuse of the other European military establishments.*

Such was the deteriorated state of the Scottish brigade, when, in 1673, Mackay was transferred to it, and began those reforms, by means of which he was afterwards enabled to restore its discipline, and recover its character among the nations of Europe.

The first service in which he was engaged under his new master, was in the year 1674, in the bloody battle of Seneff, and the siege of Grave,

* See Strictures on Military Discipline, including an Account of the Scottish Brigade. London, 1774.

where the Prince of Orange was opposed by those celebrated commanders, the Duke of Luxembourg, and the Prince of Condé, under whom Mackay had formerly served. On both these occasions he so distinguished himself, though in no higher rank than that of captain, as to attract the notice of his superiors, and lay the foundation of that esteem which he gradually acquired with the Stadtholder. The parliament of England having obliged the king to reduce his forces, the officers and men of ten of the companies thus disbanded, tendered their services to the Prince of Orange, which he gladly accepted, forming the men into a separate corps, under the temporary command of Mackay as major commandant. About this time, the lieutenant-colonelcy of one of the regiments, forming the Scottish brigade, falling vacant, two candidates started for the appointment, both excellent officers, but men of characters widely different. These were Graham of Claverhouse, then an officer in the Prince's service, afterwards notorious for his unrelenting cruelties to the covenanters in the west of Scotland, and Mackay, characterized by Bishop Burnet, as the most pious military man he ever knew. The Prince preferred Mackay, which gave such mortal offence to his rival, that he instantly quitted the service and returned to Scotland, burning with resentment against the authors of his disappointment. In 1680, Mackay was promoted to the rank of colonel of his regiment, and not long after appointed commandant of the whole brigade, which was by this time esteemed one of the best disciplined in Europe.* On the occasion of Monmouth's invasion, in 1685, King James called over the brigade to his assistance, and was so pleased with their prompt obedience to his call, and with their soldierly appearance, that he promoted

* From this period of its renovation under Mackay's command, the brigade preserved its high military character, till about the middle of the last century when it began to decline; and during these 70 years, some of the most distinguished officers in the British service commenced in it their military career. Among these may be mentioned the Earl of Portmore, and his brother Field-Marshall Collyer, Colonel Cunningham of Enterkin, the Hon. General James Murray, (brother of Lord Ellibank,) Sir Robert Murray Keith, General Simon Fraser, (killed at Saratoga,) and Sir William Stirling of Ardoch.

Mackay to the rank of major-general in his service. As matters turned out, they were not required to draw the sword, but it cannot be doubted that the presence of a body of men so highly disciplined, and so efficient, greatly contributed to the speedy suppression of the rebellion. As a farther mark of his royal approbation, the king was pleased to appoint Major-General Mackay a privy counsellor in Scotland, in consequence of which, he proceeded to Edinburgh, where he took the oaths and his seat at the council-board. He returned to London immediately, his public duties not admitting of his visiting his estate and relations in the north. The king having reviewed the brigade on Hounslow Heath, in 1686, dismissed them with letters to the Prince of Orange, expressive of his acknowledgments for the seasonable aid they had afforded him; after which they returned to Holland. In 1687, King James, alarmed by the reports of the warlike preparations on the Dutch coast, and the surmises of a projected invasion of England, again sent, to demand the return of his subjects in the service of Holland. The demand came too late, for, by his infatuated conduct, he had now forfeited the affections of his subjects abroad, as well as at home, and by his persevering devotion to the French court, excited the apprehensions of the Prince of Orange, and of the States General for their own religion and liberties. Under various pretexts, the States at first evaded, and at length, in the following year, 1688, peremptorily refused permission to the private men, but left the officers at liberty to follow their own inclinations. In the Scottish brigade, and the three English regiments in Dutch pay, there were 240 officers, of whom only 60, and these chiefly catholics, adhered to King James.* All the rest declared their unanimous re-

* See *Life of Major Bernardé*, p. 51. Rapin says that only 40 officers declared for King James. The defection of so large a proportion of the officers of the brigade, was imputed by the King, and probably not without cause, to Mackay's influence; and on this account he included his name in the list of six individuals whom he excepted from pardon. The other five were Lord Melville, the Earl of Leven, Lieutenant-General Douglas, Sir John Dalrymple, and Bishop Burnet. See *Dalrymple's Memoirs*, vol. ii. p. 104. App.

solution to follow the standard of the Prince of Orange, in order to deliver their country from the yoke of popery and of arbitrary power. The expedition consisted of 15,000 men formed into three divisions, and was commanded by William in person. They were distinguished from each other by the colour of their flags; the English and Scotch had a red flag, and was commanded by General Mackay; the Prince's guards and Brandenburghers had a white, under Count Solms; and the Dutch and the French protestant refugees with a blue flag, were commanded by Field-Marshal the Duke of Schomberg. After putting to sea, the fleet was dispersed and driven back by a furious storm from the south-west; but speedily refitted, and the wind coming suddenly round to the east they sailed again, and passed through the channel without opposition, the same easterly wind which thus proved so propitious to the Prince of Orange, having locked up the English fleet within their own ports. On this occasion the overruling providence of God was signally manifested in favour of the expedition; for if the wind had not shifted at the critical moment, and if the expedition had in consequence failed, the religion and liberties of the British kingdoms might have been buried in the same common grave. The events which followed the landing of the expedition, viz. the abdication of King James, and the transference of the crown to William and Mary, are too well known to require repetition in this brief memoir. William's measures, with regard to England, having hitherto been followed with complete success; he next turned his attention towards Scotland, where he had reason to apprehend a more formidable opposition. The long experience he had had of Mackay's great military talents, and conscientious discharge of the duties of whatever office he undertook, induced him to select this officer for the important station of commander-in-chief of the forces to be employed in Scotland; and never, perhaps, did any general enter on a more uninviting command, than that which now devolved on Mackay. The prospects before him was that of civil war, the evils of which he had too often witnessed on the continent, not to deprecate their occurrence in his native land. The majority of the Scots were presbyterian protestants, but a considerable proportion of the aristocracy, and even of the middling and lower classes not a few, were still bigoted Roman catholics, and consequently attached to the cause of the exiled monarch.

These, however, were not the only enemies with whom it was probable the new government would have to contend; such protestants, even, as held tory principles of government, or were attached to the episcopal forms of worship, being little less adverse than Roman catholics to the intended change.

During the two last reigns, especially that of James, the principal civil offices of the state had been monopolized by papists or their abettors, and at the period of Mackay's arrival in Scotland, the chief fortresses of the kingdom were also in their hands. To dislodge them, therefore, from those strongholds became one of his first and most urgent duties; but to the immediate accomplishment of this important object, his military resources were altogether inadequate. The sinews of war, money, arms, stores, and provisions, were wanting. Skilful officers too, an order of men with which Scotland once abounded, were not to be found in this her hour of need. The veterans of the Covenant, who had served in the German wars, or who had been opposed to Cromwell, were now no more; nor were their places filled up by men, the soundness of whose principles could be relied on. Such were some of the difficulties which Mackay foresaw that he should have to contend with, but these were not all. Though a native, and a landed proprietor himself, he was almost an entire stranger in Scotland, having left it at so early an age. His family connections were respectable, but situated in a remote corner of the kingdom, and though powerful over their clansmen, in their own country, possessed but little political influence. Thus unconnected, with either of the two great parties which agitated the state, he could look for no support to his measures, beyond what he derived from the legitimate influence of the high station assigned to him, and from the confidence of his royal master, which he was supposed to enjoy. Of him it might be said with truth, that he entered on the duties of his office, "*sine ira, sine studio, quorum causas procul habeo.*"

Soon after his landing in England, Mackay was seized with a severe fit of illness, from which he had scarcely recovered, when prompted by zeal for the public service he embarked for Scotland, and arrived at Edinburgh about the middle of March 1689.

King William found himself so hard pressed between the defence of his native dominions and those he had newly acquired, that the only troops he could with safety spare for Mackay, were detachments from the three regiments forming the Scottish brigade, viz. the General's own, Brigadier Balfour's and Colonel Ramsay's, amounting in number to 1100 men. Nor were these the flower of the brigade, for the king judged it expedient to retain in England the most effective portion of it, in order to strengthen his Dutch battalions. With this handful of men did Mackay proceed to Scotland, to assist in subduing a faction, which had, for the last thirty years ruled the nation with a rod of iron. There existed at this time but a very inconsiderable military force in the kingdom, Dumbarton's foot and the royal dragoons, the two most efficient regiments on the establishment, not having yet returned since they were ordered to England by King James, the preceding year.

Claverhouse, when raised to the peerage by the title of Viscount Dundee, had also been appointed to the command of the royal dragoons, but was superseded, after the revolution, by Sir Thomas Livingstone, baronet, an officer of reputation in the Scottish brigade, who accompanied King William from Holland.* Mackay brought with him a commission

---

* Sir Thomas Livingstone, after serving with great ability and zeal in Scotland, under General Mackay, succeeded him as commander-in-chief, in November 1690, and was afterwards employed in all King William's wars on the continent. Care must be taken not to confound this officer (which Mr. Chambers has most unaccountably done in his History of the Rebellion, p. 58,) with the traitor, Lieutenant-Colonel Livingstone, of the same regiment.—See page 76. In 1696, Sir Thomas was created Viscount Teviot, but dying 1711, without issue-male of his body, the title became extinct. It is to be regretted that he stained his high military charac-

as commander-in-chief from King William, but prudently refrained from exercising it, till that Prince should be invested with the royal authority in Scotland, as he had already been in England; and, in the meantime, he contented himself with acting under the orders of the convention, which commenced its sittings a few days before he arrived. By authority of that body, he issued letters of service to the Earl of Leven and Viscount Kenmore, to the Earl of Annandale* and Lord Belhaven,†

---

ter, by his conduct in the affair of Glenco. As commander-in-chief, he was the official organ through which the orders of government, for the massacre, fell to be conveyed; and it appears that he did convey them with alacrity. In his letter of instructions to Lieutenant-Colonel Hamilton, commanding officer at Fort William, dated 23d January, 1693, are these words: "I understand that the Laird of Glenco, coming in after the prefixed time, was not admitted to take the oath, which is very good news to us, seeing, that at court, it is wished that he had not taken it; so that the very nest might be rooted out: So here is a fair occasion to shew you that your garrison serves for some use. I desire you will begin with Glenco, and spare nothing of what belongs to them, *but do not trouble the Government with prisoners.*"—*Culloden Papers*, p. 19.

On the morning of 9th February 1693, these cruel orders were executed without remorse,—thirty-eight innocent individuals having been butchered in cold blood. Happy would it have been for the memory of King William, his ministers, and all concerned in this barbarous transaction, had Mackay continued in the command. If he had so continued, such orders would, in all probability, not have been issued; nor if issued, would they have been obeyed.

* Third Earl of Annandale and Hartfell. He was one of the first to join the revolution, and raised a troop of horse for its service. In 1689, he was seduced by his brother-in-law, Sir James Montgomery, to engage in the plot for restoring King James; but, soon repenting, made confession of his fault to King William, and was restored to favour. In 1701, he was raised to the dignity of Marquis of Annandale, and died, 1721, after having filled some of the highest offices in the state, during the reigns of William, Anne, and George I. He married Sophia, daughter of John Fairholm of Craigiehall, remarkable for the beauties of her mind and person, and for having been a wife and mother in her fifteenth, and a grandmother in her thirty-second year.

† John Hamilton of Biel succeeded to the title of Belhaven, on the death of the first Lord, in 1679, and distinguished himself in parliament, by his opposition to the tyrannical measures of Charles and James. Having joined the revolution, he raised in its defence, a troop of horse which he commanded at Killiecrankie, as hereafter related, and continued through life, a strenuous supporter of the religion and liberties of his country. He is the same who was after-

the two former to raise each a battalion of foot, and the two latter noblemen, each an independent troop of horse. By the same authority, he empowered the three skeleton Dutch regiments to complete their establishment to 1,200 men each,—a measure, however, which he never was able fully to accomplish, in consequence of the preference that Scotsmen felt for regiments in the service of their own country. With these levies, and the expected reinforcements from England, he proposed to lay siege to the castle of Edinburgh, which, under the command of the Duke of Gordon, held out for King James,—and to carry on those ulterior measures which he deemed necessary for the establishment of the new government. Dundee, having been denounced as a rebel by the convention, flew to arms, and repaired to the north, in order to stir up his friends in that quarter to declare for King James. Mackay felt strongly inclined to pursue him, but the other various and important duties of his station, as commander-in-chief, admitted not of his absence. He therefore ordered Sir Thomas Livingstone's dragoons, with Lord Colchester's, and Barclay's horse, from the north of England, to Edinburgh, where they arrived early in April, but in bad condition. Sir Thomas being an officer of experience, on whom he had great reliance, he dispatched him with his regiment, first to Stirling, and thence, about the 20th of April, to the shire of Angus, where Dundee's chief strength lay, with instructions to watch the motions, and, if possible, seize the person of this formidable enemy; or, at all events, so to counteract his measures, as to prevent the further augmentation of his force. In pursuance of these instructions, Livingstone formed a plan for the apprehension of Dundee, which, though conducted with the utmost prudence and secrecy, failed of success, owing to the vigilance of the latter, and his good understanding with the people of the country.

1689.

wards celebrated for his eloquent speeches against the Union. In 1708, the nation being threatened with an invasion by the Pretender, his lordship was suspected of favouring the cause, arrested, and carried prisoner to London. He was soon released, but his high spirit not brooking the indignity of being dragged through the streets like a felon, for a crime of which he was innocent, he was seized with a brain fever which brought him to his grave.

1689. Arms having thus been resorted to, the General foresaw that it was in the north the contest would ultimately be decided, and, for that reason, felt anxious to repair himself to the probable scene of action, where, he believed, his presence was more immediately required, than in the south. The Duke of Hamilton and his colleagues in the council, were of a different opinion,—being apprehensive of an invasion, and, therefore, desirous of retaining the General at the seat of government. He preferred, however, acting on his own judgment, and set out for the north, leaving Brigadier Balfour to command at Edinburgh, till he should be relieved from England by Major-general Sir John Lanier, whom he appointed to carry on the siege of the castle, now converted into a blockade.

Arriving at the town of Dundee, Mackay drew thither whatever troops could be spared from the blockade of Edinburgh castle, and the other exigences of the service, viz. the six troops composing Sir Thomas Livingstone's regiment of dragoons, and 120 of the best of Colchester's horse, with 200 foot of the Dutch brigade. He left two troops of Sir Thomas Livingstone's at Dundee, under the command of the lieutenant-colonel of the same name, who was afterwards detected in a traitorous conspiracy to deliver up his General to the enemy. With the remaining four troops of Livingstone's dragoons, and the horse and foot already mentioned,—the whole not exceeding 450 in number,—he proceeded to watch the motions of his adversary.

Dundee, though abhorred by his enemies, for his unrelenting, and sometimes unmanly cruelty to helpless old men and women, was no less admired by his friends, for his lofty bearing and chivalrous spirit; and no sooner did he arrive at his house, Glenogilvie in Angus, than he was resorted to by many of the nobility and gentry of the neighbourhood. Attended by a few of these, and seventy or eighty horsemen,—deserters from his former regiment, who had followed him from England,—he proceeded, as already mentioned, to rouse the northern shires, and especially the Highland clans, to declare for King James. Passing rapidly through Angus and Mearns, to Aberdeenshire, he held hasty conferences with the numerous branches of the powerful family of Gordon, their vassals, and dependents, and, in his own mind at least, organized an insurrection against the government. Mackay pursued, but not with the same speed, from the difficulty of provisioning, at short notice, even the small force he brought with him,—and the necessity of greater caution in passing through a country, whose inhabitants were, for the most part, unfriendly to his cause.

1689.

Before his departure from Edinburgh, the Laird of Grant waited on the General with a tender of his services, and received his instructions to repair to his extensive estates, and employ four or five hundred of his people to guard the fords of the Spey, and prevent the entrance of Dundee into his country. Mackay accordingly set out in the full belief that Grant had gone before, but now had the mortification to learn that he staid behind several days in Edinburgh, and that the precautions he recommended to him were wholly neglected. "Had he been a man of service," the General observes,* "such conduct would have been highly punishable." But as he was not a soldier by profession, and served purely from patriotic motives, it was but a venial error, though in its consequences productive of serious prejudice to the cause, enabling Dundee to cross the Spey and reach Inverness in safety.

Arrived at Inverness, Dundee unexpectedly met with Macdonald of Keppoch, a friendly chief, who came thither with a thousand of his followers, to take revenge on the inhabitants for an insult or injury he had received from them the preceding year. Availing himself of this casual meeting, he is said to have suddenly formed the project of facing about, and, with Keppoch's aid, of fighting Mackay, whom he supposed to be about this time crossing the Spey. In furtherance of this project, he despatched a letter to the magistrates of Elgin, intimating his intention of lodging in their town the following night, and requiring them to provide quarters for his troops. The magistrates, not much liking the prospect of a visit from such a number of unwelcome guests, forwarded the letter to Mackay,

* Memoirs, p. 10.

1689. then near the river Spey, beseeching him to hasten his march and anticipate the enemy, in the occupation of the quarters on which he seemed to rely. To Mackay this intelligence was not a little perplexing. He found his position now suddenly changed from the offensive, to the defensive; and saw himself reduced to the necessity of fighting an enemy more than double his number, or of retreating; an alternative, the very thought of which, to him seemed insupportable.

Recollecting, that, in war, the boldest course is generally the safest, and trusting to the protection of Heaven, he resolutely determined to meet his enemy. Crossing the Spey, therefore, he quickly advanced towards Elgin, rejoicing to find his troops animated by the same spirit; the Dutch foot keeping the horse at a trot, during a march of nine miles to the town. He arrived there in the evening, with just enough of day-light to examine the surrounding ground, before placing his sentinels, and was cordially received by the inhabitants. Next morning, he was joined by the Laird of Grant, to whom he had given a letter of service, to raise a regiment of 600 men; and who, by the whole of his subsequent conduct, proved himself a most loyal subject to William and Mary, and thus made ample amends for his former error.

Dundee not appearing, Mackay took the opportunity of spending two days in this friendly town, to refresh his exhausted troops. He also availed himself of the leisure thus afforded him, to write letters to his friends, in the shires of Ross and Sutherland, informing them of his approach, and requesting that they would bestir themselves, and meet him at Inverness with as great a number as possible of their followers. To Lord Strathnaver, eldest son of the Earl of Sutherland, he sent a letter of service similar to that given to Grant, and directed the guardians of his own grand-nephew Lord Reay, then a minor, to join him with 200, and the Laird of Balnagown with 100, of their respective clans.

Proceeding towards Forres, he learned that Dundee had altered his resolution, and that instead of marching eastward to Elgin, he had turned to the right, and taken the road through Badenoch to Lochaber. In an ordinary commander, such change of purpose would have been deemed weakness, or pusillanimity, which certainly formed no part of Dundee's character. Mackay simply says,* that Dundee, not choosing to risk an action, marched towards Lochaber. Some writers account for his change of purpose, by supposing that he believed Mackay to have been joined by his expected reinforcements; and his admirer Mr. Chambers insinuates that he was intimidated by Mackay's boldness, and judged it prudent to retire. The most probable supposition, however, because most in accordance with Dundee's character, seems to be, that the intention he announced to the magistrates of Elgin, of taking a night's quarters in their town, was a mere *ruse de guerre*, a stratagem to deceive Mackay, and divert his attention from the real object, which was, that of being suffered to march without interruption to Lochaber, to organize an insurrection in the Highlands against the new government, as he had already done in the Lowlands.

1689

It is somewhat singular, that the course which the Viscount of Dundee thus took, was precisely that which best suited the views of his rival, who was no less anxious to be permitted, unmolested, to enter Inverness, and remain there till he should have accomplished the important measures he had in contemplation. He found the magistrates of Inverness, and the inhabitants in general, well affected to his cause, and ready to adopt whatever expedients he should recommend for the defence of their town. He announced his arrival to Lord Lovat, the Earl of Seaforth, and other influential persons in that part of the country, and invited them in their Majesties' names, to meet him at Inverness, in order to concert such measures as should be judged advisable at the present critical juncture of affairs; but, with very few exceptions, they treated his invitation with such neglect, that he perceived they bore no good will to the cause.

* Memoirs, p. 16.

1689. Very different was the conduct of the leading men of the shire of Sutherland, and that of one individual of note in the county of Ross, viz. the Laird of Balnagown. Lord Strathnaver promptly joined him with 300 men of his new regiment, Lord Reay's administrators with 200 of his vassals, and Balnagown with 100, all brisk Highlanders, as the General describes them, and hearty in the cause. Of Lord Reay's men he formed 100 into an independent company, the remainder, together with Balnagown's men, he destined for the defence of Inverness, and directed that an additional number of 200 Mackays and 100 Rosses should be held in readiness in case of need; all which requisitions were punctually complied with.

It was now manifest that the General judged correctly, when he predicted, that the north was to be the theatre of the impending civil war, and insisted with his colleagues in the council, on the necessity of his repairing thither in person. He foresaw some difficulties, and experienced many more than he foresaw; yet he had the satisfaction to reflect, that his labour was not in vain. A little had been done, but much more yet remained to be accomplished, to place the government on a secure footing.

The fertile genius, and active spirit of Dundee were at work, and the effects, he feared, would soon appear in a vast accession of force to the enemies of the government. Reflecting on the utter disproportion of his present force, to the exigencies of the service, he judged it necessary to draw towards the north all the regiments that could be spared from the other parts of the kingdom. He ordered the two troops of Livingstone's left at Dundee, to join him without delay, and these to be followed by Barclay's horse, the remainder of Colchester's horse, and Sir James Leslie's foot, now the fifteenth of the British line. He wrote also to Brigadier Balfour, to detach Colonel Ramsay with 600 men, drafted from the three Dutch regiments, and order them north, for greater despatch, by the short cut on the Highland road from Athole to Badenoch. But for the better understanding of what follows, it will be necessary to advert to the intercourse which took place in Edinburgh, between the Marquis of Athole and General Mackay. 1689.

Of all the Scottish nobility, there was no individual, Dundee excepted, who, having it in his power to promote, did in fact so much to obstruct the cause of the Revolution, and the settlement of the kingdom, as the Marquis of Athole. His vassals were numerous, his estates compact, and situated in the heart of the kingdom; and his principal mansion or castle of Blair was, as it were a key, which gave him an easy and immediate passage to, or from the Highlands,—a circumstance of essential importance at the present crisis. Descended from the royal family of Stuart, the Marquis was connected by blood, alike with the late king, and the present. With the latter he had another connexion by marriage, the Marchioness being, as well as his Majesty, allied to the house of Solms;* the then head of which was one of Mackay's colleagues in command of the invading army.† With the Count, therefore, and other members of his family, the General was intimately acquainted, which furnished him with subjects of conversation interesting to the Marquis, and enabled him to answer his numerous inquiries concerning his German cousins, in a manner highly gratifying to his Lordship.

Intimacy being thus established, Mackay, always intent on the great cause in which he was engaged, embraced every opportunity of bringing back the discourse with his Lordship to the present critical state of Scottish affairs. He enlarged on the great benefit which the Marquis's peculiar local situation and circumstances enabled him to confer on his country, and took the liberty of pointing out to him the advantage

---

* The Marchioness was third daughter of James, seventh Earl of Derby, by Charlotte, daughter of Claude Duke de la Tremouille, and Charlotte Brabantina, daughter of the illustrious William, first Prince of Orange, great-grandfather of King William. Frederick Henry, his grandfather, married Emilia, daughter of John Albert, Count of Solms, a woman of distinguished merit; who, after the death of her son and daughter-in-law, the father and mother of King William, governed the principality of Orange, during his minority.

† Memoirs, p. 29.

1689. which would probably result to his family, if he cordially supported the new sovereign at the commencement of his reign. The Marquis appeared to receive these suggestions so favourably, and responded to them with such warm protestations of loyalty and affection, that Mackay was led to reckon on him as a firm friend to the new government. His son, Lord Murray, participated in the sentiments thus professed by the father, as did Lady Murray, a daughter of the Duke of Hamilton, and, like her pious mother, the good Duchess Anne, warmly attached to the Presbyterian interest.* But his conduct soon proved the fallacy of the Marquis's professions of attachment to King William. Whether from the levity and indecision of his character, or from resentment, at seeing his rival, the Duke of Hamilton, appointed, first, president of the convention, and afterwards commissioner to represent the Sovereign in parliament,—he determined neither to take his place in the convention, nor head his vassals in the field, but slunk away to England, leaving his affairs to be managed by his steward or factor, Stewart of Ballechin, a devoted partizan of the late king, and, consequently, an inveterate foe to his successor.

Dundee having proceeded to Lochaber, remained there but a few days, when he discovered that the state of his finances, as well as the condition of his horse, had been impaired by his long marches, and, in order to recruit

* Lady Anne Hamilton, eldest daughter of James, first Duke of Hamilton, who perished on the scaffold, 1649, succeeded her uncle, second Duke, who died of wounds received in the battle of Worcester, 1650, and thus became Duchess of Hamilton in her own right. She married Lord William Douglas, third son of the first Marquis of Douglas, and obtained a patent creating her husband Duke of Hamilton for life. In this manner were the families of Hamilton and Douglas connected; and on the death of Archibald, last Duke of Douglas, in 1759, without male issue, the representation of the Douglas family, in the male line, together with the Marquisate of Douglas, devolved on James, eight Duke of Hamilton, as being descended from the aforesaid Lord William Douglas and Duchess Anne. It is somewhat remarkable, that, as the Hamiltons thus became the male heirs of the Douglasses, in like manner, by the failure of the male heirs of the Hamiltons in the direct line in 1660, the Abercorn family became the male representatives of that of Hamilton.

both, he resolved to make an irruption into the low country. The en- 1689.
trance into Athole being open to him, through the good offices of his
friend, Ballechin, he made a rapid march through that district, into Perth,
surprised the town early in the morning, and, seizing as lawful prize whatever public money he could find there, took the lairds of Blair* and
Pollock,† captain and lieutenant of horse, with two foot officers, prisoners.
He carried these officers about, in an ungenerous triumph, on all his
marches, for six weeks, and then sent them to the Isle of Mull, where
Blair died, in consequence of the barbarous treatment he received. Having ranged for some days in the shires of Perth and Angus, and recruited
his horse; with the addition of some well affected gentlemen and their
servants, Dundee now returned to Lochaber by the way he came, without
opposition from the men of Athole. Such were the first fruits of the tergiversation of the Marquis of Athole; the more mature products will by
and by appear.

While Colonel Ramsay was preparing, in obedience to the orders of the
commander-in-chief, to proceed to Inverness, with 600 men of the Dutch
brigade,—it so happened, that a fleet of Dutch herring busses appeared in
the mouth of the frith of Forth, which, being mistaken for a fleet of French
transports with troops on board, caused such an alarm in Edinburgh, that

* William, fifteenth Laird of Blair, was one of the foremost to join the Revolution, and elected, in consequence, a member of the convention of estates, and of the committee for settling the government. He raised at his own expence, and commanded a troop of horse, but was unfortunately taken prisoner, as above. He married Lady Margaret, a younger daughter of William, second Duke of Hamilton, and by her had a son, William, his heir. This last having had a son who died before his father, was succeeded by his daughter Magdalene, who married Scott, advocate, second son of John Scott of Malenie. The issue of this marriage was a son, William, who took the surname of Blair, and having no heirs of his own body, settled his estate on the issue of his father, by a second marriage, from which the present family of Blair of Blair is descended.

† Sir John Maxwell of Pollock; created a baronet in 1682; chosen Commissioner for the shire of Renfrew to the Convention of Estates, in 1689; and afterwards appointed, successively, a privy councillor, a commissioner of the treasury, and Lord Justice Clerk. He married Marian, daughter of Sir James Stewart of Kirkfield, and died without issue.

1689. the council countermanded Ramsay. After the lapse of three or four days, the mistake was discovered; and the alarm in consequence subsiding, he was permitted to depart; but, in their confusion, the council most unfortunately omitted to advertise the General of his detention. Ramsay had been furnished by the commander-in-chief with general instructions for his route, but with a discretionary power to regulate his march according to circumstances.

It was calculated, that, barring unforeseen interruptions, he might reach Ruthven castle by a certain fixed day; and on that day, the General proposed to meet him there. On his arrival in Athole, Ramsay found the people of the country in arms, and their scowling looks afforded a sufficient indication of their inward feelings towards him; but, as they offered no opposition to his march, he proceeded till he came to a place* not named, within twelve miles of Ruthven castle, that is, within eighteen, according to the modern measurement. At this place he rested for the night, and early next morning, dispatched a letter to the General, advising him of his approach and intention to be at Ruthven castle the evening of the following day. His apprehensions, however, were so much excited by increasing demonstrations of hostility on the part of the Athole men, that his resolution gave way. Seeing himself thus surrounded by enemies, in a wild country, to which he was an entire stranger, and disappointed of the additional instructions he expected to receive, he judged it most prudent to retrace his steps, and return next morning towards Perth.

All this time, the General being, through the negligence of the council, left in ignorance of Ramsay's detention, impatiently expected his arrival every day, and was both surprised and disconcerted, at his non-appearance. He heard of Dundee's irruption into the low country, and of his having been suffered to pass and repass unmolested through Athole, and from thence concluded that the Marquis had thrown off the mask, and that both his lordship and his people were alike enemies to the government. Being, therefore, seriously apprehensive for Ramsay's safety, he

* Memoirs, page 21.

sent messenger after messenger to apprise him of his danger, and carry 1689. fresh instructions for his guidance. Such, however, was the disturbed state of the country, and such the hostile appearance of the people of Athole, that his messengers were intimidated, and returned to the General with their letters unopened, and without learning any tidings of Ramsay. The last messenger was intercepted by Ballechin, and detained three days prisoner in Blair Castle, his letters taken from him, and transmitted to Dundee, who was then busily employed mustering his forces in Lochaber.

The Viscount thus apprised of Ramsay's advance, and of Mackay's probable junction with him, lost no time in assembling 2,000 of his mountaineers, at the head of whom he descended from the hills, leaving orders for 1000 more to follow, in the hope of cutting off either Ramsay or Mackay, or both. He entered the heights of Badenoch, eighteen English miles west of Ruthven castle, on the morning of the 27th May, that is, the day after Ramsay should have reached the castle. Hence it appears, that if this officer had not been detained in consequence of the false alarm of the Dutch herring busses, he might have been at Inverness before Dundee could have had notice of his approach; and that even notwithstanding his detention, if he had persevered in his march, he might have reached Ruthven castle on the 26th, the same evening, as it afterwards appeared, that Dundee had quitted Badenoch. On the evening of the 27th, the General received the letters from Ramsay, already mentioned, and so prompt were his measures, that by six of the clock next morning, Sunday 28th, he was on his march to meet him at Ruthven castle, with 640 horse and foot, including 200 of Lord Reay's and Balnagown's men. Half way to Ruthven castle, he met a messenger from the commandant, with a letter to inform him of Ramsay's return, and of Dundee's entrance that morning to the heights of Badenoch.

Military history seldom exhibits a situation more perplexing, than that in which the General now found himself placed. If, turning his back on

1689. Inverness, he abandoned that town to its fate; it would soon fall into the hands of the enemy, who would speedily be joined by the Frasers, the Mackenzies, and other contiguous clans, great and small, well affected to his cause. If, on the other hand, he returned to Inverness, that important post would indeed be saved, but the southern counties would in every direction be laid open to Dundee, who would thus be enabled to cut off all communication with the government, which appeared to the General an evil of such magnitude, that he resolved to run all risks to prevent it. Instead, therefore, of proceeding as he intended towards Badenoch, turning to the left he marched down Strathspey, and in order to get the start of Dundee, in case he should bend his steps that way, continued his course twenty-four hours without a halt. For guides and provisions, he trusted to his inestimable friend the Laird of Grant, who had been already apprised by him of the probability of such a visit, either from Ramsay, or from himself.

Having advanced so far a-head of Dundee, as to be out of all danger of being intercepted by him, Mackay slackened his pace and moved slowly on, anxiously looking out for the reinforcements he had ordered to join him from the south. The first that appeared, were the two troops of Sir Thomas Livingstone's dragoons, left at Dundee under Lieutenant-colonel Livingstone, but these, instead of augmenting his strength, increased his weakness, and proved a source of much additional perplexity.

The second day after the junction of the dragoons, two deserters came in from Dundee's camp, and requested a private audience of the General. This being granted, and all present except Sir Thomas Livingstone ordered to withdraw, they informed him there were traitors in his camp, who carried on a secret correspondence with the enemy; and being desired to name them, without hesitation mentioned Lieutenant-colonel Livingstone, Captains Murray, Crichton, Livingstone, and some others. To the General this was astounding intelligence, but he was not altogether unprepared for it, having already begun to entertain some doubts of the fidelity of these officers. Affecting, however, to be incredulous, he told the deserters he believed they were spies, sent by Lord Dundee to deceive him, and that if his suspicions proved well founded, they should assuredly suffer the punishment of spies, but if otherwise, they should be suitably rewarded. They coolly replied by repeating their former assertion, adding, that they had been in private communication with the Lairds of Blair and Pollock, prisoners in Dundee's camp, who specially charged them to warn the General of his danger, in case he should, trusting to the fidelity of these men, engage the enemy. Having ordered them into confinement until the truth of their relation could be ascertained, he held a conference with Sir Thomas Livingstone and Major Mackay, the only officers of the regiment on whom he could rely; and the result was by no means calculated to allay his apprehensions. In his own mind he had no doubt of the guilt of the accused officers, but as the proofs might not turn out sufficient to insure conviction before a court martial, and as, moreover, he doubted the prudence of arresting them in the present weak state of his force, he resolved to defer that critical step till joined by his expected reinforcements.

Dundee found, on entering Badenoch, that he had missed his prey; Ramsay and Mackay having moved away in different directions. He determined, however, to pursue the latter, hoping to overwhelm him by superior numbers. Ruthven castle lay in his way, and being garrisoned by a young officer, Captain Forbes, with only sixty men of Grant's regiment, in want of provisions, Dundee took it after a slight resistance, and ordered it to be burnt. Forbes having stipulated for the liberty of himself and his men, was proceeding to the General's camp, when he was met by two troopers who challenged him with *qui vive?* and being answered *vive le roi Guillaume*, they replied that they were sent by General Mackay to get intelligence of Lord Dundee. Forbes pointed out the situation of Dundee's camp, and cautioned them against falling into the hands of his stragglers, who were at no great distance, but they, notwithstanding his caution, pursued their course. The circumstance appearing strange to Forbes, he mentioned it, while at dinner, to the General, who immediately concluded these must be some of the traitors alluded to by the deserters, which, on inquiry, proved to be the fact.

The two camps being now within a few miles of each other, the General watched the motions of the enemy with double care, availing himself, for this purpose, of the extraordinary means which Grant's friendship, and zeal for the service, placed at his disposal. Every two hours, trusty messengers were despatched to bring him intelligence, some of whom came in this evening with the report, that Dundee was in motion towards him. The General immediately calling the commanding officers, ordered them to get their respective regiments under arms, and prepare to resume their march. It could not be disguised, that this would be to retreat before the enemy; but the safety of the army rendered it necessary; for, to risk an action with such a disparity of numbers, the maxims of war, and the ordinary rules of prudence would alike condemn. To the Laird of Grant he expressed his deep regret, that circumstances compelled him to leave his country exposed to the ravages of the enemy, but added, that he hoped to return in a very few days with reinforcements, and in the meantime, recommended his giving orders to his people to remove their cattle and every article of food to the low country. The patriotic and noble minded chief, with a spirit worthy of his high station, replied, " that though all his interest should be lost thereby, he would not wish the General to make a single step to the prejudice of their Majesties' service.

As the General did not yet judge it prudent to discover his suspicion of the treachery of the dragoons, and as he had hitherto made them march in front and rear of the line, he would not alter that order, but made such a disposition of the whole as placed the suspected officers constantly under the eyes of others, on whose fidelity he could rely. That the enemy might not discover the direction he took, the General delayed his march till night. He had three ways, by either of which he could retire to avoid an engagement;—one towards Inverness; another through Strathdon, which was nearer by twelve miles, to join his succours, than the third, namely, that by Glenlivet. "By which," says the General,* "if Dundee had understood the country and his trade, to have informed himself exactly thereof, he might have gained betwixt our (the General's) party and the regiments which we expected from the south, and put the General to a hard pull; who, though he perceived the feasibility of such an accident, durst not resolve to march through an enemy's country—all papists, with an enemy four times his number in his rear." He began his march in the dusk of the evening, "and so," to use his own words, "committing all to the providence of God, (against whom there is no wisdom, nor understanding, nor counsel, can succeed,) he took his way down the river, with hungry horse and men, though resolute, particularly Colchester's horse, and the 200 fusileers, upon whom he relied most; and, marching by the house of Grant of Balindalloch, who was himself with Dundee, made no halt till he came to Balveny, where he was forced to settle himself till he should get some bread for his men, and oats for his horse. There, having met with Sir George Gordon of Edinglassie, with the country foot, he furnished him with men to send out for intelligence; of whom, he dispatched some by the way he came, and others by the way he apprehended that Dundee would labour to cut him off from his succours. They came in next morning with news that Dundee had not left Strathspey as yet: whereat the General being very well satisfied, sent nevertheless, presently again, others out the same way; and ordered a party of twelve dragoons to be sent out by the way he had marched off, being in the greatest impatience to have in some provisions and oats; which came at last about five of the clock at night. The General seeing none of those he had sent in the morning return, notwithstanding both officers and soldiers grumbled, he would not stay till they had given their horse corn, and the soldiers got some bread baked. He marched the party off in the same order he had done the day before."

After some further details, the General goes on to say, "that he continued his march till he had past the river of Bogie, where he was necessitated

1689.

* Memoirs, p. 32.

1689. to come to a halt, at four of the clock next morning—neither horse nor foot being able to march farther, and where he caused distribute the oats and oatmeal which he had got up in his former camp,—and let the horse feed upon a spot of corn in the men's hands."* Here he learned that his reinforcements would join him in the course of the day, and, therefore, after two hours rest, proceeding three miles farther to meet them, he took post at the foot of the Suy hill, where he expected his succours, and had a view, fully two miles in every direction by which the enemy could approach.

All this time, as it afterwards appeared, Dundee was ignorant of Mackay's expecting reinforcements,—a circumstance which seems strange, considering his high military character, and that his march lay through the country of the Gordons, and other clans attached to King James, and the popish interest: "but," as the General observes, "God, who overrules all the actions of his creatures, preserved singularly that small handful of men, beyond all expectation, considering the strength of the enemy, and that; of 600 men, 200 (in which consisted our greatest advantage, were they trusty to the service,) were to be considered as enemies. For, in the first place, had Dundee accepted of it, the General had engaged in action with him, in all appearance, the first day he came near, having then opinion of the dragoons, that they would fight as haply he had done, had Dundee attacked him at Culnakiell, before the spies discovered the plot of the dragoons to him. In this case, he had certainly, without a miracle, been beat, which would be naturally of sad consequence to the government. Whereby we should also learn to be modest when it pleaseth God to bless the service in our hands, which the most experienced and clear sighted in their profession will have reason to do, if they examine themselves impartially, either as to their judgment, diligence, and resolution, wherein they shall find enough to humble them in themselves, and move them to give the glory to God."*

The General having arrived at the foot of Suy hill, judging himself out of all danger from Dundee, let his men repose; and their stock of provi-

* Memoirs, p. 34.   † Memoirs, p. 35.

sions being nearly exhausted, sent to request a supply from a house in 1689. the neighbourhood, belonging to Lord Forbes. That nobleman, who was well affected to the cause, and whose eldest son, the Master of Forbes, had joined with 50 horse the preceding day, gave immediate orders for complying with the request, but before the requisite quantity could be prepared, circumstances induced the General to recommence his march. The regiments anxiously expected at length arrived, Barclay's dragoons at twelve, and Leslie's foot at six of the clock the same day. Thus reinforced, the General immediately resolved to face about and meet his enemy, and the better to conceal his design, delayed his march till the hour of ten, P. M.

He now proposed to attack the enemy in his turn, and would in all probability have succeeded, had not his traitorous officers despatched two dragoons to give Dundee warning, and these men being found concealed in the woods near the house of Edinglassie, led to further discoveries, which ended in completely establishing the guilt of Lieutenant-colonel Livingstone, and the other suspected officers. The General, upon this, ordered them to be arrested, and seized the earliest opportunity of sending them prisoners to Edinburgh, to be dealt with according to the pleasure of the government, by which means he was relieved from much disquietude and danger.* The Master of Forbes, Edinglassie, and Major Mackay, are mentioned by him as having been mainly instrumental in the final detection of the plot.

The tables were now turned on the jacobite general, for, on the day

* The traitors afterwards confessed their guilt, but how they were ultimately disposed of cannot be ascertained. A story told by one of them (*Memoirs of Captain Creichton*, p. 68), which, whether true or false, may here be mentioned as indicating the opinion entertained even by his friends, of the savage nature of Dundee. It being reported that some one or more of these criminals were to be executed, Dundee is said to have written to the council, that if a hair of their heads were touched, he would cut the Lairds of Blair and Pollock, joint by joint, and send their limbs in hampers to the council.

1689. after that on which the event just mentioned took place, Mackay advanced to Balveny, and the following day to Culnakill, from whence he had retreated five days before. Here, having got notice, that a body of the enemy, in number about 500, had assembled on the opposite side of the Spey, he ordered Sir Thomas Livingstone with a party, consisting of his own, and Barclay's dragoons, to attack them. This service, Sir Thomas, assisted by Colonel Hauly and Major Mackay, promptly performed; killing nearly 100, and would have cut off the whole, but for a mistake of his adjutant, in prematurely giving the alarm. Livingstone's dragoons behaved with the greatest gallantry on this occasion, as if desirous to wipe off the disgrace they had incurred in the late affair.

Colonel Ramsay having, as has been stated, returned to Perth, wrote to the council assigning his reasons for that step, and requesting fresh instructions. In reply, he was directed to make another attempt to join the commander-in-chief; and to enable him to do so, 100 of Barclay's dragoons, with 200 of Leven's newly raised regiment (the 25th), and 100 of Hastings' (the 13th foot), were ordered to put themselves under his command; and with this force, in addition to his original detachment of 600 men, he made his way without difficulty, through Athole and Badenoch, to Inverness. On this, as on a former occasion, the council committed an error, in issuing orders to Ramsay without communication with the General, not perhaps from intentional disrespect, but from a want of attention to that combination, and unity of design so essential to the success of military enterprise, and yet so often lost sight of by civil authorities when they interfere with military commanders.

The General remarks,* that if he had been apprised in due time of this march, he might have sent Ramsay such additional instructions, as would have made it difficult for Dundee to disembarrass himself of both, and would cause a divertion in favour of the General, then struggling with so many difficulties in Strathspey. Now, however, it afforded him

* Memoirs. p. 39.

great satisfaction to have such an addition to his strength, as would enable him to act with greater vigour and effect against the enemy. He accordingly, never quitted the pursuit of Dundee, till he had chased him from the low country, and compelled him to take refuge in the wilds of Lochaber.

Ruthven castle, as mentioned in its place, having been burnt by order of Dundee, the General now caused it to be repaired, judging that from its position, almost in the heart of Badenoch, it was peculiarly well adapted for a garrison. He gave the command to a cousin of his own, Captain Hugh Mackay, an active and intelligent young man, who proved useful to him during his late marches. From Ruthven he proceeded to Inverness, where he found all quiet; the neighbouring disaffected clans having been so overawed by the presence of the Sutherland and Ross men, stationed there to support the well affected inhabitants, that nothing was attempted against the peace of the town.

Some of the chiefs made general and vague professions of good will to the service of their majesties, but none came forward with a specific declaration of their allegiance. Lord Lovat, following the selfish and ambiguous policy of his father-in-law, the Marquis of Athole, kept aloof, and his people refused to join without positive orders from their chief. The Earl of Seaforth acted a similar part. Viscount Tarbat boasted to the General both in London and Edinburgh, of his great influence with his countrymen, those especially of the clan Mackenzie, assuring him "that though Seaforth should come to his own country and among his friends, he (Tarbat) would overturn in eight days more than the Earl could advance in six weeks; yet he proved as backward as Seaforth or any other of the clan. And though Redcastle, Coul, and others of the name of Mackenzie came, they fell not on final methods, but protested a great deal of affection for the cause."* To be a check on their proceedings, the General placed a garrison of 100 Mackays in Brahan castle, the seat of the Earl of Seaforth, and an equal number of Rosses in Castleleod, the

* Memoirs, pp. 25 and 237.

1689. mansion of Viscount Tarbat, both places of strength, and advantageously situated for watching the motions of the disaffected.

The General remained at Inverness a fortnight, during which he bestowed much consideration on the state of the Highlands. He perceived the impossibility of subduing them by the ordinary methods, in consequence of the bogs and morasses, the rugged mountains and rapid rivers, by which the country was intersected. It therefore occurred to him that the most effectual, if not the only way to accomplish the desired object, was to imitate the example of Cromwell, and erect a fort at some central point, to overawe the mountaineers and prevent their incursions into the low country, holding out to them inducements to remain at home, and guaranteeing, on condition of their doing so, the security of their possessions. Inverlochy appearing to him the situation best adapted for this purpose, he drew up a detailed plan for the erection of a fortress there. He transmitted it to the Duke of Hamilton, the king's commissioner to parliament, requesting his Grace to lay it before the council, that, if approved, immediate measures might be taken to carry it into execution, so soon as he should return to Edinburgh.

The regiments of Lord Strathnaver and the Laird of Grant were by this time nearly complete in point of numbers, but being without clothing, arms, or discipline, the General could not rely on them alone, for the security of the northern shires. All beyond the Spey, with the exception of the districts belonging to the Lords Sutherland and Reay, and to the Lairds of Grant and Balnagown, were wholly disaffected or lukewarm in their attachment to the present government. He therefore deemed it prudent to leave a strong force at Inverness, under the command of Sir Thomas Livingstone,* with authority to draw whatever succours he might require from Sutherland, and the well affected part of Ross-shire.

Having now the satisfaction to see the north in a state of comparative

* The troops left at Inverness were Sir T. Livingstone's dragoons, Sir J. Leslie's foot, with 300 of Hastings' and Leven's, and the two companies, 100 men each, of Lord Reay's and Balnagown's Highlanders.

security, and his speedy return to the metropolis being urged by the Duke 1689. of Hamilton and the council, he proceeded towards Edinburgh from Inverness on the 20th June, with the 600 Dutch foot and some horse and dragoons.

The Earl of Mar having declared his adhesion to the new government, the General, in virtue of his authority as commander-in-chief, some time before his departure from Edinburgh, directed that nobleman—as he had the Marquis of Athole, and Laird of Grant,—to take measures for guarding the passes of his country against Dundee. The Earl dying soon after, and his son being a minor, the administration of his affairs fell into the hands of persons who encouraged his people in their opposition to the new government. As Braemar house, the seat of the family, was situated far back, and might be said to cover the shire of Aberdeen, the General deemed that also a fit situation for a garrison, and sent a detachment, consisting of 100 horse and dragoons, and sixty foot, with a stock of provisions, to take possession of it. He gave the commanding officer written orders, so to regulate his march, as to arrive at the house about midnight, leaving the foot to follow; and, after posting twenty dragoons there, to proceed directly three miles farther on, to Inverey house, in which a number of Dundee's officers were said to be hospitably entertained by Farquharson, laird of that place.

This enterprise, so judiciously planned, was frustrated by disobedience of orders, followed by egregious blundering and mismanagement, on the part of those intrusted with its execution. They arrived in good time at the point of destination, but, instead of proceeding according to their instructions, immediately to Inverey, they lingered at Braemar house to refresh their horses, and thus, before reaching their ultimate point, were surprised by day-light, and missed their prey. Inverey and his guests having escaped in their shirts to a neighbouring wood, the assailants returned to the house of Braemar, where they most unaccountably laid themselves down quietly to sleep, about the doors,—leaving their horses to graze in the fields. While they were thus indulging their repose, Inverey, not finding him-

1689. self pursued, and knowing the localities, watched his opportunity, ascended some rocks behind the house, remarkable for reverberating sounds, and fired off a few musket shots, which, re-echoing from rock to rock, roused the men from their slumbers, and frightened their horses. Retreating in confusion towards the foot, they speedily disappeared; and Inverey, that he might not be again annoyed by a hostile garrison in his neighbourhood, set fire to Braemar house, and reduced it to ashes.

The General, meanwhile, was proceeding towards the south with the main body of the detachment, and had got some miles in advance, when he was overtaken by an express, with tidings of the disgraceful proceedings just related. Military men can best estimate the disappointment and mortification they excited in his breast. On public and private grounds, he felt the most intense anxiety to reach the metropolis without delay. The council urged his return—the Inverlochy project required immediate attention—he had but a day's bread for his detachment—and his own frame was so exhausted with fatigue of body, and anxiety of mind, that it was not without difficulty he could keep his seat on horseback. It is at such moments the influence of religion on the character is most clearly manifested; and General Mackay's religion was not of the inoperative kind; it pervaded the whole man, subdued a temper naturally warm and impetuous, and kept his passions under due restraint.

Without betraying any symptoms of irritation, he made a halt, and turned aside to redress this little disorder, as he terms it, foreseeing the enemy would magnify it into an affair of great importance. The person chiefly to blame, was the senior officer of the detachment, who was an English captain of dragoons, and a stranger; the next in command, was that excellent youth the Master of Forbes, who had so often signalized his zeal for the service. The General, therefore, judged this not a fit season to examine too minutely the causes of the failure, and resolved to pass it over in silence for the present. He commenced his retrograde march in the afternoon, continued it all night, and at ten next morning, joined the 60 foot he had destined for the garrison of Braemar house, together with the horse and dragoons; and as an act of severe, but just and necessary retaliation, burnt the house of Inverey. He then descended Dee side to Abergeldie, and placed there a garrison of seventy-two men, "which small number," he observes, "kept a thousand from doing any considerable prejudice to the government."

1689.

The General arrived at Edinburgh about the 1st of July, and found that the castle had, on the 13th of the preceding month, been surrendered by the Duke of Gordon, to Major-general Sir John Lanier. Previously to the departure of the commander-in-chief for the north, the convention had come to the bold and decisive vote of forfeiture against king James, and settled the crown on William and Mary; whose authority was henceforth universally acknowledged in the southern half of the kingdom. In the north, it met with opposition, which, however, by the blessing of God on the honest and indefatigable exertions of Mackay, was so far overcome in the north-eastern shires, that no farther open resistance was to be apprehended in that quarter.

The convention was now turned into a parliament, which ratified its own proceedings, in its character of convention, and nothing seemed wanting to complete the establishment of the new Sovereigns, but the expulsion of Dundee from the north-west Highlands. To the accomplishment of this object, the General directed all the energies of his mind. The demon of discord broke out in the parliament, even among friends to the revolution; and in the council there were found traitors, who revealed to the enemy its most secret deliberations. Hence the hands of government were paralyzed, and tardiness, indecision, and imbecility, characterized its measures. The Inverlochy project, which the General communicated from Inverness to the Duke of Hamilton and the council, seemed to meet with their approbation, and yet the necessary preparations for carrying it into execution, which he expected to find completed on his return to the metropolis, were scarcely begun. Instead, therefore, of immediately commencing his march towards the Highlands, as he proposed, he was detained for want of the requisite equipments, a prisoner as it were, during three weeks, in Edin-

1689. burgh; while in the meantime, he had the mortification to learn, that Dundee expected shortly to be joined by 500 auxiliaries from Ireland, and would in all probability soon invade the low country.

Under these circumstances, the General judged it prudent to abandon all thoughts of Inverlochy for that season, and limit his views to watching the motions of Dundee, and checking his progress towards the south, in the hope of being able to accomplish his ulterior objects the following year. It had been evident for some time that the Marquis of Athole had falsified his engagements to the General, and that Ballechin his chamberlain, in still retaining forcible possession of Blair castle, the key of the Highlands, acted either by positive orders from his lord, or with his connivance. On this account the General's first object was to endeavour to wrest that fortress out of the hands of Ballechin, and place a garrison there, as a barrier against Dundee.

Having about this time learned from Lord Murray, that Ballechin had supplanted him in all influence and authority over his father's vassals, and even refused him access to his father's house; the General earnestly recommended to his Lordship, to proceed to Blair without delay, and make one vigorous effort more to dislodge Ballechin, or at all events prevent the people of Athole from openly declaring for Dundee; assuring him that he should himself soon follow with his whole force. Murray accordingly repaired to Athole, but found Ballechin immoveable in the castle, and therefore, to prevent its being furnished with supplies, blockaded it with two or three hundred men, whom he gained over to his side. The expulsion of Ballechin from the castle appeared to the General an object of such importance, that he would have undertaken it in person, had he not reason to fear that his absence from the council board, at the present critical juncture, might risk the failure of his whole design. He therefore resolved not to stir from Edinburgh, till he should obtain from the council a supply of stores and provisions sufficient for the commencement at least, of his expedition.

At length he succeeded by dint of perseverance and personal exertion, and forwarded the supplies thus obtained, to Perth, which he fixed on as the place of general rendezvous. There also, he ordered the largest force that could be spared from other duties, to assemble,—and followed it himself by the way of Stirling, 22d July, to visit the castle, which he had not yet seen, and inspect the troops quartered in the neighbourhood. From Stirling, he wrote, under date 24th July, to Lord Melville, secretary of state for Scotland, resident in London, in these terms:—" I am this far towards the Highlands; it is not an easy commission the King has given me,—to keep a kingdom peaceable, when there is so much division even betwixt such as love the present government, that it hinders the necessary expedition of those things which in my judgment press most. I am afraid to be straitened for provisions in this expedition, therefore, if I cannot effectuate what I project, with God's assistance (upon whose providence I rest more than any direction or conduct of mine,) it shall not be my fault; for I am determined, God willing, not to spare my pains nor my life (which is all I have to venture,) for the advancement of so just a cause."

He found at Stirling two troops of horse and four of dragoons, which he ordered to follow him to Perth with all possible speed. Arriving at the latter town on the evening of the 24th, he devoted the following day to reviewing the troops stationed in that vicinity, and destined for his expedition.

It is worthy of remark, that the historians of this eventful period, from Balcarras down even to our own times, are for the most part either avowed Jacobites, or, to say the least, so tinctured with Jacobite principles or prejudices, as unconsciously, perhaps, to give a colouring to their narratives, injurious to the military character of General Mackay. This remark is particularly applicable to their exaggerated statements of his numbers in the memorable battle of Killiecrankie, of which we are now to attempt a description.

By some writers his numbers are stated at 6000, and by none under 4000 men. The most authentic, indeed the only authentic statement we have of the amount of his force, is derived from the General himself, whose

1689. correctness will not be questioned. He says expressly* that he took with him "six battalions of foot, making at the most 3000 men, with four troops of horse and as many of dragoons, new levies for that expedition."† He afterwards‡ specifies the battalions of foot and troops of horse he had with him, viz. his own, Balfour's, and Ramsay's Dutch foot; Hastings' (the 13th), an English regiment; Leven's,§ (the 25th;) and Kenmore's, both newly raised and incomplete. The troops of horse were Annandale's and Belhaven's; the other two, with the four troops of dragoons ordered to follow him from Stirling, did not overtake him. The two Scottish regiments of foot, as well as the horse, were not only new levies, but were also commanded by noblemen and gentlemen wholly destitute of military experience, and selected for their respective commands, solely on account of their power of raising men. Little more, therefore, than one half of the whole number could with any propriety be said to be disciplined, though by these writers, they are all represented as veteran troops.

The accounts the General received at Perth, of Dundee's growing numbers, filled him with perplexity, which was increased by the non-arrival of the six troops ordered to follow him from Stirling. He now experienced

---

* Memoirs, p. 46.

† It is impossible not to feel some surprise, that with this authentic narrative before him, and without producing any evidence to invalidate it, so respectable a writer as the late gallant and philanthropic Major-general Stewart of Garth, should reckon Mackay's force at *nine* battalions of infantry, and *two regiments* of horse. See *Sketches*, vol. i. p. 67. In the former he includes the Scottish fusileers, (now the 21st,) and Sir James Leslie's, (the 15th.) General Mackay mentions 200 fusileers, picked men from the *Dutch brigade,* whom he placed on a rising ground, under the command of Lieutenant-colonel Lauder, and these General Stewart inadvertently takes for the Scottish fusileer regiment, which is never mentioned from one end of Mackay's Memoirs to the other, and which consequently could not have been in this action. Sir James Leslie's, (the 15th,) he expressly says, (*Memoirs,* p. 40,) were left with Sir Thomas Livingstone at Inverness. The *two regiments* of horse mentioned by General Stewart, it is evident from what has already been stated, were no other than Annandale's and Belhaven's *troops,* not regiments of horse.

‡ Page 47.

§ Of Leven's and Hastings' he left 300 at Inverness. *Memoirs,* p. 40.

a renewal of those difficulties, by which he had been so much harassed 1689. on his northern campaign, and saw himself reduced to a dilemma which left him but a choice of two evils. A due proportion of cavalry he deemed essential to the success of his enterprise; and in this force he was weak, having with him only two troops of horse, and these raw and inefficient. On the one hand, therefore, if he marched on directly without waiting for his reinforcements, he must expect to be greatly outnumbered in horse by the enemy. If, on the other, he waited for the junction of the six troops from Stirling, Dundee would enter, without opposition, the country of Athole, where he would speedily be joined by reinforcements, both of horse and foot, from Angus and Mearns and all the disaffected districts in the south. To obviate such tremendous evils, he judged it to be his paramount duty to risk a great deal, and therefore resolved to proceed towards Athole without delay. His cause was that of religion, of liberty, and of his oppressed country, in behalf of which he doubted not the providence of God would ultimately interpose.

Next day, Friday 26th July, the General marched with his whole force to Dunkeld, and rested there for the night, after sending back strict orders to Perth, for the six troops from Stirling to follow him with increased speed. At midnight, he received an express from Lord Murray, communicating intelligence of the arrival of part of Dundee's force at Blair that morning, and of his having himself, in consequence, been obliged to raise the blockade of the castle, and retreat towards the pass of Killiecrankie, at the upper end of which, he left some of his adherents to guard the pass, and keep it clear. The General, though much pleased with this proof of Murray's zeal and attention to the service, had no confidence in his guards, and therefore immediately detached Lieutenant-colonel Lauder, with 200 fusileers, picked men from the Dutch regiments, to strengthen, or replace them, according to circumstances. At break of day, Saturday 27th July, he resumed his ill-fated march towards the pass, and a little below it met with Murray, who accounted for the small retinue with which he was attended, by stating that his few adherents followed the rest of the country people to the hills with their cattle, according to the custom of the country, on the approach of hostile armies. With this explanation the General was satisfied, having never expected more from Murray than that he should prevent his people from openly joining the standard of Dundee. Some of the most zealous friends of government about Edinburgh, doubted the fidelity of this young lord, suspecting him to be in league with his father; but the General, though at first he lent an ear to these suspicions, was now convinced of their being groundless, and lost no opportunity of doing justice to Murray's good faith.

At ten A.M. Mackay reached the lower end of the pass, where, having come to a halt, he despatched the Lieutenant-colonel of Leven's regiment, with 200 men, to reinforce Lauder, with orders to send back intelligence of the enemy's movements. After giving his men two hours for refreshment, and receiving a report from Lauder, that the pass was clear, he recommenced his march at twelve, and entered the pass, his troops being disposed in the following order, viz: Balfour's, Ramsay's, and Kenmore's battalions first, then Belhaven's troop of horse, followed by Leven's regiment, and the General's own, commanded by his brother, Lieutenant-colonel James Mackay; next came the baggage horses, about 1,200 in number; last of all, Annandale's troop of horse, commanded in his Lordship's absence, by a young lieutenant; and Hastings' foot, which had been left for the protection of the baggage, brought up the rear. The pass extended from two to three English miles in length, along the east bank of the river Garry, and the road was extremely narrow, confined between a range of craggy precipices, on one hand, and on the other, the river tumbling down from rock to rock, on a level, for the most part, considerably lower than the road. A handful of men, provided with a collection of stones, and stationed at intervals on the summits of these precipices, might with ease impede the progress of an army. On this account, some have wondered, that a commander of Dundee's vigilance and activity should have neglected this method of annoying his enemy. Whether he had it in his power, will by and by come under our consideration.

The General having met with no opposition in his progress through 1689. the pass, and having seen his rear fairly out of it, rode forward to examine the ground beyond it, and if within reach, to view the position of the enemy. But before proceeding farther with the movements on the side of Mackay, it will be proper that we return to Dundee, who, it will be remembered, when driven from the low country, betook himself for the third time to the wilds of Lochaber. There he remained ever since, preparing for another descent, with an increased force, to the Lowlands, and anxiously looking for his promised succours from Ireland, which at length arrived to the number of 500, under the command of Brigadier-general Canon. He took the field last campaign with only 2,000 Highlanders, but with the hope of being followed by 1000 more. On the present occasion, after having exhausted all his powers of persuasion on the Lochaber men, he could prevail on no more than the original number of 2,000 to turn out in his favour. Whatever might be said of the attachment of the Highland gentry to the cause of King James, Dundee could scarcely now disguise from himself the fact, that the lower ranks of the Gael were influenced by the sordid motive of gain, and that if he found his popularity somewhat abated, it was owing to his endeavours to restrain their plundering propensity. Be this as it may, he quitted the country, as has been stated, at the head only of 2,000 Highlanders, and 500 Irish, all equally animated with the hope of rioting on the spoils of the Lowlanders.

The Lairds of Blair and Pollock, the two unfortunate gentlemen mentioned as having been carried about in an ungenerous triumph by Dundee, during the whole of the last campaign,—were still detained by him in custody. Both were men of high birth and connexions, married, and had families at home; yet were they dragged about like felons, in this ignominious manner, and for no other reason than that they served with fidelity a sovereign to whom they had sworn allegiance. Tired of entertaining them any longer, either as prisoners or guests, Dundee, before his final departure from Lochaber, sent them to Doward castle, in the island of Mull, where they were treated with such barbarity, that Blair died in consequence,

1689. a few weeks afterwards, and Pollock recovered not his liberty till King William's government was finally established.

In Badenoch, Dundee trusted he should be joined by the Laird of Clunie, chief of the Macphersons, and by some minor chiefs in that neighbourhood, who had before been restrained by fear from declaring in his favour; and he had also some hopes of assistance from the more powerful but distant clans of Fraser and Mackenzie. Such, however, was the effect of the garrisons planted at Inverness and Ruthven castle, and of the other judicious measures adopted by Mackay before his departure from this country,—that none of these clans, great or small, ventured, from this period, to join Dundee, or give further trouble to the government. After lingering some days to no purpose in Badenoch, the Viscount lost all patience, and proceeded on his march towards Blair castle. He arrived there with his main body, on the same morning (27th July,) and from circumstances, it is probable, about the very hour that Mackay was entering the pass of Killiecrankie. His army consisted of Macdonalds, Stewarts, Camerons, and Macleans, together with stragglers from various other clans, besides the Irish brigade. The privates were, as already observed, men of predatory habits, whom, as they served without regular pay, it was not only difficult, but perhaps even unreasonable to restrain from plundering for a subsistence; and who, without such license, could not be kept together for any length of time. Of the officers, many were gentlemen of birth and education; some had seen service on the continent; a few even in the Scottish brigade; and they were in general men of high military spirit, who joined Dundee from pure affection to his cause, and from a mistaken principle of loyalty to a prince whom, though he had violated the fundamental laws, and endeavoured to subvert the established religion and liberties of their country, they, nevertheless, blindly considered as their legitimate sovereign.

Having learned at Blair, that Mackay had sent an advanced party under the command of Lieutenant-colonel Lauder, to guard the entrance to the pass,—Dundee detached Sir Alexander Maclean with 400 men, to oppose them: but, being afterwards informed that Mackay had entered the pass with his whole force, he judged it expedient to proceed thither himself, with his main body. Instead, however, of following the direct road from Blair castle, he turned to the left at Glen Tilt, and making a detour round the hill behind Lude castle, went on, gradually ascending, till he gained an elevated position near Urrard house, from whence he perceived Mackay preparing for battle on a piece of level ground below. Dundee, after surveying the enemy's lines, drew up his men in the following order :—On the right, he placed Sir John Maclean with his regiment of two battalions; on the left, Sir John Macdonald's regiment, commanded by his son, together with Sir George Berkley. The main body was composed of four battalions, being the clans of Lochiel, Glengarry, and Clanronald, respectively, with the Irish regiment, and a troop of horse commanded by Sir William Wallace. Besides these, Dundee had his own original body of horse, which, although recruited on his irruption from Lochaber into the low country, must, by this time, have been much reduced by hard service and want of forage. He had also a number of Highland gentlemen, well mounted, and fully acquainted with cavalry service.

Mackay having, as already mentioned, cleared the pass, halted with the greater part of his force on a low field near the river, till the rest should come up. He despatched Lieutenant-colonel Lauder with the 200 fusileers, to an eminence in front, in order to watch the motions of the enemy, while he himself should examine the intermediate ground, and choose the field of battle. Lauder reported that small parties of the enemy were seen advancing by the direct road from Blair, but that Dundee, with the main body, had taken a sweep round the hill, and might be expected shortly to appear on the heights to the right. This coinciding with his own observations, the General became apprehensive, that if he continued on the haugh, or flat below, the elevated position of the Highlanders might enable them to force his men over the bank into the river, in the heat and confusion of battle. To obviate this evil, he removed them to a higher piece of ground, of sufficient extent to admit of their being ranged in order of battle, and which, after due examination, he judged "fair enough to receive, though not to attack the enemy on it." He ordered every battalion to form by what he calls a *quart de conversion* to the right, upon the ground on which they stood, and ascend the hill without changing their order of march. Having seen the five battalions advance up the hill before his face, he ordered Brigadier Balfour's, as the leading battalion to take post to the left, and the rest in the order already mentioned. He then made a short speech to his men, addressing each battalion, in terms suited to their respective composition and character, and earnestly recommended to all to stand firm in their ranks, assuring them that if they did so, they should soon see the Highlanders turn their backs, but if, on the contrary, they suffered their line to be broken, they were undone; and concluded with a few short and appropriate religious admonitions to all. The enemy, from their elevated position, having a full view of the General as he moved along the line, fired several running shots, which missed him, but wounded many by his side. In order to get a surer aim, they took possession of some houses on the brow of the hill, and in front of their left wing, which induced the General to direct his brother Lieutenant-colonel Mackay, to detach a captain with some firelocks to dislodge them. The officer selected by the Lieutenant-colonel for this service, was his nephew Captain the Honourable Robert Mackay, who accordingly executed it with great promptitude and gallantry, killing or wounding some, and chasing the rest back to the main body. The General dreaded a night attack, and still more a night retreat, one-third of his men being young soldiers, who had never seen the face of an enemy in the field, and even the disciplined portion unaccustomed to the Highland mode of fighting. He therefore felt anxious to bring on the action with day-light, and hoped Captain Mackay's skirmish would have this effect; in which being disappointed, he tried various expedients to provoke the enemy to fight, but all in vain. Dundee was not to be diverted from his purpose, which was evidently to spin out the time till near sunset. During two tedious hours of a bright summer evening, both armies stood still, looking at each other. It was not therefore without the most intense 1689. anxiety, that Mackay beheld the sun sinking towards the horizon; and just as this feeling was wound up to its highest pitch, about half an hour before sunset, he perceived the Highlanders moving slowly down the hill, bare-footed, and stript to their shirts. As they descended they quickened their pace, at the same time uttering a yell,

"So loud and dread,
"That ne'er were sounds so full of woe."

Being drawn up in clans with little attention to order or regularity, their fire made but a slight impression on Mackay's men, who, marshalled in line according to the strictest rules of discipline then practised, reserved their fire till within a few paces of the enemy, when they poured it into his breast. By discharging in platoons, they were enabled to take a steady aim, and thus their fire told with dreadful effect on the thick and disorderly masses opposed to them.

At the commencement of the engagement, and for some minutes after, (for the whole lasted but a few minutes), the advantage was at least six to one on the side of Mackay; but when the Highlanders, after discharging their pieces, threw them away according to custom, and drew their broad swords, they took ample revenge. The most robust among them using the two-handed sword, gave what further impetus a savage ferocity could add to the force of this destructive weapon. They were down upon Mackay's men before these had time, after a discharge, to fix their bayonets, which, at that period, were awkwardly attached to the musket. To remedy this defect, the General invented a method,* not materially different from that still in use, which saves time, and enables the soldier to fire with his bayonet fixed.

Marvellous tales of the great muscular strength and personal prowess of the Highlanders, more resembling the fabulous exploits of the heroes and

* Memoirs, p. 52.

1689. demigods of antiquity, than the sober realities of history, have been handed down to us by the Jacobite writers of the period. Limbs lopped off,—heads cleft in two,—and bodies cut asunder by a single stroke of the tremendous two-handed sword, are among the deeds recorded of this day. If we reject such exaggerations as utterly unworthy of credit, enough will still remain to establish the extraordinary achievements of Highlanders in the field of battle, as exemplified on this occasion. The novelty of their dress, or undress, their ferocious aspect, and the hideous yell with which they advanced, struck Mackay's troops with such a sudden panic, as even the oldest soldier among them could not withstand. In a few minutes, they fell into confusion, and gave way; and the line, according to the General's prediction, once broken, decided the fate of the day.

Owing to some unexplained cause, the veteran Balfour's battalion did not fire a shot, and but one half of Ramsay's was engaged. The brunt of the action fell on the centre and right wing, more especially on Mackay's own battalion, against which, a dead set seemed to have been made by the Macdonalds, some of whom had formerly served with them in Holland. On this occasion, the Macdonalds formed the left wing of the enemy, and appear to have felt a high degree of excitement on finding themselves opposed to their ancient comrades, who, on their part, were not wanting in a corresponding emotion, and both, therefore, exerted themselves to the utmost. By the fire of Mackay's regiment, Dundee and several of the principal gentlemen of the name of Macdonald, were killed, according to the accounts of their own party.* Lieutenant-colonel Mackay, deserted by his men, was cut down by the merciless broadsword, while endeavouring to rally them, in which he was nobly seconded by his young nephew, Captain the Honourable Robert Mackay. Besides the Lieutenant-colonel, two captains and five subalterns of the Mackay regiment were killed, and two captains left wounded on the field. Balfour was also abandoned by his men, and slain. The Lieutenant-colonel

---

* Memoirs, p. 265.

of Kenmore's, a captain of Ramsay's, and many other officers not named, shared the same fate. The centre division signalized its gallantry, and its youthful commander, the Earl of Leven, proved himself a worthy descendant of the veteran Leslie. Hastings, also, on the right wing, sustained the reputation of the English lion, but all to no purpose,—so far had the panic extended.

The General observing the foot give way, ordered Belhaven's and Annandale's horse to advance, and take the enemy in flank, the one on the left, the other on the right. Belhaven promptly obeyed but had scarcely brought his men to the front of the line, in order to wheel to the left flank, when they also began to give way, and turned about. Their example was speedily followed by Kenmore's, and one half of Leven's battalion, as well as by Annandale's troop, on the right. The General, perceiving the horse come to a stand and firing in confusion, and the foot falling away from him, spurred on his charger through the thickest of the enemy, hoping the horse would be piqued to follow his example; but all without effect,—he was supported only by one of his servants, whose horse was shot under him in advancing.* Whithersoever he moved, the enemy made way for him, though alone, on which he remarks,† "that if he had but fifty resolute horse such as Colchester's with him, he had certainly by all human appearance recovered the day."

Lieutenant-colonel Lauder, who had been posted advantageously with 200 men, the flower of the army, on a rising ground in front, proved as useless as the rest; whether through his own fault or that of his men, does not appear; for the General would not scrutinize too minutely the failures of the day, as they were unfortunately too many in number. "Resolution and presence of mind in battle," he observes,‡ "being certainly a singular mercy of God, he denyeth and giveth it when and to whom he will; for there are seasons and occasions, that the most firm and stout-hearted do quake and shake for fear. As Solomon saith, "The wicked flee when

---

* The same who afterwards carried him off the field at Steinkirk.
† Memoirs, p. 56.   ‡ Memoirs, p. 56.

1689. none pursueth, but the righteous is bold as a lion ;" and though all sincere Christians be not resolute, it is because it is not their vocation; for I dare be bold to affirm, that no truly sincere Christian, trusting in God for strength and support—going about his lawful calling, shall be forsaken of him, whether military, civil, or ecclesiastic: Not that sure victory shall always attend good men, or that they shall always escape with their lives; for experience doth teach the contrary; but that God, upon whom they cast their burdens and care, shall so care for them, that they shall be preserved from shame and confusion; and that they have his promises (by whom are the issues against death, and innumerable means inconceivable to us,—to redress the disorders of our affairs,)—to support their hope and mind in the greatest difficulties: As the General confessed, that immediately upon this defeat, and as he was marching off the field, he could not cast his thoughts upon any present means to redress his breach, but recommended earnestly unto God to direct his judgment and mind to fall upon such methods, as the success should manifest him to be the chief author thereof."

Such were the reflections of this pious soldier, on an occasion which put his christian temper and patience to a severe test. After a thirty years' course of training under the most eminent masters, in theory and practice of the art of war, he had been selected for this command; and after encountering four months of the most vexatious opposition from some of his countrymen, which he at length so far subdued, as to have victory within his grasp, it was unexpectedly snatched from him through the cowardice of his men, and misconduct, or want of firmness, on the part of some of his officers, on whom he most relied. Instead, however, of giving way to censure or complaint, he endeavours to palliate, or frame excuses for those officers whom he still valued for their former good conduct.

Having passed unhurt through the crowd of Highlanders by whom he was surrounded, the General turned about to see how matters stood behind him, and was not a little surprised to find his left wing had wholly disappeared, and as it were, in the twinkling of an eye, had gone down the hill, mixt pell-mell with the Highlanders, who, yielding to their plundering propensity, forthwith made for the baggage at the river side, 1689. which, in the sequel, facilitated the escape of the fugitives. At this sad spectacle, it may easily be conceived how much he was mortified, and ashamed of the cowardice of his troops. It appeared to him at first, as if he had been left alone on the field ; but looking farther to the right, he espied a small party of red coats, which proved to be the Earl of Leven, with some of his officers and men, mixt with a few belonging to other regiments. After complimenting his lordship and his officers on their steadiness, he recommended to them to get their men as soon as possible into condition to receive the enemy, whom he expected every moment. Meantime, he galloped farther to the right, towards a part of Hastings' regiment, with which their colonel was returning to their first ground, having quitted it, as he affirmed, to pursue the enemy.

Captain Mackay presenting himself on horseback at this moment, though he had received eight broad-sword wounds on his body, the General dispatched him after the runaways, with orders to such of the officers as he could meet with, to collect, and keep their men together, till all could be re-united. He then formed a junction between Hastings' regiment and the remains of Leven's ; but observing that their officers were not able to get the men into any order, he visited a garden in the rear, in which he thought for a moment of drawing them up, in hope of succour. This idea he presently abandoned, fearing, that should succour fail, there could be no hope of escape by defending such an enclosure. While he was in this state of perplexity Captain Mackay returned, reporting that none of those to whom he had spoken, paid the least attention to him, and that all were now gone clear out of sight.*

* The author has in his possession a short MS. account of the Reay family, written by John Mackay, Esq. of Tordarroch, who died in 1768, in the 64th year of his age, and who, besides relationship, lived in the most intimate habits with his contemporaries of the family, and was therefore likely to have correct information respecting the battle of Killiecrankie. Among other things, he states that Captain Robert Mackay, third son of John, Lord Reay, having been left for dead on the field of battle, was found by Glengarry and his men, who, perceiving

1689. Hitherto the General knew nothing of the left wing, since the commencement of the action, beyond the mere fact of their utter disappearance; and having at this moment descried some men collecting at the edge of the wood, on the left of Balfour, and where Lauder had been posted, he rode towards them in the hope of their being part of the left wing, who had retired there on the descent of the Highlanders. A nearer view discovering them to be enemies, he slowly returned towards his own men, whom he directed to have special care to march off softly without precipitation or disorder; the least indication of which would encourage the enemy to attack them. If, on the other hand, they retired steadily, and with apparent unconcern, the Highlanders, it being now twilight, would suppose their numbers greater than the reality, and give them no molestation. In this manner he led them himself cautiously down the hill, and crossing the river, halted till he saw all his men over, being about 400 in number. Before commencing his retreat, he was joined by Belhaven, by his own subalterns, and those of Annandale's troop, with some men belonging to both, who proved useful as scouts on the subsequent march.

life was not yet extinguished, had him conveyed on a barn door to the nearest hut, where he remained some days, till he could be removed with safety, and was then carried to Dunkeld.

It is, by the way, not a little pleasing to find such an instance of humanity in an enemy, for such Glengarry was at that time. From this account, coupled with what has been mentioned in the text, on the authority of the General's MS., it seems not improbable that Captain R. Mackay, after parting with his uncle, fainted, from loss of blood, in consequence of over exertion, with the many and severe wounds he had received; and in this state was found by Glengarry and his men.

He was at this time captain of grenadiers in his uncle's regiment, but was afterwards transferred to the Scottish fusileers (21st foot,) in which, having greatly distinguished himself on various occasions, he rose so rapidly, that we find him, in the official army list, appointed colonel of that regiment, 13th November 1695. Having never perfectly recovered from loss of blood at Killiecrankie, and been repeatedly wounded in King William's subsequent wars in Flanders, he fell into a languishing state, for which he was ordered by his physicians to try the effect of his native air. His constitution was, however, so debilitated, that he died at Tongue, the seat of his family, in December 1696, in the 30th year of his age.

The General's next concern was how to conduct the handful of men 1689. thus preserved, and lead them in such a direction as should best secure their ultimate safety; for *sauve qui peut*, was not his maxim. He felt that should they now be suffered to fall into the hands of the enemy through any neglect, or injudicious orders on his part, it would at once lower his professional character, and injure the great cause entrusted to his care. His officers recommended, and even urged his immediate return to Perth, by the way of Dunkeld; but this route he, without hesitation, rejected, as it would expose him to the insults of his inveterate enemies, the Athole men, and to what, in his present defenceless state, he dreaded still more—the attacks of Dundee and his horse; for he knew not yet, that his noble opponent had fallen in the battle.* He resolved, therefore, to quit this part of the country, and, turning to the right, strike across the mountains to Strathtay, and from thence, towards Stirling, by the way of Drummond castle, where he had a garrison. The road to Strathtay, (if road it might be called) he was aware was difficult, if not dangerous for cavalry, but he hoped the few horse he had with him would be able singly to extricate themselves from the bogs and marshes with which it was obstructed, while, to such a large body as Dundee's comparatively was, these presented an insuperable barrier.

They had not advanced above two miles from the river, when they overtook Ramsay, with 150 of his runaways, (as the General calls them,) almost without arms, and in utter dismay, not well knowing where they were, or whither going. Joining this little party to his own, he proceeded towards a hut, in which he espied a light, and requested information from the inmates as to the localities of the country. They were at first

* Sir John Dalrymple informs us, and that too on the authority of Mackay's manuscript, that on ascending the first eminence, and perceiving there was no pursuit, the General said to those around him, that he was sure the enemy had lost their General. *Dalrymple's Memoirs*, ii. 89. Nothing to this effect is to be found in the Memoirs of General Mackay, who, on the contrary, expressly says, p. 60, "that he apprehended more the pursuit of Dundee (whom he knew not to have been killed) with his horse, than of the Highlanders, whom he knew to be so greedy of plunder that their general would not get them that night to pursue us."

1689. thrown into consternation on the appearance of men in arms, but this soon subsided, when Mackay, softly addressing them in their native language, assured them he meant no harm, and should depart so soon as he received the information he requested. This being given, and compared with his pocket map, he was enabled to form a correct idea of the country, and proceeded on his march. He then directed his course towards Weem castle, the seat of the Laird of Weem, a friendly chief, whose son, with 100 of his clan, had joined him the preceding day.*

The morning began to dawn as they approached Strathtay, and here the appearance of men in hostile array caused fresh alarm. The people of this district taking them for the opposite party, of whose habitual depredations they stood in great awe, ran to and fro, as if in danger of their lives, as well as in fear for their property. Ramsay's men being unarmed, and broken in spirit, were in their turn thrown into consternation, and dispersing, would have escaped to the hills, had not the General and his officers, with their pistols in their hands, threatened and driven them back, after in vain trying to convince them that their safety consisted in keeping together. Notwithstanding these exertions of their officers, 100 or more made good their escape, and, as it was afterwards discovered, were knocked in the head and stript by the men of Strathtay.

Before morning, the General reached Weem castle, where he and his men were hospitably entertained by the good old laird, who furnished them with such a hasty repast as their numbers, and the shortness of the time permitted. He proceeded from thence to Drummond castle, through a country in confusion and uproar; and after a short halt, prosecuted his march to Stirling, where he arrived on the evening of Monday the 29th July. During nearly sixty hours, he had been on horseback without sleep, and with but little rest or refreshment, having, besides the bodily fatigue which he endured, in common with his men, been doubtless harassed with cares peculiar to his station; for, Christian though he was,

* Memoirs, p. 61.

it is not to be supposed that he could wholly suppress the feelings of a soldier, or be indifferent to the obloquy which would attach to the name of an unsuccessful commander; and the mortification of his defeat must have been aggravated by the recollection of the ancient rivalry betwixt himself and his now successful opponent. Yet these private and selfish considerations vanished, when viewed in comparison with the detriment which the noble cause, wherein he was engaged, had suffered, and, it might perhaps be alleged also, through his misconduct. He was supported, however, by the consciousness of having done his duty according to the best of his abilities, and firmly trusted that God would in due time vindicate his own cause, by substituting more skilful instruments in their room, if he judged those at present employed unfit or unworthy.

With such reflections passing in his mind, Mackay arrived at Stirling, and there received the first certain intelligence of Dundee's death. Here we shall leave him for a while, and, returning to the field of battle, enquire into the circumstances which accompanied the termination of Dundee's career, and which have been falsified or exaggerated by his admirers, to heighten the romance of his character, and increase the stage-effect of his fall. The Author would rather decline controversy; but cannot, in justice to the subject, and in conformity with the maxim contained in the motto of this work, avoid making a few remarks on the closing scene.

Dundee was undoubtedly the life and soul of his party; and had he survived the battle, nothing would have been wanting to complete his military glory, but a good cause, and oblivion of his past misdeeds. According to the accounts best entitled to credit, he fell early in the battle; while others maintain, that he survived it so long as to write a letter to King James, communicating the intelligence of the victory. In proof of the former position, a letter is produced from the king, to Stewart of Ballechin, dated Dublin castle, 30th November 1689, that is, four months after the battle, when consequently, the true state of the facts could not fail to be known. In this letter, his Majesty alludes to the loss sustained by the death of Dundee, "*at your entrance into action.*"* The latter opinion is founded on the letter pretended to have been written by Dundee to the King, and which, unless we disregard the best cotemporary authorities, can only be considered as a clumsy forgery, got up by his blind and injudicious admirers.†

By some it has been asserted, that if Dundee had lived, he would not only have cut off Mackay's retreat, and left him not a man to tell the tale, but that he would afterwards have marched directly to the capital, and overturned the new government. This opinion has been advanced with such confidence, and so often copied by one author from another, that it has passed into an article of popular belief among the Jacobite party. On a closer examination, however, it will be found that the condition of the two contending armies was, after the battle, not so dissimilar as would at first sight appear. Of Dundee's force, more than one-third were slain on the field, to which, adding, according to the usual proportion, a greater number of wounded, fully two-thirds would be found, at the close of the action, *hors de combat*. The remaining third, be it remembered, consisted not of disciplined soldiers accustomed to obedience, but of ungovernable mountaineers, and wild Irish, both so addicted to plunder, that even in the moment of victory, they could not refrain; but in spite of their officers, quitted their ranks, to pounce upon Mackay's baggage, and before morning, wore off to the hills with their booty. It would be difficult to re-assemble men of such a stamp, and still more to bring them back to discipline and obedience to their officers.

* See Stewart's Sketches, Balcarras's Memoirs, and Collier's Dictionary.

† On the supposition of Dundee's letter being genuine, he must have breathed his last, surrounded by his friends, and doubtless amidst their tears and lamentations. Is it then to be supposed, that those friends would fail to pay to his remains the funeral honours to which he was so well entitled by his rank, and by the value of his services to the cause of his royal master? Historians do not mention any such funeral honours; and from their silence we may infer, that none such were paid. On the contrary, there is evidence that his body, after being stript by his own people, was left on the field of battle, so long that it could with difficulty be recognized, having no mark to distinguish it from that of the meanest of his followers. See *Balcarras's Memoirs*, p. 108.

A great proportion of Mackay's men, it is true, yielding to the impulse of a sudden panic, had turned their backs and fled; but there were among them many brave soldiers, who, chafed in their spirit, and burning with indignation at their disgrace, would seize the first opportunity to turn on their pursuers, and if they did not repulse them, would at least sell their own lives as dearly as possible. If, therefore, Dundee had survived, he would thus have to begin the campaign again under the same difficulties as before, while the resources of his opponent would daily gain strength, and the vigour and energy of his character more fully develope themselves. But to return to our narrative.

Notwithstanding the fatigues of the two preceding days, the General, before retiring to rest, wrote hasty letters to the Duke of Hamilton and Lord Melville, briefly stating the principal facts and circumstances of his defeat, and promising particulars in a future dispatch. He besought his Grace, and his colleagues in council, "not to be disheartened by what had happened, which with God's blessing on the means still left, would speedily be repaired;" he recommended "the setting of men quickly to work to stop the consternation of our friends, as well as the hopes and pride of our enemies;" and entreated "that the recent disaster might not in the least interrupt the session of parliament." Next morning he inspected the troops quartered in the town and neighbourhood, and soon after had the satisfaction of being joined by that excellent officer, Sir John Lanier, whom the council had sent to assume the chief command at Stirling, in case a report which had reached them of the death of the commander-in-chief should prove true. He was informed by Lanier, of the pusillanimous measures agitated in council, on receipt of the first intelligence from Killiecrankie, namely, the removal of the seat of government to the borders, or to Glasgow, and abandoning to the enemy all the country north of Tay, or even of the Forth. These propositions he utterly disapproved of; and the last excited his indignation to such a degree, that he instantly resolved, of his own authority, and on his responsibility, to reverse it; which resolution he intimated to the council.

1689. Had Dundee survived, and rapidly marched towards Edinburgh, as he would undoubtedly have done, with so many of his followers as he could collect; Mackay would in that case have deemed it his duty to follow close in his rear, with all the forces he could muster. The death of the Viscount totally changed the aspect of affairs, and put an end to all apprehensions for the safety of the government. Mackay therefore resolved to adopt a different course; and instead of proceeding to Edinburgh, returned immediately towards Perth, to stop the further progress of the Highlanders, and overawe the disaffected in the shires of Angus and Mearns. For this purpose he held a final review of his troops, on Wednesday morning, in Stirling Park, and at two P. M. was in full march on the road to Perth, at the head of nearly two thousand horse and foot.

Success in battle is sometimes the result of what, in common parlance, is termed, mere accident. A good retreat, though it may be facilitated, can never be produced by such a cause, and always argues judgment and skill on the part of the commander. During his retreat from Killiecrankie, not only judgment and skill, but gallantry also, as well as a humane and even fatherly concern for the lives of his soldiers,—were conspicuous in Mackay. He is now to appear in a new point of view, as resuming offensive operations within less than forty-eight hours from his retreat to Stirling, and displaying a promptitude of decision, and energy of action, rarely equalled, and never perhaps surpassed, in similar circumstances. Yet, this part of his conduct has been either wholly overlooked, or but slightly noticed by most modern historians. Sir John Dalrymple, after exhausting his stores of panegyric on his favourite hero, Dundee, and censuring what he thought amiss in the military conduct of Mackay,—passes over in silence what would do him honour; and after the battle, never mentions his name. Laing duly appreciates his character, and bestows on it, just, though rather concise praise. Subsequent writers, while they acknowledge praise to be due, are all (with one honourable exception) niggardly in bestowing it. Chambers, though a Tory writer, and evidently leaning to the Jacobite side of the question, enters more fully than any of his predecessors, into the merits of Mackay, and does ample justice to his military character. 1689. That it may not be supposed the Author of these sheets has been led, by excessive admiration of his excellent relative's character, to over-rate his merits, he trusts he shall be excused for quoting a passage of some length from the author just mentioned, who cannot be suspected of any undue bias.

"The Revolution party," says Mr. Chambers,* "had no cause to complain of the conduct of their own General. To do Mackay justice, he had performed all that a good leader could have performed under the circumstances, and with such troops. When all his efforts were found unavailing in battle, he had done what was next to victory,—performed a masterly retreat with the wreck of his forces. His conduct, however, after reaching Stirling, was characterized by an energy and boldness very different from what might have been expected in a beaten general. On arriving there, he learned that the convention had given orders to the various bodies of troops stationed in the north of Scotland, to draw towards the capital; and it was intimated to himself, that, if he could only defend the pass of Stirling, so as to prevent the Highlanders from coming south, though at the expense of surrendering all the north to them, he would be held as doing sufficient duty. This did not satisfy Mackay. He knew that the north of Scotland could raise an army far superior in bravery and discipline, to the south; he also considered, that, if they were permitted to take possession of such towns as Perth, Dundee, and Aberdeen, they could assume a face of government, and fairly divide the kingdom with his master and mistress. He thought it far better to hazard a good deal, for the sake of restraining the enemy to the hills. Accordingly, resolving to march back forthwith to Perth, for the purpose of facing them in their expected descent, he exerted himself during the two days following his return to Stirling, to collect all the bodies of troops which lay within reach. With such alacrity did this excellent soldier prosecute his design of marching back against

* History of the Rebellions in Scotland, p. 116.

1689. the enemy, that, on Wednesday afternoon at two o'clock, less than two days after his return from Killiecrankie, he was on the high road to Perth with a new army of nearly 2000 men. Before that evening he reached a village about half way betwixt Stirling and Perth, where he rested for a part of the night. Next day, marching towards Perth, he experienced great inconvenience from the impossibility of procuring any intelligence of the enemy, all the houses by the way being deserted by their inhabitants, who were gone in arms to join the Highlanders. "As he approached a body of about 300 Highlanders, whom Cannon, Dundee's successor, had pushed on in advance, and immediately attacking them, he killed 120, and dispersed or took the rest prisoners. An affair," continues Mr. Chambers, "reflecting so much discredit on Dundee's successor, and auguring so well of Mackay's renewed operations, was generally considered in the country as likely to check the progress of the war not a little. Accordingly, from this moment, the friends of the reformed government were inspired with fresh hopes."

In ordinary circumstances, this affair would have been viewed in no other light than as a casual rencounter between two hostile detachments, which could not be supposed to lead to any material consequences. Very different, however, in this case was the result. It revived the drooping spirits of the new government and their friends, fixed the wavering, and inspired the timid with courage. Dundee, the idol of his friends, and the terror of his enemies, whom, but a few days before, the latter every moment dreaded seeing at their gates, was now no more, while his rival, Mackay, falsely reported to be numbered among the dead, was still alive, at the head of a victorious army, and hailed by his friends as their deliverer. The effect of this altered state of affairs on the mind of Mackay himself, the pious reader alone can fully appreciate. He communicated the tidings to the council by an appropriate messenger, by Lord Belhaven, his own companion in arms, and the cousin of his Grace the high commissioner; nor did the tidings lose aught of their effect on the public mind, by the rank and character of the bearer.

Notwithstanding this partial success, the General now found his resources too much impaired, and the season too far advanced, to resume the Inverlochy project, or undertake any other enterprise of importance, during the few remaining months of the year. He therefore resolved to limit his views to the securing of the low country against the incursions of the mountaineers, and for this purpose again fixed his head-quarters at Perth, as a central position, from which to observe the motions of the enemy, till he could collect a sufficient force to oppose them. He ordered Sir John Lanier to join him, with two regiments of horse from England; he directed Sir Thomas Livingstone to hold himself in readiness to march at the shortest notice to Aberdeen; and made such other dispositions as would ensure the more speedy concentration of his force, should that measure be required.

With all Dundee's influence over the Highlanders, he never was able to assemble more than 2000 of their number at any given point, yet Cannon, though a stranger to their habits, and of a character infinitely less attractive, was now at the head of a mixed body of above 4000 men, Highlanders and Irish. The exact proportion of each cannot now be ascertained, but it seems probable that at least three-fourths were composed of the remains of Dundee's army, and fresh levies of Highlanders,* and that the rest were Irish. How this feeble commander was enabled to draw so many Highlanders to his standard, seems a mystery which the spoils of Killiecrankie, together with those expected from the ensuing campaign, may go far to explain; but if this was the magnetic force that attracted the Highlanders, they were miserably disappointed, as will appear in the sequel.

Cannon, disheartened by the check he sustained near Perth, and perceiving that, notwithstanding his superiority of numbers, he could make no impression on Mackay in that quarter, resolved to try his fortune in another. Decamping suddenly from Dunkeld, he turned round towards the north

* Macgregors, Frasers, M'Farlanes, and the Gordons of Strathdon and Glenlivet, joined Cannon in the heights of Braemar.

by the way of Blairgowrie, keeping near the Grampians, his force being composed almost wholly of foot. Mackay, without waiting for his expected reinforcements, followed in his rear with 1400 horse, leaving his foot behind, for the sake of greater despatch, and pursued his march, skirting the plains along the bottom of the hills. In this manner both parties moved in parallel directions towards Aberdeen, neither of the two evincing a disposition to quit his vantage ground, in order to attack the other. Arrived at Aberdeen, Mackay was welcomed with joy by the majority of the inhabitants, who were led to believe the Highlanders would be in their town that very night.

Here he received an express from his faithful friend the master of Forbes, informing him that Cannon had taken up a strong position on his father's grounds, where he had the Highlanders at his back, a wood to cover him, and free communication with his friends in the low countries of Aberdeen and Banff.

This intelligence made the General anxious for the safety of the garrison he had left in the castle of Abergeldie, which, should it fall into the enemy's hands, would enable him to turn with equal convenience and prospect of success, either towards Inverness or Aberdeen. He therefore sent an express to Sir Thomas Livingstone, ordering him to leave the command of the troops about Inverness to Sir James Leslie, and repair forthwith himself with his regiment of dragoons to Strathbogie. At the same time, he wrote to Sir John Lanier, to despatch Hayford's regiment in all haste, from Forfar to Aberdeen, and with these additions to his present force, he trusted he should be able to keep the enemy in check, if not wholly to overturn his designs. Meantime, he was subjected to a renewal of those fatiguing marches, and countermarches, by which he had been harassed some months before. He was kept perpetually in motion by day, and during the night lay in the fields with his men in a body, not judging it safe to separate them. The country people being attached to the opposite interest, he had no confidence in their reports, and therefore was continually sending out small parties all night, to procure intelligence as if in an enemy's country.

1689.

Livingstone and Hayford having arrived at their respective destinations, the General resolved to present a bolder front to the enemy than he had hitherto been able to shew; and with this view, despatched Sir George Gordon of Edinglassie, on two succeeding days, and by different routes, with 100 dragoons, to reconnoitre his position. This officer reported that the position was so surrounded by hills on one hand, and by woods, or by bogs and marshes, on the other, as to be inaccessible to horse. The General was therefore obliged to abandon his design, but consoled himself with the hope that want of provisions would, by compelling the enemy to quit his stronghold, soon terminate this desultory and inconclusive warfare. The event justified his expectation; for Cannon, a few days after, retreated over the mountains into the shires of Mearns and Angus, by paths inaccessible to horse. He gave notice of Cannon's motions to Lanier, who being provided with foot as well as horse, was prepared to give the enemy a warm reception, wheresoever he might encounter him.

How Cannon was enabled, during almost a month, to procure subsistence in such a country, for an army of 4000 men, seems difficult to conceive; yet that such were his numbers, is more than once affirmed by Mackay, and not denied by any writer of the adverse party.

At Strathbogie, the General having had some leisure, for the first time since he left Killiecrankie, employed it in drawing up a narrative of the battle, and transmitted it to Lord Melville. It has already been more minutely detailed in the foregoing pages; but as the reader will probably be desirous of perusing the General's modest recital in his own words, it is inserted in the Appendix. Commanders in those days had not the aid of a regular staff, such as the improved methods of carrying on war in modern times have provided. Mackay having neither adjutant, nor quartermaster-general, nor aides-de-camp, was obliged to conduct the details of the army by orders emanating directly from himself, which must

1689. have added in no small degree to the labour and difficulties of his situation.*

About the middle of August, the General received a letter from the council, expressing their wish that he should forthwith dislodge the enemy from Blair castle, and Finlarig, the seat of the Earl of Breadalbane, and place garrisons there. He replied, that he could not quit his present position, while the enemy continued together in such a formidable body, and that, as the service they proposed was of less immediate urgency, it had better be deferred for the present. If, however, their lordships continued bent on the project, he added, that they had only to issue their orders to Sir John Lanier, who commanded at Forfar, and who, after making the previous arrangements that might be necessary, would carry their orders into effect.

Instead, however, of adopting this prudent and regular course, the council, without further enquiry, or communication with either of the two Generals, thought proper to send a mandate to the Earl of Angus', or Cameronian regiment,† to march to Dunkeld, and remain there till further orders. Nothing could be more rash, or ill-advised than such a step; for, besides the irregularity of sending an order to the commanding officer

* See Mackay's Letters to Lord Melville about Colonel Hill. Memoirs, p. 320.

† So denominated, from the Cameronians, a religious sect, which, about the year 1680, separated from the main body of the Covenanters, and took its name from that of its leader, Richard Cameron, a noted field-preacher of those times. By this sect, the Cameronian regiment was raised, and of its adherents, it was at first exclusively composed. They professed great strictness of religious principle, and maintained a corresponding purity of moral conduct; but, as they held certain opinions on the subject of government, which the General deemed incompatible with military subordination, he never availed himself of their services, without urgent necessity. He therefore recommended to King William to remove them from their own country, and employ them in Flanders, where, by mixing with other troops, they would gradually correct their narrow notions. The King adopted the suggestion, and with the happiest results; for, during all his subsequent wars, no regiment in the service was more distinguished than the Cameronians, for exact discipline and gallantry in the field, as well as by correct, moral, and religious conduct.—See *Crichton's interesting Life of Blackadder*, the brave and pious Lieutenant-colonel of this regiment.

of a regiment, without the knowledge of his immediate superior, the General of the district,—it was contrary to the most obvious maxims of prudence, as well as military discipline. The village of Dunkeld was open and defenceless, situated in the entrance to the Highlands, at the Marquis of Athole's gate, and in the immediate vicinity of his people, who were the implacable enemies of this regiment in particular, as well as of the cause which they served; and the village was, moreover, fifteen miles distant from either Perth or Cupar of Angus,—the two nearest military stations from which aid could be expected in case of need.

1689.

The Cameronians obeyed, apparently unconscious of danger, and led, as it were, like so many sheep to the slaughter. They arrived at Dunkeld, seven or eight hundred in number, under the command of Lieutenant-colonel Cleland, on the evening of Saturday the 17th August, and took up their quarters in the houses of the village, or lay on their arms in the streets, during the night. Sunday, the Highlanders began to appear on the neighbouring hills, and continued encreasing in number during the two following days, after being joined by Cannon, till they augmented to four or five thousand men. Lord Cardross* arrived at the same time, with

---

* John, seventh Earl of Marr, lord high treasurer of Scotland, being in great favour with James VI., was, in 1606, created by him, Lord Cardross, with remainder to his third son, Henry, who accordingly succeeded the Earl as Lord Cardross, in 1635, and was father of Henry, the second Lord Cardross mentioned in the text. This lord was educated in the love of liberty, and the strictest principles of religion, by which his family was distinguished. Becoming obnoxious to the tyrannical government of Charles II., on account of the protection he afforded to oppressed Presbyterian ministers, he was heavily fined, and imprisoned from 1675 to 1679. After his release, he was still exposed to such continual vexations, that he fled for refuge to Carolina, where he settled a colony, which being destroyed by the Spaniards, he returned to Europe, and took shelter in Holland with many of his persecuted countrymen. In 1688 he accompanied the Prince of Orange to Britain, raised a regiment of dragoons, at the head of which he served, as above mentioned, and obtained from the Scottish parliament some compensation for his losses and sufferings. He enjoyed much favour with King William, who appointed him a privy councillor, and general of the mint, which offices, however, he did not long enjoy, having died in 1693, aged 44, of complaints brought on by his sufferings. His son, third lord Cardross, on the death of James, eighth Earl of Buchan, (second son of the

1689. three troops of dragoons, and two of horse,—having been detached by Colonel Ramsay in aid of the Cameronians; but, being afterwards peremptorily recalled by that officer, he reluctantly returned to Perth,—thus leaving the Cameronians, in all human probability, devoted to destruction. Nor was this all: Lanier being ordered by the council to put himself at the head of the force destined against Blair castle, advanced to Cupar of Angus in his way, and there met an express from Ramsay, informing him of the approach of the Highlanders towards Dunkeld, and of the perilous situation of the Cameronian regiment, and requesting his instructions in consequence. Lanier most unfortunately deferred replying till he should himself arrive at Perth, which he expected to reach next morning. He reached it accordingly, but too late, alas! for this gallant, and apparently devoted regiment, which was at that very time engaged in mortal combat with an enemy five times its number. The battle lasted from seven in the morning of Wednesday the 21st, till eleven A. M.; and, though consisting rather of a succession of personal conflicts than of a regular action, has been considered one of the hardest fought, and most desperate recorded in the annals of the seventeenth century. Victory at length declared in favour of the Cameronians, but was dearly purchased with the loss of the gallant Lieutenant colonel Cleland,* Major Henderson, and many other brave officers and men. When all was over, the survivors devoutly sang a hymn of praise and thanksgiving to the God of battles, to whom alone they ascribed the glory of their victory. Cannon, though not mentioned as having been present in the action, must have exercised the functions of commander, as he was stated by some of the prisoners to have made strenuous, though unavailing efforts to induce the Highlanders, after their retreat, to renew the attack. During the last month's campaign, he had

treasurer Marr) without issue, succeeded to that earldom, which has accordingly been borne by his descendants ever since.

* For an account of this distinguished young officer, and eminent christian also, see *Crichton's Life of Colonel Blackadder,* p. 95.

been gradually sinking in the estimation of his army; and now, by his 1689. pusillanimous conduct, drew on himself their contempt.

It thus appears, that a rash order of the council, which had well nigh led to the destruction of a brave regiment, and nearly converted Dunkeld into another Killiecrankie, was by the providence of God so overruled, as to produce a very different result, and may be regarded as one of the causes which contributed to the stability of King William's government.

The General, having a second time provided for the security of the northern counties, left them under the charge of Sir Thomas Livingstone, and returned to the south by the way of the coast, being unable, as already mentioned, to follow Cannon over the hills with his horse. He arrived at Perth about the end of August, and a few days after proceeded to Blair, with a competent force to execute his long-meditated design of planting a garrison there. He had reason to fear the Athole men would, in order to frustrate his intention, set the castle on fire, and therefore caused proclamation to be made, that if they did so, he should not leave a house standing between Dunkeld and Blair, and should burn and destroy their corn. This threat had the desired effect, and prevented great distress to the families of these deluded men themselves, as well as annoyance to the General. The Athole men had been the chief authors of his losses and disappointments during the summer; but now that they were at his mercy, he shewed himself willing to forgive the past, and receive into the King's peace, all who submitted themselves and delivered up their arms. Having taken possession of the castle without opposition, he garrisoned it with nine companies of foot, and ordered it to be fortified with a breastwork and pallisade. Incessant rains prevented his proceeding, as he intended, to Finlarig, and obliged him to return to Perth, whence, in obedience to commands from his Majesty, he despatched the regiments of Lanier, Hayford, and Hastings to the west, in order to be shipped for Ireland, and those of Colchester and Barclay, for better quarters and forage to England. The King, having concluded a treaty with his Danish Majesty, in virtue of

1689. which, the latter engaged to furnish a thousand auxiliaries, who were to be landed at Leith, the General received the royal commands to make the necessary arrangements for their reception, and conveyance in like manner to Ireland. Contrary winds, however, detained them at first in their own ports for several weeks, and afterwards obliged them to land in different parts of England.

All active operations in the Highlands being now at a stand, in consequence of the extraordinary floods; the General employed this short interval of leisure in visiting Edinburgh, to confer with his colleagues on the present posture of affairs. During his stay there, the Earl of Breadalbane presented himself to take the oath of allegiance, and give bail for his appearance; an example which was speedily followed by the Earls of Southesk, Strathmore, and Callander, and by the Lords Livingstone and Duffus. The extensive possessions of the first mentioned nobleman gave him considerable influence in the country, and being of an intriguing disposition, he was universally regarded as the chief fomenter of the present troubles in the Highlands. The submission, therefore, of such a personage as the Earl of Breadalbane, was to the General a source of peculiar satisfaction; the more so, perhaps, as he suspected that, if not produced, it was at least accelerated by the surmise of the garrison intended to be placed in his house. The rains having somewhat abated soon after his return to Perth, he detached Lord Cardross, with 200 men, to the head of Loch Tay, and his Lordship, without opposition, established himself in garrison at Finlarig. Drummond castle had been already secured, and smaller garrisons having now been planted at Weem castle, Cambusmore, Cardross, and Drummakill, the chain of communication was completed, from the remotest extremities of Perthshire to the town of Inverness.

Having thus shut up the Highlanders in their hills, his next care was to make such a distribution of his forces in the low countries, as should most easily enable him, in case of a sudden emergency, to assemble a sufficient number at any given point, to repel their incursions. While deliberating on this subject, he was thrown into considerable perplexity by a letter from Lord Melville,* secretary of state for Scotland, resident 1689. in London, under date 5th October, intimating that the King, apprehensive of the parliament withholding the necessary supplies, had resolved to reduce some of the Scottish regiments, both of horse and foot, and therefore desired to be informed which of the standing regiments were judged least serviceable, that these might be disbanded.

Against this proposition, the General took the liberty of warmly remonstrating, and pointed out, in forcible terms, the danger of reducing a military establishment, already inadequate to the various duties to be performed, especially at the present critical juncture, when the divisions in parliament and the council were likely to revive the hopes of the enemy, and stir them up to fresh insurrections; adding, that though the newly-raised regiments had not yet attained any high degree of discipline, their very name was sufficient to keep in awe, men who would otherwise throw off the mask, and openly join the enemy. If, however, his majesty still adhered to his purpose, he humbly requested to be informed what regiments it was his pleasure to keep up, that he might make his arrangements for winter quarters accordingly. Receiving no reply, he wrote again and

* Lord Melville was the representative of an ancient and most respectable family, many individuals of which had filled high offices in the state.

George, the fourth Lord, born 1636, was educated in the strictest principles of the presbyterian religion and forms of worship, to which he adhered so firmly, that he became obnoxious to the late sovereigns, and found it necessary to retire for safety to Holland. There he joined Monmouth, came over with him on his rash expedition to England, from whence, escaping for his life, he fled again into Holland, and remained there till 1688, when he accompanied the Prince of Orange to England, and obtained an act of the Scottish parliament for restoring his estates, which had been forfeited. During the whole of that reign he enjoyed an extraordinary degree of favour and confidence; having at one and the same time been secretary of state for Scotland, and high commissioner to the parliament; and afterwards successively keeper of the privy seal, and president of the council. His eldest son, Lord Raith, as deputy treasurer, had for many years the entire management of the revenue; and his second son, who became Earl of Leven in right of his mother, was colonel of a regiment, and governor of Edinburgh castle; and would have succeeded, or even supplanted, General Mackay in the chief command, had his father's ambitious schemes succeeded.

1689. again to Lord Melville, urging and reiterating the necessity of an early communication of his Majesty's resolution, but apparently without making any impression on the secretary's mind. Of these letters, copies or large extracts are inserted in the Appendix, to which the attention of the reader is invited, and particularly to the letters of 21st and 31st December, which breathe a spirit of the most ardent piety towards God, as well as of affectionate zeal for the interest of his earthly sovereigns.

Finding he could elicit nothing satisfactory from Lord Melville, the General addressed himself to the Earl of Portland, but for some time with no better success. At length, after three months' delay, a reply was re-
1690. ceived in the month of January; but one little calculated, either in form or substance, to soothe his wounded feelings, or avert the evil which he deprecated. It announced an instrument, under the royal sign-manual, appointing three commissioners to disband certain regiments of foot, and troops of horse, and remodel those which remained. The establishment of foot at this time, consisted of nine regiments; of which, three were ordered to be reduced, viz. those of Marr, Blantyre, and Bargeny; a new regiment was to be formed of the men thus disbanded, the command of which was to be given to Colonel Cunningham; and a company was to be added to each of the seven regiments, which should then form the new establishment. All the independent companies were at first to be in like manner reduced, but the order was subsequently rescinded. The existing troops of horse and dragoons, were, after being remodelled, to be formed into two regiments, each consisting of three troops, and command-ed, the horse by the Earl of Eglington, the dragoons by Lord Cardross. The Master of Forbes was to be appointed lieutenant-colonel, Sir George Gordon of Edinglassie, major of Eglington's horse, and of Cardross' dragoons, Jackson lieutenant-colonel, and Guthrie major, but without a troop, that being assigned to Sir Patrick Hume of Polwarth.*

* One of those illustrious patriots who, by their vigorous opposition to the tyrannical mea-sures of the two royal brothers, made themselves obnoxious to their vengeance. Sir Patrick

It might naturally be expected, that the execution of these orders would 1690. be entrusted to the commander-in-chief, to whose department it properly belonged, or, that if commissioners were to be appointed, he should be placed at the head of the list. Instead of this honour, the first place was assigned to the Earl of Leven, the youngest colonel in the service, but second son of the lord secretary, while the rear was brought up by the veteran generals, Mackay and Munro.* At such an indignity, most general officers would have taken fire, and instantly resigned the chief command; Mackay felt the indignity as a man, and an officer, but bore it as a christian, and a patriot, choosing rather to stifle his private feelings, than weaken the hands of government, by disputing about precedency at such a crisis; and accordingly proceeded to execute the task assigned to him, without betraying any symptoms of dissatisfaction. He could not, however, now disguise from himself, the alteration which he had for some time suspected in his Majesty's conduct towards him, nor help being sensibly affected by it. During seventeen years that he had been in the service of the States General, he received repeated marks of favour and confidence from the King, as Prince of Orange. He had the honour of being selected for the command of the third division of the invading army. On landing in Scotland, he was invested with the chief command of the forces in that kingdom; and though unsuccessful at Killiecrankie, he could safely appeal to the present state of the King's affairs in that country, contrasted with the state in which he found them, as a proof that he was not wholly unworthy of the confidence of his sovereign. Notwithstanding these services, he now found, not only his recommendations, but even his opinions on professional matters disregarded, and that confidence which he had been accustomed to experience from his Majesty, transferred to another.

was in consequence obliged, in 1684, to fly with his family to Holland, where he continued in great poverty till the revolution of 1688, when he came over with the Prince of Orange, had his forfeiture rescinded by act of Parliament, was raised to the peerage, by the titles of Earl of Marchmont and Baron Polwarth, constituted high chancellor, and died in 1724, in his 84th year.

* For an account of Monro, see note p. 76.

1690. Even in early youth, King William had given proofs of superior capacity. After crushing a domestic faction, he delivered his country from the yoke of France; he attacked Louis the XIV. in the plenitude of his power, and never rested till he organized that great confederacy, which, in the end, humbled the pride of the *grand Monarque*. It is, therefore, a curious phenomenon in the history of the human mind, that a prince who had achieved these mighty deeds, should now suffer himself to be guided by the counsels of such a puny politician as Lord Melville, or by those of a statesman, how able soever, yet so noted for tergiversation and perfidy, as Viscount Tarbat.* These two lords, at their outset in life, held political principles, and formed political connexions, diametrically opposite to each other; but they were led by circumstances to coalesce; and during the remainder of their lives, mutual interests held them together, and cemented

* Viscount Tarbat, so created 1685, was the son of Sir John Mackenzie of Tarbat, baronet, and grandson of Sir Roderick Mackenzie of Cogeach, knight, who was the second son of Colin Mackenzie of Kintail, and brother of the first Lord Kintail. The Viscount was a man of superior talents and accomplishments, which he prostituted at the shrine of power, to aggrandize himself, by enslaving his country. He made his first appearance at court, soon after the Restoration; and having the advantage of a prepossessing figure, and good address, was considered one of the most rising young men about court. He had a taste for literature and science, was one of the original members of the Royal Society, and contributed some valuable articles to the earlier volumes of the Philosophical Transactions. Happy would it have been for his fame, had he confined himself to such pursuits, but in an evil hour he plunged into the vortex of politics, and associating himself with some of the worst men of those bad times, made shipwreck of his reputation. His first political connexion was with Middleton, for the purpose of overthrowing Lauderdale's administration; but being foiled in this attempt, he turned round, and made his court to the man whom he had endeavoured to destroy. Through Lauderdale's influence, he climbed his way to place and power, with such success, that during the last years of Charles's, and the whole of James's reign, he had the chief management of Scottish affairs, but was dismissed from all his employments at the Revolution. Such, however, was his flexibility of principle, that he was found among the foremost in making advances to King William, who would gladly have availed himself of his talents, and taken him into his service, but for the odium attached to his name, on account of the obnoxious measures of the two former reigns, in which he had so large a share. Nowise discouraged by the coldness

their union. Tarbat having been a participator in some of the most obnoxious measures of the late governments, had good reason to apprehend
danger from the scrutiny of parliament; and therefore it was his obvious
policy to throw obstacles in the way of its meeting. Melville, not having
engaged in public affairs during the two former reigns, and being irre-
proachable in his private life, had no such fears to influence his conduct;
but, like most other ministers, he would gladly be freed from the constant
inspection of parliament; and he was besides, a mere tool in the hands of
his cousin Tarbat,—a craftier and more able politician than himself. A
striking feature in Melville's character, was an inordinate desire to mono-
polize places of power and emolument in his family; and to the gratification
of this passion, he foresaw that the presence of parliament would prove an
obstacle. For these and other reasons, he co-operated with Tarbat in his
intrigues to prevent the assembling of parliament, and to counteract the
measures of the General to facilitate its meeting.

Between such men and Mackay, there could be no community of senti-
ment or interest. They pursued their own selfish measures; he aimed at
nothing, either for himself or his family; and his sole end and aim was the
public good. The only relative of his own whom he recommended for

1690.

with which his advances were at first received, he feigned the deepest contrition for his past errors, and so far overcame William's scruples, that he restored him to his former post of clerk register, in which situation, he was accused of having repeatedly falsified the records of par- liament. At the accession of Queen Anne, he was immediately sent for to court, appointed secretary of state, created Earl of Cromarty, and had his pension, with all the iniquitous grants of former reigns confirmed to him. He died at New Tarbat in 1714, in the 84th, or, according to some, in the 88th year of his age. It is an invidious, and to a mind of any gen- erosity, a painful task, to revive the remembrance of blemishes in the characters of men long since deceased, but it is due to the truth of history, and in the present instance, to the charac- ter of General Mackay, to speak out. During the whole of the time Mackay commanded in Scotland, the Lords Melville and Tarbat endeavoured to undermine his influence with the King, and secretly counteract his measures for the public good, in which they were cordially joined (as will presently appear) by Lord Breadalbane.

1690. promotion, was his gallant nephew, Major Mackay; and, notwithstanding the acknowledged merits of that excellent young officer, he was disappointed of this promotion, through the secret influence of the cabal. As commander-in-chief, it was alike the right and the duty of the General to recommend, in all cases of vacancy in the army; and, though he made it a point of conscience to attend to the claims of the most deserving only, his recommendations were, through the same sinister influence, often disregarded.

Towards the close of the campaign, he transmitted to Lord Melville, for the consideration of his Majesty, a request for leave of absence to visit his family, for a few months during the winter, which he conceived would, at that season of the year, in no way impede the public service. This request, in itself so reasonable, was strengthened by the consideration, that he had grounds for believing Major-general Sir George Munro of Culrain would have been, by this time, appointed to a seat at the council board;* yet it was refused, through the insinuations of Melville and Tarbat, who represented to the King the necessity of keeping Mackay at his post during the winter. Gladly would they have seen him removed altogether from his present high station; but so long as he held it, they were anxious to prevent an interview between his royal master and himself, rightly judging, that, to obtain such interview, was one great object he had in view when he solicited leave of absence.

Lord Melville had already frustrated the General's endeavours to convey his sentiments in writing to the King, and now succeeded, for the present at

* Much inconvenience having been experienced from the want of a military man to advise with the council on military matters, during the occasional absence of the commander-in-chief, it was suggested by Mackay that Major-general Sir George Munro of Culrain, should, for this purpose, be appointed to a seat in the council board. The suggestion having been favourably received by the King, who was no stranger to Munro's high military character,—Mackay had reason to suppose the appointment would, by this time, have taken place. Munro was a veteran officer, who had served with reputation in the German wars, as well as since then, in Ireland, and now lived in retirement on his estate in Ross-shire.

least, in cutting off all hope of a personal interview between them. The General, however, was not discouraged, and resolved to make one attempt more to communicate with his Majesty, through the medium of the Earl of Portland, whom he believed to be sincerely attached to his royal master's interest, how much soever he might sometimes mistake the means of promoting it. After referring to what he had already written more at large on the subject of past miscarriages, he gave the Earl plainly to understand that "his continuing in command of the forces in Scotland, could not but prove prejudicial to the King's service, because his secretary, and others of his faction, were his enemies, and having more credit than he with the King, would labour to be revenged of him, to make the service fail in his hands. And therefore, if the King did not judge him capable to give his Majesty solid information of matters, and propose right methods to establish his authority in that kingdom, it were the interest of the service, as well as the General's desire, to be removed out of that command, being unwilling to hazard his reputation, though obscure in the world, where he had so little prospect of advancing the service, so long as those who could be most helpful to him, proved his greatest obstacles."

Portland, having set out for Holland, before this letter arrived, it was received by Melville, and carried by him to the King, who appears to have in this manner learned for the first time the causes, and full extent of Mackay's dissatisfaction; and immediately wrote to him desiring to know what further measures he would recommend, for subduing the Highlanders. In obedience to this command, Mackay sent his Majesty a full statement, and detailed explanation of his views. He represented that, as the Highlanders from the greater hardiness of their habits, made better soldiers than the peaceful Lowlanders, ever since the cessation of the border wars; it would be easy for what party soever in the state had the command of them, to give serious annoyance to their lowland neighbours, and when opposed to the existing government, oblige it to keep up a large military force, ready at all times, and on every point, to repel their incursions.

* Memoirs, p. 79.

1690. This had been particularly experienced in the last, and probably would be, in all future campaigns, so long as the Highlanders continued, as at present, opposed to the government. To guard against this evil, the most efficacious, as well as the cheapest method, appeared to him to be the erecting of a fort at Inverlochy, which would have the effect of overawing the Highlanders, and of thus preventing their sending reinforcements to Cannon, or to whatever other general happened to command on the part of the abdicated family in the low country; being assured that on condition of their remaining quietly at home, they should not be molested by the garrison.

For further security, the General recommended that three frigates, or small armed vessels, and transports for conveying troops with stores, provisions, and building materials, should be fitted out; which, after the fort was erected, might be employed in scouring the inlets, with which the islands and adjacent coasts were indented, and thus keep a constant watch over the motions of the inhabitants. On these and other adventures of his proposed measures, he enlarged in his letters to the King and the Earl of Portland, but "by the multitude of his Majesty's other affairs, or haply not judging those of Scotland of so great importance, with insinuations of persons who gave him other notions of them, the General received no return to his propositions and frequent letters, which made him so chagrined and impatient that he declared that he would not continue a minute in that command, seeing plainly nothing to be expected but the loss of his reputation with the service thereby, (wherewith, as to the judgment of the vulgar, he was intrusted,) and would lie under the blame of its miscarriages, though in effect, it was never seen that a man hath been employed in a service of that importance so little trusted by his master, as he discovered himself to be by the King; which could not but be very sensible to him, considering that his Majesty thereby must either question his fidelity, or his judgment and capacity. Nevertheless, he overcame all at last with patience, in the firm expectation that God, (without whose providence he had not been pitched upon for that service, when he was so very unfit for any by his great sickness, who overruleth the destiny of the least of his creatures, much more that of kingdoms, and in whose presence he served that protestant interest in uprightness, and self-denyed sincerity) would bless his endeavours, and overcome by his providence those difficulties which he foresaw to his great discouragement, had he not been supported by that hope."*

There were two routes, either of which might be chosen for the expedition to Inverlochy,—one by Athole and the heights of Badenoch, another by sailing there from Greenock round the west coast. The former, though shorter and more direct, was impassable from want of roads and provisions, before the middle of June; whereas, the latter would be open at any time after the end of March; and on that account was recommended in preference by the General in his letters to the court. These, however, being treated with the usual neglect, he had recourse to another expedient, and moved, in council, that a detachment of 600 chosen men should be embarked at Greenock on small armed vessels, victualled for three months, which should serve the double purpose of carrying implements and materials for building the fort, together with stones and provisions for the support of the garrison, and supply of the expected frigates after their arrival at Inverlochy. Their lordships assented, and wrote to Lord Melville, approving of the new plan, and soliciting the means for carrying it into effect, which were accordingly promised; but this, like other promises, appears to have been no more thought of, so powerful was the sinister influence of the faction behind the throne.

The General having had occasion to be in the west country about this time, to see the Danish horse embarked for Ireland, had an interview with the magistrates of Glasgow, to whom he communicated his difficulties in carrying on the service, particularly the Inverlochy expedition, and requesting their aid. This patriotic body, setting a noble example of disinterestedness to the other corporations of the kingdom, immediately complied, and engaged to furnish, on their own credit, ships, stores, and pro-

* Memoirs, p. 81.

1690. visions, with a variety of other articles necessary for the expedition. These would, in all probability, have been neglected, had it been left to the government, whose duty it was to supply them; and thus a month at least would have been lost, and the design frustrated.

Finding, on his return to Edinburgh, no reply from the court to his last representation, he felt not a little chagrined, but was not to be diverted from his purpose, judging that, engaged as he was in the cause of religion and liberty, it would be a dereliction of duty to desist while even a possibility remained of attaining his object. He therefore resolved to make one attempt more to open the eyes of the King and his ministers to a sense of the danger of thus continuing to neglect his Scottish affairs, particularly during his Majesty's intended absence in Ireland. This, and similar arguments, the General urged in strong terms, "being willing" (to use his own words) " that his free and hard language might have one of two effects,—either that the service be better provided for, or himself removed from the command; though he rather desired the former, because he was sensible that another of much more capacity and knowledge could not comprehend that sort of service, nor execute the designs which he had formed, so well as himself: for, besides that he had been already twelve months engaged against the enemy; being a Highlander by birth, and of a family which had formerly special correspondence and good understanding with all the Highlanders now in rebellion, he had better ways to know their numbers, interests, and inclinations, and so more able to take sure measures than others."*

Whether any, or what effect the freedom of this letter produced, cannot now be ascertained, as the General's Memoirs terminate at this period; but that it did produce some effect, may be inferred from a fact incidentally mentioned in a fragment appended to the Memoirs, from which it appears that he received about this time, by special order from his Majesty, a remittance of L.4000 in aid of his expedition.

While his letter, to which this was a reply, was on its way to London,

* Memoirs, p. 87.

Lord Melville arrived at Edinburgh, and it seems no breach of charity to 1690 suppose that if he had remained near the King, the remittance had never been made. He came down from court decorated with an earl's coronet, and invested with two of the highest dignities in the state, that of commissioner to represent his Majesty in parliament, and that of sole secretary of state for Scotland; at the same time that his eldest son, Lord Raith, was at the head of the treasury, and his second son, the Earl of Leven, colonel of a regiment, and even then aspired to the chief command of the forces. The new Earl thus became more than prime minister of the kingdom, engrossing in his own person, or in his family, such an accumulation of places of power and emolument, as has never, perhaps, fallen to the lot of any other individual.

So many honours conferred on the lord secretary, augured ill for the General's measures, as they indicated the increasing influence of the faction opposed to him. Though not deeply skilled in the classics, he had read and studied the book of nature, and in it found such sentiments as these, *tu ne cede malis, sed contra audentior ito ;* and *justum et tenacem propositi virum,* &c. Encouraged by such maxims, and supported, above all, by his firm persuasion that the blessing of Heaven would, in answer to the many prayers daily offered up by protestants throughout all Europe, finally enable their cause to prosper in Scotland, to which all good protestants now looked with an anxious eye.

The General took the earliest opportunity, after his arrival at Edinburgh, to pay his respects to his Grace the commissioner, and notwithstanding what he knew of his ill disposition towards himself and his measures, communicated to him, without reserve, the designs he had formed for subduing the Highlanders. One of the chief matters of detail discussed at their conference, was the appointment of a commissary of stores and provisions. Many inconveniences had been experienced in former campaigns, from the want of such an officer; and great advantage was found to result, even at the close of the last campaign, from the appointment of an officer thoroughly qualified for the situation. He

1690. therefore moved in council, that the same gentleman should be re-appointed, but was overruled—his colleagues having, out of deference to the commissioner, left the nomination to his Grace; who, notwithstanding the General's repeated remonstrance, suffered five or six weeks to elapse before he made up his mind, and at length appointed a creature of his own, wholly unfit for the duties of the office. To this person the General immediately handed over the L.4000, remitted to him by the King, some weeks before, to prevent the possibility of suspicion of its misapplication in his hands. Such a manifestation of integrity on his part, being, at the same time, an act of conciliation towards the commissioner, might have been expected to abate somewhat of his Grace's hostility; but far from producing such an effect, it seemed rather to sharpen it into rancour. Before proceeding farther with our narrative, it may therefore be proper to endeavour to trace this unfortunate difference between the secretary and the commander-in-chief to its origin, which was as follows:—

Soon after Mackay's first arrival in Edinburgh, he had an interview with Tarbat, at which was discussed the subject of the disaffection of the Highland chiefs, its causes and consequences, with the most likely means of putting an end to it. Tarbat declared himself decidedly of opinion, that their disaffection proceeded neither from the love of King James, nor from the hatred of William's cause, but solely from such self-interested motives as generally influence the conduct of the greater part of mankind. Between the Earls of Argyle, he observed, and the neighbouring chiefs, Macleans, Macdonalds, &c. there had existed feuds of long standing, which were exasperated during the reign of Charles II., by the grants of the Argyle forfeited lands to some of the chiefs; and as the present Earl attached himself to the cause of William, and accompanied him from Holland, it was of course concluded that he would now have interest with his Majesty, to obtain a resumption of the lands in question; and hence the apprehensions of the chiefs.

Tarbat therefore suggested the idea of buying off Argyle's claims, and distributing money among the chiefs, which would have the effect of quieting their fears, and reconciling them to the new government. This appearing to the General a rational plan, he communicated it to Portland, and Portland to the King, who, in consequence sent down instructions to Melville for carrying it into effect. The person selected for conducting the negociation, was the Laird of Calder, a Campbell unfortunately by name, and a relative of the Earl of Argyle.* The chiefs therefore, having no confidence in his impartiality, declined treating with him; and thus the project fell to the ground at that time, but was now revived, and strenuously supported by Melville and Tarbat.

The General, though at first favourable to the measure, now opposed it; the experience of the last twelve months having convinced him of the utter inefficacy of all such schemes, and of the mercenary motives by which their abettors were actuated. Melville, though a man of mean abilities, and contracted views, was nevertheless ambitious of the character of a statesman, to which he had no just pretensions. He looked forward to the prospect of placing his son Leven, at the head of the Scottish army; preparatory to which, that young lord was most indecently placed before the Generals Mackay and Monro, in the commission for remodelling it. To him it was a motive sufficient for opposing the plan of subjugating the Highlanders by force, that it had been proposed by Mackay; and he favoured the other, because, if it succeeded, he would himself have the credit of its success, and would thus find it easier to undermine Mackay, and pave the way for his son's elevation to the chief command. Tarbat encouraged Melville in his extravagant notions of his own importance, well knowing that in his hands he was but a puppet, which he could move at pleasure; that if the plan of buying off the Highlanders with money succeeded, he should participate with Melville in its advantages; and that if, on the other hand, King James's party finally prevailed, he could with truth allege, that it was owing to Mackay's scheme of coercion having been frustrated through his and Melville's advice.

Having been dismissed, as already mentioned, from all his employments

* Memoirs, p. 19.

1690. at the Revolution, he had not yet succeeded in being restored to royal favour, notwithstanding the impression his insinuating manners and fascinating address, had made even on the cold and phlegmatic temperament of William. But though apparently excluded from council, he might be said to be present at its deliberations, and even to dictate its proceedings,—in the person of his cousin and representative Melville; thus occupying the unconstitutional, and, in a free state, the dangerous position of an irresponsible minister of the crown.

The most important question agitated in council after Melville's arrival, was that regarding the best method of subjugating the rebellious clans. The General inflexibly adhered to his Inverlochy project, and plan of coercion connected with it; this was vehemently opposed by Melville and Tarbat, who supported the opposite measure, of purchasing the allegiance of their chiefs with money.

To carry this last measure into effect, the junta proposed to send a private agent into the Highlands, with powers to treat with the chiefs for laying down their arms, and submitting to the government. The person selected for this negociation, was a certain Colonel Hill, who had commanded at Inverlochy, under Cromwell, and who, from his superior sagacity and long residence among the Highlanders, was supposed a fit person to treat with them. Having been accordingly sent for to Edinburgh from Ireland, where he had for some time been employed, after many conferences with the two lords, which were carefully concealed from the General, he was privately despatched by them to the Highlands, and so well was the secret kept, that he had been eight days gone from Edinburgh, ere the General was aware of his departure. He returned, however, sooner than was expected, having totally failed in accomplishing the object of his mission, and from that period became a convert to the superior efficacy of Mackay's plan, fully convinced, that without force, no impression could be made on the Highland chiefs.

This opinion coming from a man perfectly disinterested, and so well qualified by his local knowledge and experience, to form a correct judgment on the subject, confirmed the General in his opinion of the soundness of his own views. He therefore resolved on making a last attempt to open the eyes of his sovereign, to a juster apprehension of his true interests, and for this purpose to send an intelligent and confidential officer, thoroughly acquainted with his designs, to Chester, where his Majesty was expected to arrive, about this time, (18th May,) in his way to Ireland; and such an officer he fortunately now had on his staff, in the capacity of adjutant-general. It will be recollected, that one of the grievances he had to complain of, during his last year's campaigns, was the want of a regular staff, particularly of an adjutant-general, to manage the details of the army; and having had experience of the qualifications of Captain Hill of Leven's regiment, he recommended that he should be appointed to that office. This was accordingly complied with; it being one of the few instances in which his recommendations were attended to by the government; and Hill's conduct since his appointment, fully justified the choice. It was this officer whom he selected for the delicate and important mission to the King, in which, also, Hill acquitted himself to his entire satisfaction. He proceeded to Chester, without delay, furnished with plans of Inverlochy, and maps of the adjoining districts, with every other document requisite for the elucidation of the subject of his mission.

1690.

No sooner had Hill set out, than Melville and Tarbat, dreading a renewal of Mackay's influence with the king, took the alarm, and in order to counteract him, despatched to Chester no less a personage than the Earl of Breadalbane,* lately associated as the third member of their triumvirate, trusting

* George, sixth Earl of Caithness, being a weak man, and involved in pecuniary difficulties, sold his title and estate to his principal creditor, Sir John Campbell of Glenorchy,—reserving to himself his life interest in both. After his death, Campbell, having obtained a royal patent recognising his right to the peerage, assumed the title of Earl of Caithness; but this being afterwards set aside, at the instance of George Sinclair of Keiss, heir-male of the family,— Campbell had interest at court, 1681, to get another patent creating him Earl of Breadalbane. He divided the estate into lots, which he sold by degrees, and thereby greatly enriched himself. Returning to his own country of Breadalbane, and being a man of intrigue, he contrived to sow the seeds of dissension among his neighbours, and engaged them in expensive law-

1690. that his high rank, and vast possessions in the Highlands, would give weight to his representations. In this, however, they found themselves deceived; for the King now began to awaken from the dream into which he had been lulled, through the suggestions of his false councillors; he saw his error in withdrawing his confidence from his old and faithful servant, Mackay, and, even at the eleventh hour, resolved to retrace his steps.

The mind of King William, though one of no ordinary capacity, appears sometimes to have been distracted with the multiplicity of his cares.

suits, which ended in their finding it necessary to sell their estates to him, at an undervalue, thus greatly enlarging his already extensive territories. He hated the Macdonalds, particularly the unfortunate Laird of Glenco, and was alleged to have devised the insidious measures which led to the fatal massacre. Criminal proceedings, on account of this transaction, were instituted against him in parliament, which, however, he found means to elude, and was never brought to trial. He is also said to have been the original author of what has been called, Tarbat's plan for buying off the Highland chiefs; and it was to him its execution was ultimately committed. Connected with this subject, a curious anecdote is related in Sir John Dalrymple's Memoirs. A sum of £12,000 having been remitted to Breadalbane, for the purpose just mentioned, he was called on for an account of its expenditure, some years after, by the Earl of Nottingham, and made this characteristic reply,—"the Highlanders are quiet, the money is spent, and between friends, this is the best way of accounting for it." Though at heart, no friend to the Revolution settlement, he never avowed any hostility to it, till 1715, when, in the eightieth year of his age, and last of his life, he sent 500 of his vassals to join the Earl of Marr. John Mackay's characters, though sometimes overcharged, must have had their foundation in truth; and having besides been expressly drawn up for the information of the princess Sophia, are entitled to some credit. Of Breadalbane, he says, that he was "grave as a Spaniard, wise as a serpent, cunning as a fox, and slippery as an eel. No government can trust him, but where his own private interest is in view," &c.

Such was Breadalbane, a large participator in Melville and Tarbat's bitter enmity to Mackay, and their persevering coadjutor in factious opposition to his measures. Of these lords, Melville, Tarbat, and Breadalbane, the two last were born commoners—all the three died Earls; while Mackay, notwithstanding his important public services, lived and died a commoner. It is probable, however, that he too, in spite of their enmity, would have died an Earl, had he survived his last campaign, as, in that case, it was King William's intention to raise him to the peerage, by the title of Earl of Scoury. It pleased God to order it otherwise; and thus, if a pun might be pardoned on such an occasion, Mackay could say at his departure, "me nemo ministro fur erat, atque ideo nulli comes exeo."

Neither he nor his favourite minister, Portland, ever understood the affairs of Scotland, or duly appreciated their importance, and they therefore surrendered themselves the more readily to the guidance of Melville and his faction. Hence that procrastination and indecision so inconsistent with the general character of William, but which too often may be perceived in the administration of his Scottish affairs. The film now dropt from his eyes, he resolved to change his measures accordingly; and having once done so, inflexibly adhered to his purpose. He dismissed Hill, with peremptory orders to the council to supply the General with men, money, ships, and provisions, with every thing, in short, which he should judge necessary, not only for his projected expedition, and the building of the fort, but also for the ulterior measures which he recommended.

Nothing could be more complete, or more gratifying to Mackay, and mortifying to the pride of the faction opposed to him, than the victory which he thus obtained; and he was too experienced a tactician not to follow up and improve it without delay. Thus armed with the authority and express commands of his Sovereign, which he knew, his enemies dared not openly oppose, he proceeded with alacrity to complete his preparations, and gave immediate orders for the mustering of the forces destined for his expedition. Having appointed Perth as the first place of rendezvous, he proceeded thither, on the 18th of June, and on the 22d began his march through Athole towards Badenoch. Arriving there on the 27th, and being joined by reinforcements from Inverness, he advanced towards Inverlochy; and on the 3d July reached that place without opposition, at the head of an army of about 3000, horse and foot.

Here he found before him a small armament, consisting of three frigates, and 600 soldiers, (as already mentioned,) under the command of two active and intelligent officers, Major Ferguson,* and Captain Pottenger

---

* Ancestor of the present Laird of Kinmundy. He afterwards rose to the rank of Lieutenant-general, and served with reputation in Marlborough's wars. It is related of him, that, before he attained to this rank, having been appointed to guard a party of prisoners, superior in number to his own, to a place situated at a considerable distance, he fell on the

1690. of the navy, who, notwithstanding the £4000 paid over by the General into the hands of the commissary, were detained five weeks at Greenock for want of supplies, so that they arrived at Inverlochy only a few days before him. They were, however, furnished with an ample stock of provisions, and materials for building the proposed fort, which henceforth was to be called Fort William, in honour of his Majesty. The General was not altogether satisfied with the situation of the old fort, it being commanded by a hill in the near neighbourhood; but as the foundation of the walls still remained, and as no better situation could be found, he contented himself with repairing the old fortification. Such was the alacrity of the two branches of the service, that they vied with each other under the immediate eye of the General, and in eleven days erected works which he judged sufficient to defend the garrison against any attack of the Highlanders. On the 17th of July, while in the act of fitting out a small squadron to cruise among the islands, and watch the motions of the inhabitants, he received a letter from the council, communicating in exaggerated terms the disaster which had befallen the English fleet, with their apprehensions of the enemy landing in the sister kingdom, and for these reasons ordering his immediate return with the army. This sudden call gave him no surprise; and indeed he was prepared for it, well knowing the disinclination of the commissioner and the council from the first towards the Inverlochy project. He promptly obeyed, and the very next day commenced his retrograde march, leaving behind him 1000 men in the garrison, with a sufficient stock of provisions and materials for completing the works. On the 20th, he arrived in Badenoch and proceeded by easy marches to Perth, which he reached without encountering any obstruction from the enemy.

The idea of erecting a fortress at Inverlochy, originally projected by the sagacity of Cromwell, and now revived and more completely executed

following curious, but effectual method of securing them. He ordered the latchets of their breeches to be cut, which obliged them to march with one hand behind to keep them up.—See *Mackay's History of the Clan Mackay*, p. 464.

by Mackay, has been productive of results far beyond what could have been anticipated. It may be considered as the first of a series of coercive measures, which, by breaking the predatory and lawless habits of the Highlanders, gradually prepared them alike for civilized warfare and for the arts of peace. The military roads commenced by government, soon after the rebellion of 1715, opened up their country to strangers, and introduced a civilizing intercourse between the mountaineers and their southern neighbours. The salutary measure suggested by Lord President Forbes, of abolishing the hereditary jurisdiction of the feudal chiefs over their vassals, which was happily carried through in 1748, gradually brought both under subjection to the authority of law. Lord Chatham accelerated their civilization, by throwing open to their chiefs the gates of military preferment, and thereby amalgamating them with their fellow subjects, of the same rank in the south. " I sought for merit" (said that great statesman and orator, in his speech on the repeal of the stamp act,) I sought for merit wheresoever it could be found. It is my boast that I was the first minister who looked for it, and found it in the mountains of the north. I called it forth, and drew into your service a hardy and intrepid race of men; men who, when left by your jealousy, became a prey to the artifices of your enemies, and had gone nigh to have overturned the state, in the war before the last. These men, in the last war, were brought to combat on your side; they served with fidelity, as they fought with valour, and conquered for you in every quarter of the world. Detested be the national prejudices against them; they are unjust, groundless, illiberal, unmanly."

It may be added, that ever since this wise act of Lord Chatham's administration, disloyalty to the house of Hanover has been gradually disappearing in the Highlands, and is now wholly extinct.

The good effects of the minor garrisons which the General had sprinkled over the borders of the West Highlands, together with his other judicious measures, had already begun to appear, and would by this time have been still more conspicuous, but for the secret counteraction, or the languid support he experienced from his colleagues in the council. To this

1690. cause must be ascribed, the studied delays which retarded the sailing of Ferguson and Pottenger's armament, and which, by thus leaving the coast defenceless, afforded King James an opportunity of throwing in reinforcements from Ireland. In one of these, Major General Buchan came over with forty officers, and a commission to supersede Cannon in the chief command. He landed in the month of March on the Isle of Mull, that focus of disaffection to the new government, and proceeded to Lochaber, expecting to be joined in considerable numbers by the Highlanders of that district, but regretted to find that their loyalty had much abated since last year. They were chagrined at the repeated disappointment of their hopes of aid from the exiled monarch, and could scarcely consider the handful of men he had sent over with Buchan, as redeeming his royal pledge. They knew, from experience, the incapacity of Cannon, and placed no confidence in Buchan. On the other hand, they now learned to appreciate more justly than heretofore, the vigilance and activity of Mackay. They were aware of his intention to plant a garrison in the heart of their country, which filled them with immediate apprehensions for the safety of their dwellings, and would ultimately, they foresaw, put an end to their plundering occupation; and hence the tardiness with which they joined Buchan's standard. That commander resolved, therefore, to quit the west coast, and try his fortune in the east, in the hope of finding more loyalty among the Gordons and the other clans well affected to his cause, in the shires of Aberdeen and Banff. The garrison in Blair castle excluded him from the usual route through Athole, and left him none other than that by the way of Badenoch and Strathspey, in which direction accordingly he marched at the head of about 1200* Highlanders and Irish, and arrived at Cromdale in Strathspey, on the 30th of April.†

* The Highlanders were Macleans, Macdonalds, Macphersons, Camerons, and Grants of Glenmorriston.—*Shaw's Province of Moray.*

† In marching through Strathspey, the Highlanders plundered the country, and in passing towards Strathbogie, burnt the house of Edinglassie, for which Sir George Gordon, the proprietor, made severe reprisals; having, on their return, seized and hanged eighteen of their

Sir Thomas Livingstone, who commanded at Inverness, and was 1690. specially charged with the duty of watching the motions of the rebels, had instructions from the commander-in-chief, to hold himself in readiness to take the field against Buchan, so soon as he should hear of his being in motion. He accordingly marched towards Strathspey with about 1200 horse and foot, and so accurate were his calculations, that he reached Cromdale the day after Buchan's arrival in that quarter. For this accuracy, he was indebted to intelligence concerning the motions of the enemy, which he received from an officer who commanded a company of Grant's regiment in Balloch castle, now castle Grant, principal residence of the Grant family, near Cromdale. This officer, though young in the service, with great judgment and presence of mind, locked the gates of the castle the day he expected Livingstone, to prevent the egress of some country gentlemen and their followers, who had taken refuge there on the approach of the enemy, and who, if now permitted to depart, might, even without any ill intention, be the means of informing Buchan that Livingstone was at hand.

The last-mentioned officer, finding himself, in the dusk of the evening, within two miles of Balloch castle, and his men weary after a long and fatiguing march, would gladly have remained there for the night, had the ground been convenient for encampment. Between him and the castle, there lay a difficult pass, which he would have hesitated to enter in the darkness of night, and without more precise knowledge of the position of the enemy, had he not been persuaded thereto by one of his officers, who undertook to be his guide, and on whose fidelity, as well as knowledge of the country, he could rely. Having, accordingly, entered the pass, he had the good fortune to clear it at two, next morning, and was speedily joined by Captain Grant, the commandant, who pointed out the camp lights of the enemy, at a moderate distance, on the other side of the Spey,—and volunteered to

number on the trees in his garden.—*Grant's edition of Shaw's History of the Province of Moray*, p. 270.

1690. guide him by a covered way, down the river side, to a ford where he could cross unperceived.

Livingstone having inquired, whether his men were willing to endure a little more fatigue, rather than lose the favourable opportunity now presented to them, of attacking the enemy; they unanimously responded, that they were, and requested to be led immediately to the charge. Their brave commander joyfully complied; and, after giving them half an hour for refreshment, conducted them across the river without opposition. What follows is borrowed from an author, of whose powers of description, the reader has already had a specimen. " As Livingstone," says Mr. Chambers, p. 131, " moved forward from the bank of the Spey, he observed the Highlanders at length begin to bestir themselves, and even to move off in little parties, towards the hills. Immediately galloping up with his horse, and with a band of Highlanders,* who are said to have run with even superior speed, he attempted to get betwixt them and the hill, so as to intercept their flight. The Highlanders, roused suddenly from their beds, and without any clothes, were observed, through the misty dawn, running in all directions throughout the streets of the village, and the level grounds in the neighbourhood; some perfectly panic-struck, and disposed to get off on any terms, but the greater part fighting stoutly with sword and target, as they retired. Livingstone's troops, horse and foot, mingled fiercely with them, and did great execution. * * * * * *
The very commanders themselves, the redoubted Buchan and Cannon, were almost as much taken by surprise; and the one had only his shirt and night-cap, while the other was without sword, hat, and coat. At length, after fighting their way across the plains, the mountaineers reached the bottom of the hills, which they forthwith began to ascend with wonderful nimbleness. A dense mist happened at the time to hang a good way

---

* The Highlanders here mentioned were the Mackays,—brisk Highlanders, (to use the General's phrase) whom he had taken into the service the preceding year, and formed into an independent company, of which he gave the command to his cousin, Hugh Mackay, younger of Borley, grand-uncle of the writer of these pages.

down the steeps; and in its dim bosom the naked Highlanders escaped from the chase of the pursuing horse, like men received up into the clouds." Mr. Chambers adds, that a considerable number were slain on both sides, in which however, so far as regards Livingstone's side, he must be mistaken. General Mackay expressly states in his Memoirs,* (which were doubtless drawn up from Livingstone's official report,) that he lost seven horses, but no men; and that of the Highlanders, about 400 were killed or taken prisoners. But for the fog, the loss of the latter would have been much greater, as they were hotly pursued by Livingstone, and his spirited young major the Honourable Æneas Mackay, with their dragoons, followed by the main body both of horse and foot.

1690.

The General, who, in his Memoirs, never fails to draw the attention of his reader to the overruling providence of God, whenever it appears to him to interpose in behalf of his cause, observes on this occasion that such interposition was signally manifested; and this remark he grounds on the three following considerations. First, the prudent foresight of the young officer commanding in Balloch castle, who, to prevent the transmission of intelligence to Buchan, concerning Livingstone's near approach, ordered the gates to be locked the day he was expected. Secondly, Buchan's ignorance of Livingstone's being so near, which induced him to commit the egregious blunder of quitting the strong ground inaccessible to horse, which he occupied in the morning, to spread himself on the plain below, where horse could act with effect; being thus led as it were like an ox to the slaughter. Thirdly, Livingstone's uncertainty, both as to the exact situation of his enemy, and the difficulties of the pass, which, had he been fully aware of, he would not, even under the guidance of an officer in whom he confided, risk entering it at the dead hour of night, and yet if he had not so risked, he would have foregone the advantages of his bloodless victory next morning.

Here then were three individuals, Grant, Buchan, and Livingstone, of whom two at least, if not all, were unconnected with each other, and yet

* P. 96.

1690. we have seen them acting in concert as if they had been previously leagued to accomplish a common design ; in so much, that if any one of the three had acted differently, the design must have inevitably failed. If Grant had not locked the gates of the castle, intelligence of Livingstone's approach would in all probability have been conveyed to Buchan, and have put him on his guard ;—had not this General imprudently quitted his strong ground, Livingstone would not have ventured to attack him at such a disadvantage ;—and, finally, had the latter, from what motive soever, declined to enter the pass at midnight, he could not possibly have overtaken Buchan in his bed. All the three, therefore, may be considered as so many links of the chain, by which the unseen hand of Providence conducted the enterprize.

After this disgraceful defeat, the Jacobite commanders, with the wreck of their forces, broken and dispirited, retreated as they best could to their fastnesses in the hills, and were no more heard of, till Mackay was occupied at Inverlochy; to whose history we now return. They seized the opportunity of his absence, to steal through by-ways into the low country, with about 200 horse, consisting partly of gentlemen and their servants. Buchan took the direction of Aberdeenshire, Cannon that of Stirling, after being joined by three or four hundred Rannoch men, addicted to plunder.

This fresh irruption, together with the apprehension of a rising on the borders, gave great alarm to the commissioner and the council; who, though they had a large disposable military force at their command, took no steps to check the progress of the marauders, but tamely suffered them to rob the houses of the friends to government, within four miles of Stirling.*

Such was the state of affairs when the General returned to Perth from Inverlochy, and found himself involved in various perplexities. In the *materiel* of the army, there were several wants and defects, which he saw and felt, but had not the power to remedy. During his absence, many

* Memoirs, p. 109.

things were neglected, which he expected to find prepared for the accommodation and refreshment of his troops, exhausted by fatiguing marches, and incessant labour, in the wilds and moist climate of Lochaber. A commissary-general had been appointed some months before, but the provision department was still so much neglected, that Perth, though the principal military station in Scotland, was unable to furnish even a few cwts. of biscuit, till procured from Dundee. On the 28th July, the General wrote to the council, as follows:—" Your Grace and Lordships should consider that it is an unsupportable burden to me to have the care of those things, for 'tis impossible for me to exercise my thoughts effectually how to dispose the forces to the most advantage to the service, if I be obliged to give directions for, and solicit all things that may be found requisite for the particular detail and economy of them; therefore, to make the service go on well, it ought to be made as easy for any who happen to have the chief command of the forces, as possible; otherwise he shall necessarily neglect the chief part and end thereof, which is to contrive how to make use of them to the most advancement of the service. Your Grace and Lordships, therefore, should establish the committee of war, which I proposed, to inspect the letters and propositions which I have written, and hereafter may happen to make or write, that no delay be made in the things essential to the present service and juncture; for, though I have the design and will, —I thank God for it—good and sound in this matter, my spirit and body cannot support the weight of all; and necessarily many things must be neglected, if I should be charged therewith."*

The King was now in Ireland, and had recently gained the battle of the Boyne, which gave the first deadly blow to the cause of James, and promised the final expulsion from his throne, of that infatuated monarch. To complete the subjugation of that kingdom, much, however, yet remained to be done; which the General foresaw would probably require the withdrawing of some more English regiments from Scotland; and though the statements of the

* Memoirs, p. 341.

1689. commissioner in his last conversation* on that subject, were doubtless exaggerated, England could not be said to be free from all apprehension of a French invasion. Hence a double duty now devolved on the General,—that of keeping his forces in such a compact state, as to be removable to England with the least inconvenience, in case of a sudden call from the Queen, who had been invested with the regency during the King's absence; and that of completing the reduction of the refractory Highlanders.

To the latter, as his more immediate duty, he would have first directed his attention, had he not been prevented from taking the field, by want of provisions. It was of the utmost consequence, to have correct information as to the probability of an invasion, that he might regulate his measures accordingly. He could not rely with implicit confidence on the statements of the council on this subject, and therefore wrote to his old friend, the Earl of Marlborough, for information and advice, but received no answer, owing to that celebrated commander being called to Ireland about this time.

Buchan, as already mentioned, took the direction of Aberdeen, with a few horse; but, having been chased from that shire by the master of Forbes, fell back on Cannon, whom he met retreating from Stirling; and, after uniting their forces, they re-entered Aberdeenshire together. Here they were joined by Farquharson of Inverey, with five or six hundred Highlanders; and thus reinforced, they left 160 men to block up and starve the garrison of Abergeldie,—descending with the rest to the low country, where they expected to be joined by gentlemen favourable to their cause. They were, however, opposed by the master of Forbes, and Lieutenant-colonel Jackson; but these officers, deceived by a stratagem of Buchan's, were led to believe his numbers greater than the truth, and retreated with precipitation towards Aberdeen. The Jacobite commanders pursued, and

* The General having waited on the commissioner to take leave, previously to his departure for Inverlochy, his Grace spoke of plots hatching against the government, and reiterated his disapproval of withdrawing so large a portion of the military force to such a distance as Inverlochy, at the present juncture, when the kingdom was threatened with a French invasion, &c.

were joined in the pursuit by several noblemen and gentlemen of that county, who had not till then openly declared themselves.

1690.

The General receiving notice of this mischance, despatched Colonel Cunningham with a strong detachment of horse and foot, to join Jackson, but found that the enemy, emboldened by success, advanced so far as to prevent the junction of these two officers. Without waiting, therefore, any longer for the expected despatches from Marlborough, he marched northward himself, at the head of Livingstone's dragoons and 1400 Dutch foot, in all haste, without baggage or provisions. Arriving at the castle of Aboyne, he left Cunningham there to cover the march of Jackson, and turned aside himself to relieve the garrison of Abergeldie.

Inverey, true to his cause, and nowise intimidated by the severe retaliatory measure, which the General judged it his duty to inflict on him a few months before, boldly came out with 200 Highlanders, trusting the roughness of the ground would impede the advance of horse. Major Mackay, however, with 60 dragoons, promptly defeated him, killing or taking prisoners almost the whole of his party, the brave laird himself escaping with his life, though he had been under the horses feet, and left for dead on the field. The General then proceeded to relieve his garrison, and victualled it without further opposition. He respected the intrepidity of Inverey, but considered it necessary, for the safety of the garrison, to burn and lay waste the surrounding country for several miles, a measure from which his nature recoiled, but which was nevertheless sanctioned by the laws of war, and justified by the circumstances of the case.

After he had thus provided for the security of Abergeldie, and was preparing to march in another direction, he received such intelligence concerning the motions and probable designs of Buchan and Cannon, as induced him to follow them immediately into the shires of Moray and Inverness. Leaving his foot behind, with orders to return to Aberdeen for provisions within three days, if not previously called for by him, he pursued with his cavalry alone. Passing rapidly through the intermediate

1690. shires of Banff, Moray, and Nairn, he arrived within a few miles of the town of Inverness, when he was believed to be fully occupied in Aberdeenshire, and not the least suspicion entertained of his approach.

He found the enemy posted near the town, waiting for the junction of the Earl of Seaforth and his followers, from the opposite shire of Ross, to commence the meditated attack on the garrison. His unexpected arrival disconcerted their schemes, and threw them all into a state of confusion and alarm. Buchan and Cannon suddenly decamped, and retreated with precipitation by the north side of Lochness into Lochaber; nor did they venture ever after to shew their faces in those parts.

Seaforth had come down from his usual residence at Brahan castle, to another mansion of his near Chanonry, full of hopes from the prospect of his junction with his auxiliaries. Intimidated, however, by Mackay's sudden appearance, and Buchan's retreat, he lost all hopes, and sent two of his friends to the General with offers of submission, and whatever security might be required for his peaceable conduct in future. The General replied that he could accept no other security than the surrender of his person, and conjured him to comply, as he valued his own safety, and the preservation of his family and people, assuring him that in case of his surrender, he should be detained in civil custody at Inverness, and treated with the respect due to his rank, till the pleasure of the government should be known. Next day, the Countess-dowager* presented herself, accompanied by the Laird of Coul,† to plead for a mitigation of the terms proposed to her son; but finding the General inflexible, she yielded, stipulating only that, to save her son's credit, the arresting party should be sent during the night, to give the appearance of his being taken by surprise.

The General promised compliance; and in order the more clearly to demonstrate his kindly feeling towards the Earl, sent the party under the

---

* Isabella, third daughter of Sir John Mackenzie of Tarbat, sister of George, first Earl of Cromarty, and widow of Kenneth, third Earl of Seaforth.

† Sir Alexander Mackenzie, the second baronet of the family, ancestor of the present Sir George Stuart Mackenzie of Coul.

command of his nephew, Major Mackay, second cousin to the Earl. 1690. Before morning, however, his lordship changed his mind, and declined to fulfil his promise of surrender, on the plea of ill health, and inability to endure confinement. The General provoked and irritated by such vacillating conduct, declared that, if he did not forthwith surrender according to his promise, he should, in conformity with his instructions from the council, enter his country with fire and sword, and seize all property belonging to himself or his vassals, as lawful prize.

Lest it should be suspected, that this was a threat not intended to be executed, he immediately ordered the three Dutch regiments from Aberdeen to Inverness, and resolved to go himself with a competent body of horse and foot, withdrawn from that garrison, to take possession of Brahan castle, the principal seat of the Seaforth family. He also wrote to the lords Sutherland and Reay, and Laird of Balnagown, to send 1000 of their men, who were to be commanded by Major Wishart, a discreet and experienced officer, well acquainted with the country, to quarter on the more remote Highland estates belonging to Seaforth; and to take, burn, and destroy, should it be necessary to have recourse to that dreadful extremity. These rigorous threats had the effect of opening the eyes of the hitherto misguided Earl, who, almost at the last hour, surrendered, and thus relieved the General from the most painful duty, perhaps, he ever had to perform.

It had been his lot to witness, and sometimes even to be a reluctant actor in similar scenes, on the Continent; but the sufferers were entire strangers to him. Here the case was different; for, though not immediately connected with the Seaforth family himself, some of his near relatives were, both by the ties of kindred, and of ancient friendship. For these, and other reasons, it may be conceived, what joy, and thankfulness to Providence, he felt for the result of this affair, which at once relieved him from a distressing dilemma, and promised to put a speedy period to his labours in Scotland.

From the commissioner and council, he received a letter, communicat-

1690. ing in flattering terms, their approval of his proceedings, and authorizing him, either to detain the Earl in custody at Inverness, or send him prisoner to Edinburgh. He preferred the latter; and on the 7th October, ordered the Earl to be conveyed under a proper guard to the seat of government. He was lodged in the castle, and remained there in close confinement till January 1692, when he was liberated on bail under certain restrictions, and not long after followed King James to France, where he died in 1701.

The author of this feeble attempt, to do that justice to the military character of General Mackay, which has hitherto been either denied to, or withheld from him, cannot conclude this narrative of his proceedings, in terms more appropriate than those of an author, from whom he has already so often borrowed, and who, notwithstanding certain lurking partialities to the opposite cause, never mentions the name of Mackay, (one or two instances excepted) but in terms of the highest praise. "It was now evident" says Mr. Chambers,* "that the war was expiring. To complete the depression of the jacobite party, King James lost Ireland on the 1st of July, by his celebrated defeat at the Boyne; and Mackay, about the middle of the same month, planted an overwhelming garrison at Inverlochy. The friends of the exiled Monarch then fairly gave up heart. Overhung by ships on their coasts, by garrisons in the bowels of their country, and large detachments of regular troops at all its extremities, they were forced to remain perfectly still, at the immediate hazard of life itself, or of drawing down a vengeance, almost as much to be deprecated, upon the heads of those defenceless persons, in whom they were interested. Utterly despairing of any redemption of their affairs by external succour, they at length, early in 1691, sent the Earl of Dunfermline to King James, with a request that he would permit them, by a temporary and visible acknowledgment of the new government, to preserve themselves in the meantime, and retain that strength which might afterwards be employed in his service, at a more befitting opportunity. The distressed Monarch quickly gave them the license they wanted; and accordingly, commissioners being ap-

* P. 132.

pointed by King William to receive their submission, they held a meeting 1690. with them at Achalader in Glenorchy; where in consideration of certain indemnifying sums being disbursed to them, as a compensation for their resignation of the Argyle, and other estates, they agreed to live as peaceable subjects to the sovereign *de facto* receiving from him in return the usual protection of the state, and continuing to enjoy all their valued patrimonial privileges. Before the end of January 1692, all the heads of clans had ratified their submission in terms of this treaty."

Having thus concluded our narrative of General Mackay's military operations in Scotland, it is impossible to refrain from expressing our surprise, at the very limited support he received from the aristocracy of the kingdom. The south, and south-west, being well affected to the Revolution, his operations were chiefly confined to the Highland shires of Perth, Inverness, Argyle, and part of Stirling; and to the east coast extending from Dundee, to the town of Inverness. In all of these he remarked "an amazing degree of apathy and indifference," to the recent deliverance which God had wrought for them, from the greatest of all evils, temporal and eternal slavery, the least whereof was sufficient to make the heathens venture all, rather than submit to it. But Scotland was at this time sufficiently prepared for the yoke, both by the Popish design, for the introduction whereof the laws must needs be removed out of the way, which proved an obstacle; by the clergy, who, to favour such designs, must be chosen such as would preach what might serve to the purpose, and by the ministers of state, particularly the secretaries, who follow closely (and refine at every change, according to the capacity of the person,) upon Lauderdale's maxim of governing that kingdom by absolute power."

That the degree of amazement the General expresses was not excessive, will appear if we take a retrospective survey of his progress through the country, and mark the names of the few patriots who supported him, as well as those of the principal persons who were opposed to him. In Perthshire, the Marquis of Athole, at first a doubtful friend, afterwards an avowed and most formidable enemy; Breadalbane, a secret foe,

1690. dangerous from his extensive territorial possessions, and dark insidious character; Perth and his brother Melford, King James's most confidential advisers. The only individual of any note, who favoured the revolution in this county, was the Laird of Weem,* who being a proprietor of the second class, for that very reason deserved the greater praise for his independent patriotic spirit, especially, surrounded as he was by Athole, Breadalbane, and other powerful neighbours, deeply engaged in the opposite interest. Nevertheless, he risked his all, and sent his son with 100 of his clan to join the General the day before the battle of Killiecrankie. The circumstance is expressly stated in the Memoirs, though passed over in silence by the General in his account of the battle, probably from these Highlanders being undisciplined, and therefore unfit to be posted in the line, though usefully employed with the baggage in the rear.

From Dundee to Aberdeen, there were few Roman catholics, but many of the protestant episcopal persuasion, so lukewarm, however, in their attachment to the protestant interest, and liberties of their country, that not a single individual of their number espoused the cause of the revolution, but looked tamely on, awaiting the result. To such a degree did this cautious and frigid policy prevail, that even in the neighbourhood of the town of Dundee, where the interest of the great idol of the Jacobite cause might be supposed to have been the strongest, it does not appear that any considerable number were induced to follow his standard.

The shires of Aberdeen and Banff, being chiefly attached to the Romish faith, and under the influence of the potent house of Gordon and its numerous adherents, were of course hostile to the revolution, and from them, therefore, the General could expect nothing but the most determined opposition. The lower orders were either besotted with the episcopalian doctrines (to use a phrase of Chambers) of passive obedience and non-resistance, or had no zeal of any kind, except for the preservation of their worldly goods; but the nobles and higher ranks in general, were

* Ancestor of the present Sir Neil Menzies, Bart.

filled with the most rancorous hostility to the protestant doctrines and their abettors.

From this remark, however, must be excepted the Master of Forbes* and Sir George Gordon of Edinglassie,† the only individuals in this district who gave support or even countenance to the General. The former met him when he crossed the Dee, with forty gentlemen, his friends, and three or four hundred of the lower orders, who, however, (to use the General's words,) looked so little like their work, that he dismissed them for the present, with an expression of thanks for this testimony of their zeal for the protestant religion. To what has been already stated concerning the services of the master of Forbes and those of Edinglassie, we need here only add, that during the whole of this arduous contest, they displayed the most unwearied perseverance, disinterested zeal, and devoted attachment to the cause in which they were engaged, sacrificing, or risking without scruple, in its defence, person, house, and lands. The Forbes family were among the most ancient in the peerage of Scotland, but their estate—never proportioned to their high antiquity—had, during

---

* Honourable William Forbes, eldest son of William, eleventh Lord, succeeded his father in 1691.

† Sir George Gordon of Edinglassie and Carnusie, knight, was the second son of Sir John Gordon of Park, bart., a branch of the Huntly family. Sir George being a man of competent fortune and considerable talent, was in 1681 appointed joint sheriff principal of the shire of Banff with Sir James Baird of Auchmedden; and having, as already mentioned, early declared for the revolution, continued during life one of its firmest supporters. Mackay in his Memoirs and Correspondence, frequently mentions the powerful assistance he received from this patriot; and warmly recommended him to the favour of the King and his ministers; in consequence of which, he was appointed to command Annandale's vacant troop, and afterwards to the majority of Eglington's regiment of horse, of which his friend and coadjutor, the master of Forbes, was Lieutenant-colonel. He died in 1690 or 1691, and was buried with funeral pomp and solemnity,—his remains being accompanied to the grave by his troop, dressed in mourning, and by a considerable number of his friends and neighbours. He left two sons, whose issue in the male line, is extinct; and several daughters, the eldest of whom, was the mother of Lord Braco, afterwards Earl of Fife; and from the other daughters are descended several respectable families in the shires of Aberdeen and Banff.

1690. the two last reigns, been greatly reduced by fines imposed on them, for their attachment to the cause of civil and religious liberty. The last remnants of their former greatness were the superiorities of their own, and some of their neighbour's lands, and of these they were stript by the overgrown power of the Gordons.

The life and fortune of the Duke of Gordon being, in consequence of his late conduct, at the mercy of his sovereign; it therefore occurred to the General, that a fit opportunity was now furnished of rewarding the loyalty of Forbes, by compelling his Grace to restore to him the superiorities, of which he had been unjustly deprived. He accordingly suggested to his Majesty, and recommended to his ministers, the adoption of this, or some such measure, but, so far as appears, without effect.*

Come we now to the shire of Moray, in which Sir Ludovick Grant, the high-principled chief of that clan, stood alone; but being himself a giant, sustained with Atlantean shoulders, the weight of the good cause in the province of Moray, comprehending the shires of Moray, Nairn, and that part of Inverness in which his extensive estates were situated.

The shire of Inverness at that time abounded, as it still does, more than any other county, in Highland chiefs, most of them Roman Catholics, and of course, devoted to the cause of the exiled monarch. The only family mentioned by the General, as being friendly to the new government, was that of Forbes of Culloden—a family not of long standing in the county, nor possessed of an extensive estate; yet such was the moral influence of their hereditary talents and virtues, that in the course of a few generations, they acquired a degree of consideration and authority, not only in their own country, but throughout all Scotland, such as was not exceeded by that of any of their compeers. The first laird of Culloden of the name of Forbes, died in 1654, the second in 1688,† and the third in 1704; all the

---

* See Memoirs, passim.

† Captain John Forbes, of Grant's regiment, the officer mentioned, p. 73, as having led to the detection of the traitor Livingstone's plot; was the second son of John, the second laird of Culloden. This second laird having made himself obnoxious to the Jacobite party, his lands

three being members of parliament, and ranged on the popular side. John, the fourth laird, was many years a member of the Scottish and British parliaments, in which he maintained the true whig principles of his predecessors; and in 1734, was succeeded by his brother Duncan, then lord advocate, afterwards Lord-President of the Court of Session, the incorruptible patriot, senator, and judge. To this truly illustrious man, more perhaps than to any other individual, the nation owes its escape in 1745, from the then again threatened yoke of Popery and arbitrary power.

1690.

After this digression, which it is hoped the reader will pardon, we proceed with the enumeration of the few remaining friends from whom the General received support. The greater part of the population of Rossshire, had long since renounced the errors of popery, and professed the Reformed religion. In the western division however, the Romish faith still lingered, and even of those who relinquished it, not a few adopted the episcopal persuasion, and, together with it, still clung to the doctrines of passive obedience and non-resistance. This part of the county being, besides, almost the exclusive property of the Lords Seaforth and Tarbat, and the clan Mackenzie, no aid could from them be expected by the General. In the eastern division, the protestant doctrines and presbyterian forms of worship had already taken deep root, and were warmly supported by the Lairds of Foulis and Balnagown, the two principal proprietors. Sir John Munro of Foulis and Sir George Munro of Culrain, being connected by blood with the General, he promised himself their cordial aid; but from some cause, which the writer cannot explain, the former, not choosing to follow the example of his ancestors, stood aloof on this occasion, and left the Laird of Balnagown the undivided honour of vindicating, in this shire, the religion and liberties of his country.

We now pass over to the county of Sutherland, where the General

---

of Culloden were ravaged by Buchan and Cannon, and the damage having been estimated at £54,000 Scots, parliament, in 1690, granted the family a perpetual licence to distil whisky duty free, on their barony of Ferintosh; which immunity they continued to enjoy till 1784, when it was redeemed by the British parliament for £20,000 sterling.

1690. drew his first breath, and from whence he now derived his firmest support. Besides the supplies of men sent to him at Inverness, by the Lords Sutherland and Reay, their lordships formed an impenetrable barrier between him and the Sinclairs under the Earl of Caithness, who being ill-affected to the new government, would, had they been permitted to join the Mackenzies, have paralyzed his measures on that side. Fortunately, in what direction soever they should move, towards the Mackenzies, they would be intercepted either by Lord Sutherland or Lord Reay, and they therefore remained at home. Between the families of these two lords, there had been feuds, which were happily terminated in 1589, by a marriage between Hugh Mackay of Farr or Strathnaver and Lady Jane Gordon, eldest daughter of Alexander, eleventh Earl of Sutherland, but they were unhappily revived in the succeeding generation, by jealousies fomented, if not excited, by their common uncle Sir Robert Gordon of Gordonston. Donald, the first Lord Reay, inherited a large estate, which, by his wild and eccentric schemes of ambition, he greatly impaired. George, third Lord, having succeeded, in nonage, to the wreck of his paternal estate, William, the fifteenth earl of Sutherland, generously forgetting old differences between the families, took a friendly interest in the education of his young cousin, by which he profited so much, that he became, in due time, a considerable proficient in literature and science, and was admitted a fellow of the Royal Society. He died in 1748, in the seventieth year of his age, and having thus been contemporary with the fifteenth, sixteenth, and seventeenth earls of Sutherland, and with the Lord-President Forbes; he enjoyed the rare felicity of having co-operated with those eminent persons in bringing about the revolution, and in suppressing the rebellions of 1715 and 1745.

The war having at length been happily concluded in Scotland, the rebellious chiefs having laid down their arms, and all the kingdom acknowledging the authority of their Majesties William and Mary, the General announced to the council his intention to resign the chief command, so soon as he could obtain his Majesty's permission. This produced a change in the conduct at least, if not on the dispositions, of some of his colleagues, who had hitherto most strenuously opposed his measures. Instead of that factious spirit which had for some time characterised their opposition, they now seemed desirous to retrace their steps, and atone for past errors, by cordially adopting his suggestions. In a letter, under date 7th September, addressed to him by the council, they signify their entire approval of his distribution of the forces, and of his proceedings in regard to the Earl of Seaforth, as already detailed; adding, that they had sent directions to the Earls of Drumlanrig and Argyle agreeably to his wishes, and conclude as follows: "By this you may understand, the council have readily complied with the overtures proposed by your former letters, as the best for ordering the forces here, so that if any thing different from this hath been insinuated, it must certainly have proceeded through mistake. All possible care is taken to provide Fort William with meal and other necessaries, according to your advice. This, by warrant and in name of the council, is signified to you by your assured friend and servant. Sic. Subr. HAMILTON, P."

The King too, seemed to participate in the feeling which generally prevailed, as if due respect had not always been paid to his recommendations, various instances of which have been pointed out in the course of this work. From the following passage in the privy council records of 6th November, it would appear that both his Majesty and their Lordships of the council, seemed to vie with each other in demonstrations of respect for his suggestions. "Major-General Mackay acquainted the board, that he is now designing to wait upon his Majesty, before he go for Holland, and that the Earl of Portland has wrote a letter to him in French, which was read, signifying he had communicated the line he had received from the major-general to his Majesty, and that his Majesty would send a commission for commanding, in absence of the major-general, which the said Earl believed would be in favour of Sir Thomas Livingstone; and in respect, the said commission was not yet come, the major-general moved that the board might appoint one to command until

1690. the commission should arrive. The council left this wholly to the major-general, to name the person until the commission come." On the 10th, accordingly, his Majesty's commission was received, appointing Sir Thomas Livingstone commander-in-chief, in room of General Mackay, till further orders; an appointment which, as it took place in consequence of his recommendation, cannot be doubted to have been highly gratifying to the General.

The magistrates and town-council of Edinburgh, were suspected of disaffection to the government, yet even they, came forward on this occasion, to testify the high opinion they entertained of the eminent talents and virtues, public and private, of General Mackay, and of the moderation with which he had exercised his command. They voted him the freedom of the city, and gave him a public dinner, to which the nobility and principal gentry of the town and neighbourhood were invited.

About the end of November, having obtained his Majesty's leave, he resigned his command in Scotland, and prepared for his final departure. Testimonies in his favour so ample, and coming from so many different quarters, though grateful to his feelings, could not wholly obliterate the remembrance of the many mortifications he had to endure while he held this command. He was about to quit, therefore, his native land with no very favourable impression of the character of his countrymen, those especially of the higher ranks, among whom he had experienced so much duplicity, selfishness, and want of public principle.

From the words "till further orders" in Sir Thomas Livingstone's commission; it might be inferred that it was intended he should, either the following spring, or at some future period, resume his command. That this idea was in contemplation with the King, is not improbable, but that it never received his own assent, seems certain from various passages in his Memoirs, and annexed correspondence. In the former,* he expresses himself thus. " All these considerations made him (Mackay) look upon Scotsmen of those times, in general, as void of zeal

* P. 77.

for their religion, seeing all men hunt after their particular advantages, 1690. and none minding sincerely, and self-denyedly, the common good, which gave him a real distaste of the country and service; resolving from that time forward, to disengage himself out of it as soon as possible he could get it done, and that the service could allow." It was not however, on public grounds alone, the General's distaste of his native country was founded. Considerations of a private and personal nature coincided, and of these the chief probably was the murder of his two elder brothers, already mentioned; which being still unavenged by public justice, made on his mind an indelible impression to the prejudice of his countrymen. Being a man of warm affections, attached to his family, his friends, and his country; it is not to be supposed that he would have remained twenty-one months in Scotland, and at different times, several weeks at Inverness, within fifty miles of his own estate, and the abode of his near relatives, without visiting them, had not some cause of a very peculiar and delicate nature interposed.

At length this brave Christian soldier bade a last adieu to the country of his birth, and proceeded to London, where he had an interview with his Majesty, which, let us hope, for the honour of the sovereign, was gracious, and such as his faithful services deserved. He accompanied the King to the Hague, and spent the winter with his family in Holland.

Frequent meetings of council were summoned by the King, to deliberate 1690-91. on the measures of the approaching campaign in Flanders, at all of which Mackay assisted, it being intended that he should serve as a lieutenant-general, under his Majesty's immediate command. This arrangement was afterwards changed, and Ireland, on account of his superior skill in the attack and defence of fortified places, was chosen for the scene of his future operations. The change was the more agreeable to Mackay, as it would place him next in command to Field-marshal Schomberg,* now Duke of Leinster. He would have preferred a campaign in Flanders, but readily

---

* Son of the veteran, Marshal Duke of Schomberg, killed in Ireland the preceding year.

1691. acceded to the new arrangement, Leinster, being an officer of reputation, and moreover, his own personal friend.

In pursuance of this arrangement, Mackay immediately returned to England, and was waiting, together with Leinster, for a favourable wind, to pass over to their duty in Ireland, when the King arrived in London, after having made an unsuccessful effort to relieve Mons. Here his Majesty appears to have completely altered his previous arrangements. The Baron de Ghinkel, who had served the preceding year under the elder Schomberg, and, after the death of that great warrior, under Count Solms, was now appointed to succeed the latter in the chief command. Next came the Duke of Wirtemberg, and M. de Schravemor as lieutenant-generals, the former in command of the infantry, the latter of the cavalry, with Mackay, the Marquis de Ruvignie, a French protestant refugee, Talmash, and Tettau, a Dane, as major-generals.

By this disposition, Mackay, instead of one foreign officer, was to have three placed over his head; and after having been nominated by the king in council, second under Leinster, one of the first generals in Europe, was to serve under de Ghinkel, a man who had a name in arms yet to acquire, and two other foreign officers, whose pretensions, though respectable, were in no degree superior to his own. This was an indignity, which it may well be conceived, he found hard to brook; and it was aggravated by the consideration, that the Earl of Marlborough, who had been appointed major-general the same day with himself, by King James, was now promoted to the rank of lieutenant-general, while he saw his own services apparently overlooked.

So many repeated slights and indignities, from a prince to whom he was so warmly attached, were too much for flesh and blood, and required all his christian philosophy to enable him to endure them with patience. He felt them as a man and soldier, but bore them like a christian and a patriot, stifling his feelings, lest the great cause in which he was engaged, should be injured, by the vindication of his private wrongs. He wrote, however, to the Earl of Portland, that, if it pleased God, he 1691. survived this campaign, he should seek a master who would more duly appreciate his services. At his audience of leave, the King said nothing to him on Irish affairs, "*il ne me dit le petit mot*," and dismissed him without a single word of explanation or apology for the past. With every allowance for the cold and phlegmatic temperament of King William, it is impossible to refrain from expressing our disapprobation of such treatment of an old and faithful servant, so self-deniedly (to use his own word) devoted to his interest.

Notwithstanding the victory of the Boyne, and the subsequent successes of King William in the north of Ireland, the kingdom was far from being reduced as yet under his authority. The great mass of the population were ignorant and bigotted papists, of course attached to the late monarch, and had recently been joined by strong reinforcements from France, under the command of St. Ruth, a general of reputation. To expel the one, and subdue the other, were to be the objects of the ensuing campaign.

About the beginning of May 1691, Mackay passed over to Ireland, to enter on the duty now assigned to him. On his arrival at Dublin, he found de Ghinkel before him, and the other general officers at their respective posts,—all preparing to open the campaign. The army consisted of about 20,000 men, of five different nations; English, Scotch, Dutch, Germans, and Danes; and, besides the general officers already mentioned—of whom no more than two, Mackay and Talmash, were British—there were three other foreign officers of rank; La Meloniere, a Frenchman; the Count of Nassau, a Dutchman; and the Prince of Hesse Darmstadt, a German. In councils of war, the general officers had occasional differences of opinion, which they supported sometimes even with warmth; but, to their honour be it recorded, these never interrupted the public service, nor disturbed the harmony of their private meetings.

On the 29th May, Mackay quitted Dublin and arrived at Mullingar on the following day about noon. This place was one of great importance, being the only depot of arms, and provisions hitherto established out of Dublin, and yet he found it almost entirely without defence. He therefore, took the liberty of earnestly recommending to de Ghinkel, to cause the detachments of infantry stationed there, to throw up breastworks, so as to render it in some degree less liable to insult. Little in his opinion seemed necessary, to give it a respectable appearance in the eye of an enemy, who had, for a considerable length of time suffered it to remain unmolested so near him, though garrisoned by no more than 300 effective men. After bestowing some labour on this place, although it was still very inadequately enclosed, it was resolved, on the arrival of General Douglas,* with the northern corps of the army, to march to the attack of Ballimore, with a body of from nine to ten thousand men, before the Duke of Wirtemberg had moved from Clonmel with the southern division.

To this resolution, framed on a contempt of the enemy, more than on any sound principle in warfare, Mackay urged the solid objection, that St. Ruth, being at the head of a force superior to their's united, it left it at his option to advance between the two divisions, and force the one or the other, perhaps both in their turn, to engage at a disadvantage. He was, besides, still in possession of all the bridges and fords on the Shannon, and could therefore, in the event of their advancing, throw himself on Mullingar, by the passage that best suited him, and thus intercept their communcation with Dublin, the main source of their supplies. The opinion prevailed, however, which represented the Irish commander as little inclined to enterprize, and Ballimore was immediately attacked, and taken after a slight resistance; the defences of the place being bad, although the natural position was strong.

After the capture of Ballimore, a council of war was assembled, to determine whether the Duke of Wirtemberg should be ordered to advance to meet the main body, or remain at Ballibeg, six miles from the bridge of Banagher, where the passage of the Shannon was to be attempted. The majority of the generals were for leaving him there, in order to save

* The Generals Douglas and Kirke, not agreeing among themselves, were withdrawn from Ireland, and sent to Flanders.

a counter-march, but Mackay brought forward so may well-founded arguments for an opposite course, that the Duke was ordered to advance, and the junction fixed to take place four miles from Ballimore, on the road to Athlone. This was a large and well-fortified town, situated on the banks of the river Shannon, fifty-five miles west of Dublin. It was divided by the river, into two unequal portions, or towns, the larger, defended by a garrison of native Irish, with St. Ruth behind, at the head of a French army of 25,000 men, and the river face was protected by works erected in the preceding year, under the eye of a French engineer officer, then in the service of King James, but who had since deserted from him.

Mackay's opinion, recommending the immediate junction of the two divisions of the army, having at length been adopted, both moved simultaneously,—the one from Ballimore, the other from Streamstown, and marched next day in a body to within two miles of Athlone. Early on the following morning, the attack of this place commenced by Major General de Tettau, advancing with four regiments of infantry, and some cavalry, in order to dislodge the enemy from the advanced works and defiles in front of the town, while Mackay brought up the remainder of the infantry to their support, in the event of their requiring aid; but they succeeded in driving into the body of the place, all the force opposed to them, without assistance. A battery of eight twenty-four pounders was then erected, with which, by 5 P. M. the second day, a practicable breach was made; and it was therefore determined to proceed forthwith to the assault, although from the battery to the breach, a distance of 300 paces, there was little or no cover.

The command of this service devolved on Mackay, as the major-general of the day, having under his orders brigadiers Stuart and Witkinhoff. After making all the necessary arrangements for the attack, he had just placed himself on the battery to see the issue, when he observed that the advanced party had missed its way and halted. He therefore instantly hastened to Brewer's regiment,* and taking by the hand the first captain

* 12th foot.

he came to, shewed him the right way to the breach. Brigadier Stuart also observing, that the lieutenant leading the grenadiers, was killed, and that the lieutenant-colonel at the head of the whole party, had received a wound, which brought him to the ground, he proceeded with his regiment,* straight to the breach, where they arrived at the same time with Brewer's; and having cleared it, their united force, in spite of a desperate resistance on the part of the enemy, soon drove them to the extreme end of the bridge between the two towns.

In order to secure the possession of what had thus been gained, lodgements were now made against the bridge, and against a ford immediately below it, by which a portion of the routed enemy had been observed to retire. No measures had previously been taken for this purpose, nor had any arrangements been made for proceeding to attack the west town; although it is evident, this would have been the time to force the passage of the Shannon, had Athlone been the point fixed on for making the attempt.

De Ghinkel naturally wavering and irresolute, was so distracted with the multiplicity of his councils, that he could not come to any definite project; and was continually changing his mind, according to the opinions of those with whom he had last consulted. To assist his judgment, he had recourse to repeated councils of war, which, however, served only to bewilder him the more; their advices being as many and various as were the advisers. The heavy cannon having arrived, it was placed in battery, and produced considerable effect on the defences of the opposite town; but no decisive plan of attempting the passage had been arranged; almost every general in the army appeared to have his favourite project, till at length they seemed reduceable to the three following, viz. to force a passage by means of a bridge of pontoons above the stone bridge, by this bridge itself, or by the ford below it.

Each of these plans had its respective abettors. Mackay stood alone in disapproving of all the three,—of the first and second as impracticable, of the third as hazardous in the extreme. He was overruled, however,

* 9th foot.

by an overwhelming majority, which included the commander-in-chief, 1691. and it was resolved to make the attempt, beginning with the first plan proposed. On trial, that was abandoned; the ground on the opposite side being found firm in one place only, and this place strongly guarded by the enemy.

The stone bridge consisted originally of three arches, all of which were broken down by the Irish, to prevent the entrance of the assailants. The two next the English side were now repaired, and beams thrown across the third arch, to be planked at the moment of intended attack; but when this critical moment arrived, and the advanced party were waiting for orders to storm, a grenade thrown from the Irish side, set fire to the wooden work, which, in a few minutes consumed the whole, and thus the labour of nine days was lost. The intended attack from this point was abandoned of course, and the troops, after being ordered to hold themselves in readiness for another, returned to their quarters sullen and dejected, from this disappointment of their hopes. To stimulate their exertions, money had been distributed among them in the morning, which coming to the knowledge of the Irish, they taunted them during the night, by repeatedly calling out, to enquire what value they had given their officers for the bounty they had received.

A council was summoned in the afternoon, to consider what steps should now be taken. The members gave their opinions *seriatim*, and agreed that the ford below the stone bridge was the most eligible point of attack. In opposition to this determination, Mackay again stood out alone, insisting that it was contrary to the acknowledged maxims of war, to risk the safety of an army, by attempting the passage of a deep and rapid river, in the face of strong works, backed by an enemy of superior force, who would not fail to take advantage of his position: that in the few cases wherein such attempts had succeeded, it had been owing to surprise, the proper moment for which, on this occasion, had been lost; and, finally, insisting that should the attempt fail, the consequence would be the unavoidable retreat, ruin, and disgrace of the whole army. In-

1691. stead, therefore, of a ford so full of difficulty and danger, he pointed out two others, viz. Meelick, a few miles below, and Lanesborough, about an equal distance above the town, either of which would be found safer, and more practicable. The majority, however, adhered to their original opinion, and the following day was fixed on for the attack. Late at night, Mackay had a private interview with the commander-in-chief, at which he stated some further considerations, in confirmation of the plan he had recommended, offering his services to conduct the passage, and reiterated his former arguments with such effect, that he parted with de Ghinkel, believing him to be a convert to his opinion. But when the morning came, the characteristic doubts and hesitation of the latter returned, and he reverted once more to his favourite ford.

There were in the army four major-generals of infantry, viz. Mackay, de Ruvignie, Talmash, and Tettau, among whom it had been settled, that each should command a day in turn; and agreeably to this arrangement, it was Mackay's tour of duty to command this attack. De Ghinkel, however, under pretence of employing the same officers and men as on the former day, according to the general orders already issued, but in reality, from a secret disinclination to entrust the command to an officer who disapproved of the measure, attempted to substitute Major-General Talmash in his room; but Mackay boldly asserting his right to the post, alike of honour and of danger, the commander-in-chief yielded. This being communicated to Talmash, he requested permission to accompany the attacking party as a volunteer; a request to which Mackay would not accede, judging it imprudent to engage more than half the major-generals of infantry in this enterprize, when there might be so many occasions hereafter for their services.

The Shannon was passable only during the heat of summer, and even then but for a space barely sufficient to admit of twenty men abreast. The ford was rugged and full of large stones, so slippery that they caused the men to stumble almost at every step. Two thousand men were destined for this daring, if not desperate enterprize, forming six regiments, one of which was Mackay's own, commanded by his gallant nephew,

Lieutenant-colonel the Hon. Æneas Mackay, so often already distinguish- 1691.
ed.* The men being paraded, Mackay addressed them in terms suited
to his own religious character, and their peculiar circumstances, standing as they did at present, perhaps, on the brink of eternity. He exhorted them to keep steady, and, as much as possible, well closed while in the water, so as to issue out to the attack in a dense mass; representing to them, at the same time, the all-important necessity of making a vigorous onset, for on this almost alone (humanly speaking) hung the issue of the contest,—the smallest check on such occasions, generally proving fatal.

After seeing the advance enter the water, led by Colonel Gustavus

* This being the last time Æneas Mackay's name will occur, a few additional particulars concerning him and his brother Robert, may here be introduced. On the death of their father, they were both sent, at an early age, to Holland, to be educated for the military profession, under the eye of their uncle General Mackay, who, in due time, procured commissions for them in his own regiment; and their attention to the studies and duties of their profession, afforded favourable indications of their future character. Of Robert's short, but brilliant career, a few notices have already been given. The first mention we find of Æneas, is in 1688, when, having come to Scotland, as Captain Mackay, to visit his family, or probably also on a secret political mission from the Prince of Orange, he was arrested as a suspicious person, and confined prisoner in the castle of Edinburgh. Here he lay, in close custody, at the Revolution, when he was released, and soon after promoted to the majority of Livingstone's dragoons. He served constantly with that regiment during the years 1689 and 90, and greatly recommended himself by his vigilance and activity. Being re-appointed to his former regiment as lieutenant-colonel, in 1691 he passed over with it to Ireland, and commanded it on the passage of the Shannon, and at Aughrim. Next year we find him in Flanders, and at the head of his regiment in the battle of Steinkirk. He succeeded his uncle as colonel of the regiment, and in 1695 was promoted to the rank of brigadier-general, in which he continued to serve with distinguished reputation till 1697, when having received many severe wounds, he was ordered to Bath for the recovery of his health, and died there. A monument is erected to his memory in the cathedral of that city. Thus lived, and thus died under the age of thirty, these two gallant brothers, of wounds received in the service of their country, and like the chevalier Bayard, " Sans peur, et sans reproche." To their excellent mother, Barbara Lady Reay, the bereavement was the more severe, as she had some years before lost her eldest son Donald, master of Reay, by an accidental explosion of gunpowder, and now had no other son left for the solace of her widowhood.

1691. Hamilton,* and the gallant young Prince of Hesse Darmstadt;† he stationed an aide-de-camp on the bank, to repeat his instructions to each regiment as it entered the river; and matters being thus arranged, fearlessly plunged into it himself, the water up to his waist, under a hot fire of grape and musquetry, from which, however, through the mercy of God, he escaped himself unhurt, with the loss of no more than fifty of his men! So soon as they reached the opposite bank, the soldiers, animated by the example of their commanders, scrambled up the breach as they best could, one helping another, but scarcely knowing how they were enabled, either to pass the river, or enter the town. Having gained the summit, they formed into two divisions, one of which, led by Mackay, took to the right, and the other, by Tettau, to the left, both scouring the ramparts, and driving all before them, till they met on the opposite side of the town, to the utter dismay of the garrison as well as of the inhabitants. Of the former 1000 were slain, though no quarter was refused, and within an hour from his entering the river, Mackay was in complete possession of the town. Having secured the guns on the land side, he turned them against the astonished St. Ruth, who never dreamed of the passage of the Shannon being forced, or of the town of Athlone being taken in such a manner, and would scarcely believe the intelligence, till he had occular demonstration of its truth.

The success of this bold and hazardous enterprise, while it places the gallantry and conduct of the General in a conspicuous point of view, by no means invalidates the correctness of his previous opinion against it; for had it failed, which, but for the misconduct of his adversary it was more likely to have done,—to say nothing of the loss of lives,—the want of provisions must have compelled de Ghinkel to raise the siege, and retreat with disgrace.‡

The capture of Athlone having been thus happily effected, (2d July)

---

* Of 20th foot.   † Colonel of 6th foot, killed at Barcelona, 13th April 1705.

‡ One of the highest military authorities of the day, Field-marshal the Duke of Berwick, who had himself inspected the localities, speaks of the attempt to force the passage, as being

the enemy was permitted to retire unmolested, de Ghinkel being unable to make an immediate pursuit, for want of ammunition; besides which, he now felt the fatal effects of his negligence at the commencement of the campaign, in not establishing magazines nearer than Mullingar. St. Ruth encamped at Ballinasloe, where, after many changes of purpose, and frequent deliberations as to the route to be pursued, the Dutch General at length marched towards him; upon which, the other took up a strong position three miles farther on, near the village of Aughrim. Here, on being followed up, he showed a disposition to take advantage of the ground, and remain firm, after his advanced piquets had been driven in from the heights in front of his camp.

A skirmish now took place between the Irish outposts and Cunningham's dragoons, who had been sent forward to dislodge the former from some garden ground, which it was deemed expedient to be occupied by the left wing of the British, and more than a mile distant from the enemy's right. The enemy appearing to support their skirmishers, Eppinger's regiment in the first place, and then—seeing the Irish still disinclined to give way—the whole left wing was ordered forward to occupy the disputed ground. This occasioned a movement in the enemy's camp, as if they were withdrawing from the left, in order to

ridiculous; and gives it as his opinion "that, if St. Ruth had done his duty, the result could not fail to have been different."—*Berwick's Memoirs*, vol. i. p. 90. "This," says Bishop Burnet, "was executed by Mackay with so much resolution, that many ancient officers said it was the gallantest action they had ever seen."—*History*, vol. iii. p. 108. According to Smollett, "there never was a more desperate service; nor was exploit ever performed with more valour and intrepidity."—*History*, vol. i. p. 120. Winne writes as follows: "this might have been reckoned among those rash actions which are more for astonishment than imitation."—*Hist. of Ireland*, vol. ii. p. 326. The author of the Life of King William, after describing the passage of the Shannon, adds that "the beseigers now found more obstruction from rubbish, and stuff beaten down by their own cannon, than from the enemy; which made the soldiers curse and swear bitterly, and gave occasion to that excellent person, Major General Mackay, to tell them, 'they had more reason to fall upon their knees, and thank God for the victory; and that they were brave men, and the best of men, if they would give up swearing.'"—*Life of King William*, p. 305.

1691. strengthen their right, which made Mackay observe to the General, that less marked demonstrations had often led to a general action. He at the same time proposed to him, as his right was covered by a marsh, that he should transport some of his cavalry from the right to the left, where the ground appeared better adapted to cavalry movements; adding, that in order to prevent the enemy employing all his cavalry with his right, it would be well to cause a few batallions of his own right, to move down towards the marsh, which separated it from the enemy's left, as well to dislodge some of his out-posts, as to determine, if all the ground that appeared inaccessible were really such. To this General de Ghinkel replied, by ordering him along with the Major-generals de Ruvignie and Talmash to proceed to the right wing, to take the command, and act as the nature of the ground and other circumstances should require.

In accordance with this order, Mackay sent forward some batallions of the first line of the right wing; on which, the enemy in front retired towards a castle which covered his left. He examined the ground, and found that he could draw up about four battalions in line upon it, which force was immediately brought forward under the fire of the enemy's cannon, and some squadrons of cavalry distributed behind. He then caused a rivulet on his left to be sounded, in the event of requiring to extend his front in that direction; and, ordering up twelve field pieces to silence the three by which his advanced line was incommoded, he judged it expedient to suspend further measures, as the skirmish on the left had led to no ulterior operations on that side of the field; and the main portions of two armies there opposed to each other were still a full mile asunder. In order, however, to satisfy Major-general Talmash, who would have him here advance against all rule, Mackay now sent an aide-de-camp to the General, demanding to know whether he deemed it expedient to attack, that both wings might in that case act in conjunction. De Ghinkel being then either much occupied, or undecided, replied, that he was to act as he saw fit; being sent to a second time about 5 P. M. he came himself to the right, and it was arranged, that he should immediately advance with the left, and when Mackay saw that wing sufficiently approached to the enemy, 1691. the general attack was to take place. About two hours afterwards, judging the left wing to be far enough advanced, Mackay ordered four regiments, those of Earle, Brewer, Herbert, and Crichton, to advance on the left of the four already brought up, with strict injunctions to halt, after taking possession of the hedges beyond the bog in their front, till further orders, or until they perceived the force on their right gaining upon the enemy. He then advanced himself, with the regiments of Kirk,* Gustavus Hamilton,† Bellasis,‡ and Lord George Hamilton,§ and drove the enemy from the first and second lines of hedges in front, and from right and left of the castle of Aughrim,—ordering these regiments to draw up there, while he looked around for a passage for de Ruvignie with the cavalry. In the meantime, the four first engaged regiments, forgetting their instructions, pursued the routed enemy beyond all the lines of hedges, and were in their turn taken in flank, and overthrown; as was also the second brigade of the right, which the Prince of Hesse had brought forward without orders; and on seeing this reverse on the right, several regiments of the left wing began to give way. Mackay now saw that the only chance of arresting defeat, was by endeavouring to turn the flank of the pursuing enemy. He therefore addressed the commanding officers of the regiments of cavalry immediately about him, and entreated them—for the honour of the English nation, the interest of religion and liberty, and all they held sacred—to rush forward for this purpose without delay; for he observed that the route of the infantry made them hesitate. The Oxford regiment, however, soon led the way, and was immediately followed by the regiments of Villers‖ and Leveson,¶ with de Ruvignie at their head. The enemy, aware of this design, attacked them before they had completely formed, after passing the defile, and succeeded in driving back some; but Mackay pushing forward others to their support, they held

* 2d. † The 20th. ‡ 22d. § Afterwards Earl of Orkney.
‖ 2d or queen's dragoon guards. ¶ 3d dragoons.

1691. their ground. Still, fearing they might eventually be overpowered, he ordered a lieutenant-colonel to pass with his squadron to take the enemy in reverse, at a spot more exposed to the fire of the castle, than that where the others had passed. This lieutenant-colonel, whom (perhaps to spare some fair name) he does not further designate, answered, if he wished him to pass there, he must shew him the way. Mackay, though he severely rebuked the officer, saw it was not a time to weigh the rules of discipline, and instantly putting himself at the head of the squadron, cried, "follow me then." He leapt the ditch in front; his horse bogged on the opposite side, and he was thrown from his seat. Not a man of the squadron took the leap after him, but all retiring, left his groom to remount him; in his leap back he was more fortunate, having escaped unhurt, amidst a shower of musketry which his awkward position had drawn on him from the castle. From this untoward spot, he hastened to the defile, where the other cavalry had passed, and advancing up the rising ground where the infantry got the first check, observed a fresh squadron of the enemy bearing down upon the cavalry. He ordered Wousely's horse to advance slowly to meet this squadron, their ranks well closed, to show a steady front, and not to fire. Wousley obeyed with coolness and gallantry, and the enemy turned back. Mackay then made sign to some corps he saw in confusion, to rally behind Wousley, and he himself advanced to the height, with the three or four squadrons around him.

The infantry, in the meantime,—recovered from their confusion on the pursuing force being checked by the first advanced cavalry—soon took order, and regained their lost ground, and advanced in their turn on the enemy, along with the cavalry; the whole being now re-enforced by the regiments of Bellasis and Lord George Hamilton. Kirk's regiment, however, and Gustavus Hamilton's on the extreme right, being obstructed by gardens and fences, could not at this time advance; and the force within the castle seeing only these two regiments now opposed to them, made a sally, and would have overcome them, had not General Schravemore perceived their danger, and sent a few squadrons of fresh cavalry to their succour. By this timely aid, they beat off the assailants, and took the castle.

1691.

While all this was going forward on the right, the left wing of the army remained, in a manner, inactive, after being relieved by the altered state of the right, from the check they suffered at the commencement of the engagement; de Ghinkel contenting himself if he could sustain his infantry with the cavalry—of which force he had far the greater portion—until he should learn how the day went forward on the right. The view of that side of the field was interrupted by rising ground; but being now informed that the right wing was carrying all before it, he set forward his cavalry, and the enemy in his front were soon thrown into confusion. Mackay perceiving this, from the high ground he had just attained, and having now no longer anything to apprehend on his own side of the field, pushed forward with all the cavalry he could immediately collect, to cut off the retreat; and by this movement, the slaughter of the enemy was greater opposite the left wing than in his own front—although it was undoubtedly to the right wing, the glory of the day was chiefly due. The death of St. Ruth is a circumstance, however, not to be overlooked in accounting for the victory: he fell by a cannon-ball, before the commencement of the general attack, which did not take place till near seven o'clock in the evening. Mackay pursued the routed cavalry for a distance of four miles, until darkness and want of guides obliged him to return.

These are the leading particulars of the memorable battle of Aughrim, which, together with the capture of Athlone, gave the finishing blow to the cause of King James in Ireland. The reader cannot fail to observe that Mackay, although only fourth in the order of rank on these two important occasions, appears to have influenced the issue—on the latter by his counsel, and on both by his conduct,—more conspicuously and more directly than any other general officer in the army. At Aughrim, he had to contend against the indecision of de Ghinkel, the rashness of Talmash and the Prince of Hesse d'Armstadt, and against the most fatal, the most mortifying of all

1691. difficulties,—the absolute cowardice of an officer at the head of a portion of the troops under his command.

The following day, the whole army encamped a mile beyond the field of battle, on the road to Loughrea, where they remained three days for a convoy of provisions. Detachments were sent from this post to seize the castle of Banagher, and to occupy the pass of Portumna; and the army was then marched to Loughrea, without any fixed design, and from Loughrea to Athenry, where it was determined, that, on account of the abundance of forage which Athlone afforded, the whole cavalry, with the exception of twelve squadrons, should be encamped near this place, under General Schravemore; while the remainder of the army was to invest Galway. Mackay, who was not present at the council where this project was arranged, represented to de Ghinkel, the impolicy of thus dividing his force, before his heavy artillery, or his provisions reached him. Another council was then summoned, but the original decision was adhered to, in spite of all Mackay could advance against it, and it was therefore fortunate that, instead of eighteen regiments of which the garrison was said to consist, there were in effect no more than 1500 armed men in the place.

It does not appear that, during the few remaining weeks of the campaign, Mackay continued to act the same prominent part which he had hitherto sustained; and as the object of this work is to relate the events of the war, in so far as he was personally concerned, and no farther, it is judged unnecessary to pursue the details to any greater length. Suffice it to say, that soon after the battle of Aughrim, Galway and Limerick were successively invested and taken, after a vigorous resistance. The latter capitulated on the 3d October, and to the instrument of capitulation, the name of H. Mackay is affixed, together with those of Generals de Ghinkel, Schravemore, Talmash, Porter, and Conningsby.

By this treaty, the Roman catholics were secured in the exercise of their religion, and in the enjoyment of such privileges as were consistent with the laws of Ireland, or as they did enjoy in the reign of Charles II.;

all the Irish then in Ireland, in the service of James, were to be pardoned, their estates and effects restored, and their attainders and outlawries reversed; and, finally, all those who inclined to go to France, were to be landed there with their effects, at the expense of the King of England.

1691.

The war being thus happily concluded, which delivered these kingdoms from the threatened yoke of popery and arbitrary power, and established William and Mary on the throne, it may safely be affirmed, that Mackay contributed, under providence, as much, if not more than any other individual, to bring about this happy consummation. He was not, however, rewarded with any of those earthly distinctions which usually attend the performance of such important services as he had rendered to his king and country, while de Ghinkel and de Ruvignie were raised to the honours of the Irish peerage, the former by the title of Earl of Athlone and Viscount Aughrim, the latter by that of Baron Galway. It is true, it was intended by King William, that, had it pleased God to prolong Mackay's valuable life, he too should be ennobled, and the intention was announced in a demi-official government paper of the day, styled, "Proceedings of the States;" but the only thing, in the shape of reward ever bestowed on his family, was the giving of a company, in the Scottish brigade, to his only son, then twelve years of age.

King William had, during the whole course of his reign, been charged with an undue partiality to his Dutch generals and courtiers; and on this occasion, the honours bestowed on de Ghinkel and de Ruvignie in preference to Mackay and Talmash, caused general discontent throughout the army.

In the month of November, the foreign troops employed in Ireland, were either returned to their respective homes, or together with a large body of British, conveyed to Flanders. There William, ever on the watch to frustrate the designs of the arch-enemy, alike of the protestant religion and the liberties of Europe, had already formed the nucleus of that grand army, with which, in the following year, he took the field against Louis the XIV. To enable him to carry his designs into execution, he

1691. had great reliance on the supplies both of men and money, which he had reason to expect from his newly acquired British dominions. In forming his arrangements for the ensuing campaign, his Majesty nominated Mackay to the command of the British division of the confederate army, with the advanced rank of lieutenant-general.

Discoursing one day with the Marshal Prince of Vaudemont, on the subject of his British generals, the king asked the Marshal what he thought of them. The answer was, Kirke has fire, Lanier thought, Mackay skill, and Colchester bravery; adding, that the Earl of Marlborough possessed all these qualities united. Vaudemont might with equal truth have said, that Mackay possessed not only the single quality of skill, but all the other qualities enumerated, in a degree not inferior to any British general of that day, Marlborough alone excepted; and even as to Marlborough, it is worthy of remark, that this illustrious commander had not yet had many opportunities of displaying those transcendent talents in the art of war, which he manifested at a subsequent period of his life. Mackay and he had been, as already mentioned, in their youth friends and fellow-soldiers, and both had attracted the notice of their superiors so equally, that they attained the rank of major-general on the very same day.

Not having had the accidental advantages enjoyed by Marlborough, Mackay's rise was certainly more due to his merit alone than Marlborough's, which might in part, at least at this time, have been attributed as much to his fine figure and captivating address, which gained for him the favour of the court, as to his merits, great as they were justly acknowledged to be. While a field officer, Mackay had seen greater variety of service, and in the rank of major-general, had been more distinguished, particularly in the Irish campaign, in which his conduct having been witnessed by so many foreign officers, spread his fame throughout all Europe. Marlborough's renown was as yet chiefly confined to acts of gallant daring, as those displayed at Nimeguen and Maestricht; for, during his campaign in the south of Ireland in 1690, although he took Cork and Kinsale in a space of time, which in those days might be considered

unprecedentedly short, it does not appear that he had many obstacles to 1691.
surmount in his success. Had he been cut off in this, his first command, while the affair of Walcourt was his sole trophy as a general; his name would certainly not have been handed down to posterity as a military man, with a lustre in any degree superior to that which may with justice be claimed for Mackay, at the close of his less fortunate, and shorter career in arms.

It was perhaps with a view to select among his British generals, an individual to place at the head of the troops of that nation, now to be engaged on the continent, that the King held the conversation just mentioned with Vaudemont; and it is probable the opinion of the marshal would do no more, than confirm his Majesty's own choice of the Earl of Marlborough, had he not at this very time fallen into disgrace at court. It therefore must have been owing to this circumstance, as much as to his own well-earned reputation, that this distinguished command was conferred on Mackay; for it was the appointment, which, of all others the aspiring Sarah Jennings, Countess of Marlborough, would have coveted for her husband; and that it was given to Mackay is a striking proof of the high estimation in which his military character was held by King William, himself a competent judge of military merit.

With all Mackay's piety and Christian humility, it may be supposed how much he was gratified by an appointment so distinguished, more especially after the slights and mortifications of the three preceding campaigns; and the Christian reader will readily believe, that he was earnest in supplicating the direction and blessing of the Almighty, on the important charge which he was now to undertake. By what means it was brought about, is not known to the author; his utmost researches having failed, in filling up the chasm in the personal history of Mackay, from the conclusion of the Irish war, to the commencement of that of Flanders. He trusts however, that when the treasures of the state-paper office at Whitehall, and the archives of the Hague shall have been unlocked, and fully laid open to the scrutiny of a Coxe, or other biographer, competent

1692. to the task of clearing up mysterious passages in the political history of that period, it will be seen how many more difficulties Mackay had to contend with, than are generally known, and how numerous and important the sacrifices of personal ease and interest, he made to the public good.

William being now left at liberty, to give his undivided attention to the grand confederacy, of which he had himself been the prime mover, against the ambition of Louis, repaired to Holland early in 1692. While he was mustering his forces at Louvain, Field-marshal the Duke of Luxembourg laid siege to Namur with an army of 120,000 men, and was speedily followed by the French King himself, accompanied by a magnificent cortege of the princes and princesses, lords and ladies of the court, wives and mistresses indiscriminately, together with a troop of comedians, opera-dancers and singers. Namur had always been considered one of the strongest fortifications in Europe, and it had recently been strengthened, with additional works under the inspection of Cohorn, a famous Dutch engineer, who was now employed in its defence. To him was opposed, Vauban, a French engineer of still greater celebrity, whose works at Lisle and Tournay, have always excited the admiration of competent judges.

The spectacle thus exhibited was novel and imposing, inasmuch as the two most powerful Monarchs of Europe headed their respective armies, while the two greatest engineers perhaps the world had ever seen, put forth their utmost efforts of genius and science combined, in opposition to each other. Cohorn being unfortunately wounded during the seige, the star of Louis prevailed, and Namur was forced to surrender, after an obstinate defence under the very eye of King William, who found himself unable to raise the seige.

Louis elated beyond measure with his success, returned in triumph to his capital, to receive the compliments and flatteries of his courtiers and poets. William mortified, but nothing disheartened by a check so severe, resolved to give battle to the enemy, in the hope of retrieving the disgrace which his arms had thus sustained. He had an army of 80,000 men, all fresh troops, while the French, though flushed with success, were considerably weakened by the fatigues of the siege.

1692.

Descriptions of battles, are seldom intelligible to ordinary readers, especially when unaccompanied with plans; and the accounts of the historians of those times are, from their very minuteness, confused and contradictory.

The French being posted near Steinkirk, William quitted his encampment during the night of 2d of August, and arriving there early next morning, spent some hours in reconnoitring the ground, and marshalling his troops. He had for his second, the Count of Solms, (a name of ill omen,) and under him, the Duke of Wirtemberg and the Elector of Bavaria, with Mackay at the head of the British infantry. Solms was jealous of Wirtemberg, hated the English, and presumed on his relationship, and influence with his royal cousin, the King. Wirtemberg, being pressed by the enemy, sent to the Count for succour, which the latter affecting not to understand, either wholly withheld, or delayed to grant, till it was perceived by the King, who immediately issued the most peremptory commands to the Count, to withhold no longer the required aid. He obeyed, but, in a tone of insolence, said to those around him, "Let us see what sport these English bull-dogs will afford us." Both horse and foot had been called for, but he sent only the former, who could not act on account of the ground, and he ordered the foot to halt, which they continued to do, until put in motion by the King himself, by which means precious time was consumed, and the battle was lost.

Others allege that orders were sent to Mackay by mistake, to move to the right instead of the left, and that being killed in this movement, his death proved the loss of the day. According to Bishop Burnet's History of his Own Times,* "Mackay being ordered to a post which he saw could not be maintained; he sent his opinion about it, but the former orders were confirmed: so he went on, saying only, The will of the Lord be done." And the words with which he gave utterance to this pious ejaculation, are the last which he is recorded to have spoken.

* 8vo Edition, p. 170.

1692. In this desperate action, 5000 men, on the side of the confederates, are said to have been killed or wounded, and of these 3000 Scots and English, in obedience to a rash and criminal order of Count Solms. Among the killed there were, besides the brave Lieutenant-General Mackay, (for so he is usually denominated,) Sir Robert Douglas, Sir John Lanier, the gallant Earl of Angus, in his twenty-third year, Colonel Hodges, grandfather of Colonel Gardiner, Colonel Roberts, and many others of inferior rank.

Mackay being mortally wounded, his servant leaped up on horseback behind, to conduct him to the rear, but before he reached it the vital spark had fled. The servant was of the same name and country with his master, and attended him through many a bloody campaign. The King, to testify his approbation of his faithful services and tried attachment to his master, gave him a regimental quarter-master's commission, in which situation he acquired such a competency, as enabled him to lay the foundation of a respectable family now existing in the Highlands. His Majesty attended Mackay's funeral, and so soon as his remains were laid in the grave, exclaimed, "There he lies, and a braver or better man he has not left behind him."

Conversing some days afterwards on the subject of the battle, and the characters of the officers who had fallen, he expressed deep regret for the loss of a particular individual, whom he named. A person present ventured to observe with surprise, that his Majesty did not mention, his old and faithful servant, Mackay; to which the King replied, "the individual I spoke of, served me with his soul, Mackay served a higher master and has his reward."

The foregoing details, meagre though they be, will enable the intelligent reader to form a just estimate of the intellectual and moral qualities of Mackay's mind, and to these details will be added the testimony of Bishop Burnet; who, during his exile in Holland, previously to the revolution, was intimately acquainted with him, and had good opportunities of knowing the estimation in which his character was universally held.

"Mackay," says the Bishop, "a general officer who had served long in Holland with great reputation, and who was the piousest man I ever knew in a military way, was sent down to command the army in Scotland. He was one of the best officers of the age, when he had nothing to do but to obey and execute orders, for he was both diligent, obliging, and brave, but he was not so fitted to command. His piety made him too apt to mistrust his own sense, and to be too tender or rather fearful in any thing where there might be a needless effusion of blood."*

In the same volume† will be found his account of the battle of Steinkirk, from which that inserted in this sketch is partly taken. The Bishop then proceeds, "Mackay was a man of such strict principles, that he would not have served in a war that he did not think lawful. He took great care of his soldiers' morals, and forced them to be both sober and just in their quarters. He spent all the time, he was master of, in secret prayer and in reading of the scriptures. The King often observed, that when he had full leisure for his devotions, he acted with peculiar exaltation of courage. He had one very singular quality; in councils of war he delivered his opinion freely, and maintained it with due zeal, but how positive soever he was in it, if the council of war overruled it, even though he was not convinced by it, yet to all others he justified it, and executed his part with the same zeal, as if his own opinion had prevailed."

Of Mackay's military talents, we have here much well-merited praise, so that according to the Bishop, he was esteemed one of the first officers of the age. The value of the praise, however, is diminished by the restricting clause which limits its application to the condition of his being employed in a subordinate capacity, where he had nothing to do but to obey and execute orders, and on this gratuitous assumption, the learned prelate declares him "unfitted for command." How an officer of such a character, as is here described, could with any propriety be denominated "one of the first officers of the age," seems difficult to conceive, and the Bishop's character of Mackay is therefore in so far inconsistent with itself.

* History, vol. iv. p. 47.   † Page 170.

The first cause assigned for the alleged unfitness for command, is his "being too apt to mistrust his own judgment," which is not only unsupported by any evidence, but is at variance with known and admitted facts.

Did he distrust his own judgment immediately after his defeat at Killiecrankie, when in a state of mind little calculated to inspire self-confidence, he acted in opposition to the opinion of his officers, (who recommended his returning by the nearest route to Perth,) and wisely preferred the circuitous route across the mountains to Stirling? Did he manifest any distrust of his own judgment, when, on arriving at Stirling, exhausted in mind and body, after a distressing march of forty-eight hours, he rejected at once the pusillanimous proposition of the council, to abandon to the enemy all the country north of Tay, and remove the seat of government to Glasgow? Did he betray any symptom of the weakness imputed to him, when before retiring to rest that night, he wrote letters to the council, disapproving of the measures he understood they had proposed, and when acting on his own responsibility, he hastily assembled an army of 2,000 men, with which he marched back to Perth, on the second day after his return to Stirling to check the progress of the enemy? Could any commande have displayed more presence of mind, more decision, more vigour and energy of character, than Mackay exhibited on this occasion.

Let us follow him to Ireland, and observe his firmness in strenuously maintaining his own opinion in councils of war, even when opposed by all the other members. Not to repeat what has been already fully stated, respecting the passage of the Shannon, the seige of Athlone, and the battle of Aughrim, it is enough to say that on these occasions, Mackay displayed all the qualities which are required to constitute a consummate commander, that it is impossible to peruse the history of the Irish campaign, without being of opinion that de Ghinkel and he ought to have changed places.

The second cause of Mackay's alleged unfitness for command, is his "piety," which is represented as making him "too tender, or rather fearful in any thing, where there might be a needless effusion of blood." Such a weakness as is here supposed, would not only have unfitted him for a subordinate command, but have even wholly disqualified him for the military profession. It was Mackay's peculiar felicity, that all the wars in which he had been engaged, at least after he entered the Dutch service, were just and necessary wars, undertaken solely for the defence of the protestant religion, and the liberties of his country, or of Europe. In wars of this description, the most scrupulous piety could not object to the shedding of blood, when necessary to the defence of the most sacred rights, and carried no further.

The opinion therefore, advanced by Burnet of Mackay's unfitness for command, in consequence of his being too apt to mistrust his own judgment, and of his piety preventing the due performance of his military duty, when closely examined must fall to the ground. Nothing, it is believed, could be farther from the good Bishop's intention, than to misrepresent Mackay, or advance what would tend to lower his military character, in the estimation of posterity; and yet that he has done so, is clear from what has now been stated.

By contemporary historians, Mackay's character as a commander, is always mentioned with high respect; and it was not until the publication of Burnet's history, the first edition of which appeared in 1725, that his fitness for command was ever called in question. What could have prompted this excellent prelate to write in such unguarded terms, concerning the character of a general officer, who had rendered such important services to his country, and for whom he himself, in particular, entertained such a high respect, is not easy to conceive, unless we suppose him to have written under the momentary influence of that constitutional *etourderie* for which he was so remarkable. Be this as it may, the unfavourable opinion he has recorded, has been faithfully copied without examination, by recent writers of all parties, and has thus done an injury, now perhaps irreparable to the character of this brave soldier and excellent man.

Having thus endeavoured to vindicate Mackay's professional character as a soldier, let us now consider his piety as a Christian, a subject concerning which there can be no difference of opinion, as it was the feature of his character, which most distinguished him from other military men. At what particular period his religious impressions commenced, cannot now be ascertained, none of his private letters being extant, so far as is known to the author. That he was a man of the most ardent piety, is evident from his public correspondence—of which numerous specimens have been printed for the Bannatyne Club—from the testimony of Bishop Burnet, and from the universal voice of tradition, both in this country and in Holland, where his memory is still cherished with reverential remembrance. Of his attention to preserve strict discipline, and the exercise of religious duties, among the men under his command, a striking proof has lately been brought to light, and rescued from oblivion, by the learned editors of an edition of his Memoirs, presented to the Bannatyne Club. It appears that, not long before his death, Mackay had drawn up a code of regulations for the army, contained in a book entitled, "Rules of War for the Infantry, ordered to be observed by their Majesties' subjects, encountering with the Enemy upon the day of Battel. Written by Lieutenant General Mackay, and recommended to all (as well Officers as Soldiers,) of the Scots and English Army. In XXII Articles. Published by his Excellency's Secretary." " The conclusion of that work," it is observed by the learned editors alluded to, " exhibits in a singularly beautiful and interesting manner, this part of his (Mackay's) character. ' Lastly, when all dispositions are made, and the army waiting for the signal to move towards the enemy, both officers and soldiers ought seriously to recommend, together with their souls and bodies, the care and protection of the cause for which they so freely expose their lives, to God, who overruleth the deliberations and councils, designs and enterprises, of his creatures, and on whose blessing alone, the success of all undertakings doth depend ;—which they may do in these, or the like words :

A PRAYER.

'O, almighty King of kings, and Lord of Hosts, which, by thy angels thereunto appointed, doth minister both war and peace. Thou rulest and commandest all things, and sittest in the throne judging right; and therefore we make our addresses to thy divine Majesty in this our necessity, that thou wouldest take us and our cause into thine own hand, and judge between us and our enemies. Stir up thy strength, O Lord, and come and help us, for thou givest not always the battle to the strong, but canst save by many or by few. O, let not our sins now cry against us for vengeance, but hear us, thy poor servants, begging mercy, and imploring thy help, and that thou wouldest be a defence for us against the enemy. Make it appear, that thou art our Saviour, and mighty deliverer, through Jesus Christ, our Lord. Amen.'"

It was a common saying among the Dutch soldiers, that General Mackay knew no fear but the fear of God. Such popular sayings are commonly founded in truth, and that it was so in the instance before us, the reader, it is hoped, will readily believe. It appears from the uniform tenor of Mackay's life, that he had the fear of God continually before his eyes, and that he not only habitually regulated his own conduct by the precepts of the gospel, but also was at pains to enforce obedience thereto among the officers and soldiers under his command, for whose moral and religious, as well as military conduct, he felt himself to a certain degree responsible.

In the sublime scripture doctrine of a particular providence, (to use an expression of Professor Dugald Stewart's) he was a firm and practical believer, and embraced every opportunity of inculcating the doctrine on his men. Every bullet, he used familiarly to tell them, had its billet: and if, as our Saviour himself has told us, without the permission or appointment of our heavenly Father, not even a sparrow falls to the ground, how much less a human being destined for immortality!

From this doctrine, he derived never-failing support in the hour of need, being fully persuaded, that all the events of the present life, great and small, prosperous and adverse, are under the guidance of unerring wisdom and goodness. Animated by this conviction, he cut his way, unsupported and alone, through the opposing ranks of the Highlanders at Killiecrankie, claimed the post of danger, because the post of duty, at Athlone, and plunged into the Shannon, regardless of the perils of fire and sword; rushed into the thickest of the fight, and turned the battle, at Aughrim, and finally, at Steinkirk, in obedience to the rash and criminal order of his immediate superior, cooly marched on to certain and instant death, with this ejaculation in his mouth, "the will of the Lord be done."

Such was General Mackay. From men, he did not receive those rewards which his services merited; but he knew his record was on high, and that with his last breath, he might confidently adopt the triumphant language of the Apostle, and exclaim, " I have fought a good fight, I have finished my course, I have kept the faith: Henceforth there is laid up for me a crown of righteousness, which the Lord, the righteous Judge, shall give me at that day."—2 Tim. iv. 7, 8. " Mark the perfect man, and behold the upright, for the end of that man is peace."—Psalm xxxvii. 37.

APPENDIX.

APPENDIX.

No. I.

MAJOR-GENERAL MACKAY, TO LORD MELVILLE.

From the Head of Strathspey, the 13th June 1689.

My Lord,

Since I find that there are some apprehensions of invasion from Ireland, I will dispose myself for the south with a part of the forces I have here by me, which joined me within few days; the rebels are entered Lochaber again, where I judged it not for the service to follow them, because here there are no good ways to be furnished over all with provisions, and without them no regular body of forces can subsist together. I leave Colonel Livingstone and Sir James Leslie with their regiments in and about Inverness, with 200 of my Lord Leven's, till they be relieved by three companies of Leslie's, which are coming down from Berwick. I can assure your lordship, had I not been here to oppose the rebels these two times they descended since my north coming, that the most part benorth Tay had been by this in open rebellion against his Majesty and the present government; what shall now be the turn of affairs when I go south, I cannot as yet judge, but I hope God will complete the deliverance which he hath wrought thus far for his oppressed people, and make the reign of our present sovereign abound in prosperity and peace. I judge that it may be prejudical for the present service, that there is no fund of money in Scotland, at least for the punctual payment of his Majesty's forces upon the English foot; withal the officers not receiving payment of a long time, occasions some grumblings among them, which your lordship may take your own way to represent. I sent the party of my Lord Colchester's regiment of horse south already; the officers and troopers are very well affected to the service, but they lost many horses, which I hope his Majesty will consider; for, though there hath been no great bloodshed, they have done good service, to be of the number of little more than 400, which, by God's direction, broke the measures of a disaffected numerous people, and 200 of those discovered after to be partly infected and corresponding with our enemies, not to us, therefore, but to God (who hath hitherto blessed the just arms of our sovereigns) be the praise. If assistance from Ireland could be hindered, I question not but those Highlanders would soon weary of it, but as long as they have any hopes of that, they will not be so fond of propositions, because they will judge themselves in bad circumstances with the present government, by what they have done already. The Marquis of Athole doth not play fair, for his country is very disaffectedly disposed. I hope you shall take measures to keep from us such as would augment our troubles. Tarbat hath not done, in my opinion, neither what he ought and could do, neither among his own relations or others with whom he had great credit. I am still of opinion, that an act of indemnity would do much to quiet the spirit of such as fear after reckonings. A great part of the Lord Lovat's men have been with the rebels at this time. In all the north, I know of no families we can make state on, except my Lords Strathnaver, Reay, and Forbes, with the Laird of Grant, and a gentlemen of the name of Gordon, entitled Edinglassie, Sheriff of the shire of Banff, is very forward and zealous for the present government. I will essay Lochiel yet once, though I have no great opinion of his sincerity. There hath been a flying report this day, as if some vessels were come to Inverlochy, but no assurance as yet thereof. Your Lordship may rest fully assured, that, by the strength of the Most High (in whom I trust, and not to mine own understanding or direction) I shall do faithfully as before God, all that lies in me for the advancement of their Majesties' service, and maintenance of the protestant religion, without the least self-regard, having no other ambition than the seeing of that interest once well established and secured. I shall add no farther, than that I am unfeignedly, my Lord, your Lordship's most humble and obedient servant, H. MACKAY.

APPENDIX.

FROM THE SAME TO THE SAME.

Inverness, 14th June 1689.

MY LORD,

Being in haste when I wrote my last from the head of Strathspey, I forgot to mention the Laird of Balnagown, the chief of the name of Ross, who is a man of good following, and hath testified all the zeal and forwardness which could be expected of the most and best affected for his Majesty's service, and the present government. Upon my desire, the committee of estates did send him a commission of sheriff principal for the shire of Ross, and because I know that others who are neither so capable to do his Majesty's service nor to exercise that charge, will be putting in for it, I judged it expedient to advertise your Lordship, that he may be continued therein by his Majesty, it being an affront instead of favour, which he deserves, by his readiness to all things that I command him for his Majesty's service, if he should be put out. Next Seaforth he is the considerablest man in Ross for the matter of following, so I pray your Lordship may represent to the king that he may be continued, for none other can take so ill the not getting of it as he the being put out of the possession of it. I have sent to Lochaber to know what the rebels are adoing, they are separate once as my former did mention; all the forces I had north after the junction of Ramsay and the two English regiments, would make little more than 2000 men, and the combined Highlanders can make 3000, besides as many more that would quickly join them, if once they had some advantage. The Highlanders are absolutely the best untrained men in Scotland, and can be equalled to our new levies, though they were better armed than they are, particularly those Highlanders we have in head. I will nevertheless labour to settle things, so that the general interest of the service may be secured here, though I, with a party of the foresaid troops go south, but some particular men may come to suffer, particularly the Laird of Grant, at whom they have great prejudice, as well as at the rest of our friends, but he lies the most exposed of all, but if the whole be saved, the particular breaches may be easily made up. I shall be obliged to stay some few days here, both that I may consider what places are most expedient to be taken in possession, and that the noise of my sudden march from this, bring not the rebels so quickly together again, to fall down upon these countries, though I leave double the number of regular forces of what I had against the same enemy; so I hope things may be well enough secured, if nothing come from Ireland. God I hope will put a happy end to all, to his glory and the security of his salutary truth, to us and our successors under the government of their Majesties, and theirs. I am, my Lord, your Lordship's most humble and obedient servant,

H. MACKAY.

P. S.—A place of security made at Inverlochy for a garrison of 600 men, (which cannot be undertaken without former provision of things necessary, and six weeks sure time to end it) would, (with a small body of the like number at Inverness) make those Highlanders as peaceable as Moray.

EXTRACT OF A LETTER FROM THE SAME TO THE DUKE OF HAMILTON.

From Badenoch, a mile from the Rebel's Camp, 1689.

One thing I can assure your Grace, that Ramsay's not joining me hath extremely altered the face of affairs, for otherwise I could easily have beat or chased the rebels, without the least hazard of the service, being fortified with such a body of foot, whereas, now I find them lodged where my horse can be of no value to me, and all the old foot we have is but 200, so that without a manifest hazard to the service, I cannot resolve to attack them there, the more that they are, by all information I can get, considerably the strongest, which I would not value, if I could bring them to plain ground. The rebels expect the junction of the Athole, Mar, and Badenoch men, besides Breadalbane, Macdonald of the Isles, Macleod, the Mackenzies, and Caithness men, if things go favourably for them. The Marquis of Athole might have done much, to have prevented all this disorder, if he had been so much for the protestant religion, and the interest of King William and Queen Mary, as his Lordship was pleased to protest more than once, solemnly to me; and I believe my Lord Tarbat doth not so much as he should, either for disposing well his own family, or other Highland chiefs, by whom his advice is of great esteem. God forgive them that would bring in popery and the violentest of all persecutions, (French and Irish) upon these nations. Now, I have given your Grace a full detail of the state of affairs in the north. Besides, that little good is to be expected of all benorth Tay, all the well affected families being in small numbers besides the others, I am informed Mar's men have disobeyed his order to take arms for the government. The 600 men under Ramsay, if they had joined me according to direction, had prevented disorders, which haply 10,000 men will have enough ado to quiet, if they of the contrary party understand to serve themselves of the occasion. To remedy those disorders so much as possible, I have ordered north Sir James Leslie's regiment of foot, and Barclay's of dragoons; therefore if the state of affairs require others in their place, your Grace may desire Sir John Lanier to call for so many. My opinion is, that a good body be lodged at St. Johnston, and another at Dundee, whereof a party of horse in both places; and that the house of Blair of Athol be garrisoned; for if they should offer to hold it out, it may be forced by a pettard, whereof we brought some from England. When your Grace and the convention shall have read this letter, I pray you send it to court, that his majesty may see how things stand, as they appear to me at present, declaring before God, that I have no prejudice against any man, otherwise than that I cannot dissemble what I think amiss of men's carriage in such a just and christian cause, for which we ought to esteem it a happiness to sacrifice all temporal considerations freely and cheerfully. I am, &c.

H. MACKAY.

FROM THE SAME TO LORD MELVILLE.

Edinburgh, the 20th July 1689.

My Lord,

The Master of Forbes, who since my going north, hath given singular proofs of his great zeal and affection for their Majesty's service, hath represented unto me, that during the two late reigns, the Duke of Gordon hath got from my Lord Forbes, his father, the superiority of a great many of his own and his friends' lands, which the said Lord parted with, rather than be in disputes with the said Duke, in a time when he himself and his family were looked down upon, as not ready in all things to comply with the designs of those times. Therefore, since the said Duke's life and fortune are at his majesty's pleasure, he judgeth it not unbecoming to labour, by a mark of his majesty's favour, (which I can assure your Lordship, he deserves as much as any I know in Scotland) to have the superiority of all his own and his friends' lands, which he do hold of the Duke of Gordon, to the end he may be in better capacity to appear more formidable for their majesties' service; which consideration, with the credit to depend of none but the king, is the only reason of his solicitation, and my earnest entreaty that your Lordship, (when the king, in his own time, may judge fit to restore the Duke of Gordon, and pardon his former faults) would have the goodness to order matters so, that his Majesty may gratify so worthy a person with the grant of so reasonable a demand, which is more for his Majesty's service than any advantage to him, for it will not be ten pieces yearly in his pocket. I wish the Duke of Gordon's family well, because of an ancient friendship betwixt it and ours; but I prefer such as are zealous for the protestant interest, and the advancement of my master's service, (of which I may call myself now a competent judge, having tried the pulse of most men in the north) to any consideration of particular friendship. It is a thing in the king's hand, and which he may do with all the justice in the world, and will not lessen the Duke of Gordon's estate; and you know, my Lord, that it is fit such persons as venture freely and cheerfully life and fortune for his Majesty's service, should receive some marks of his royal favour, particularly when it can be done at so cheap a rate. I find this parliament not like to jump with the intention of the king. I believe their greatest grudge is at my Lord President of the Session, and his son, for ought is pretended as yet, for some of them have been speaking to me of the matter. The Lord Advocate, and your son the master, have this evening been consulting with me, whether to evite one of two inconveniences, (that is to check his Majesty's choice of ministers, or to hinder the settlement of the kingdom in civil and church government) it were not necessary that his Majesty should bestow something upon Duke Hamilton, which might attach him wholly to his Majesty's interest, who certainly, if he be faithfully informed, will never strike or screw up the royal prerogative beyond the just limits established by law; but it is not fit nor safe he should part with what the law provides him to. The most newly levied forces are of the west countries, and those who are contrary to their principles, and apprehend the rigour of their government, we have no great reason as yet to lay much stress on. Therefore, if the commissioner can remove difficulties betwixt the king and his parliament, I think a good charge should be well bestowed upon him, and if thereafter he should not be found so serviceable, the king is always master of his favours. For certainly there is a great inconvenience, in my opinion, to be expected from proroguing the parliament, without settling either of a church government or a College of Justice, and no less from continuing of them in a cross humour. How far their pretensions do consist with law, I am ignorant of, but one thing I believe, that if this parliament, by a mutinous disposition of some leading member, should obtain their end, it might prove of bad example; but certainly if they had right on their side, it were worthy the greatness of the king to give their claim a favourable hearing. Therefore, my Lord, I pray you to have a special care his Majesty be put upon nothing that may seem to be a ground of aspersion to the enemies of his government, for his Majesty is supposed, by such as appear against his instructions, a stranger to your constitutions; and though in my judgment, their heats and delays of the matters of greatest moment be inexcusable, I find them nevertheless always making great protestations of affection and fidelity to his Majesty's service. The officers of dragoons, which I sent here prisoners, have confessed guilt, and throw themselves at his Majesty's feet, confessing their lives and fortunes to be at his royal pleasure, so that all their hopes are in his Majesty's clemency, particularly Colonel Livingstone, whose greatest guilt seems to lie in the concealing of the plot of others, for none doth testify that ever he consented to join the enemy; but though his Majesty should incline to pardon them, I would be of opinion they should be secured till things be better settled in the kingdom. I do not know if I can be present at the council of war, for I sent the forces which I design against the rebels on their way so far at St. Johnston, and shall follow them by the way of Stirling, to see that place and the importance thereof, where I leave a good body of forces ready to march where his Majesty's service shall require, with Sir John Lanier and Balfour to command them. It were fit the twelve troops newly levied were regimented. Annandale and Ross seem to be the expectants, they are both pretty men and were forward to settle the crown upon their Majesties; what may be their reason to join with the jangling party now I cannot tell; haply this mark of his Majesty's favour might break them off. There are several express boats sent to Loch Foil, to advertise his Majesty's ships there of the invasion by their negligence made by those three ships. I cannot learn by the report of such as came from Belfast, that there is great appearance of the coming of any more; a couple of frigates upon this north coast and towards the Isle of Sky, would contribute much to subdue the rebellion. I am, my Lord, your Lordship's most humble and obedient servant,

H. MACKAY.

APPENDIX.   147

THE DUKE OF HAMILTON TO LORD MELVILLE.

Holyroodhouse, 28th July 1689.

My Lord,

On Friday last Major-General Mackay marched from St. Johnston with about 4,000 foot, four troops of horse and dragoons, and was at Dunkeld that night, where he received intelligence that Dundee was come to Blair in Athole; he marched on Saturday towards him, and within two miles of Blair about five at night they engaged; and several inferior officers and soldiers that are come here this evening, give us the account, that after a sharp engagement, Dundee being much stronger, the Major-General was quite defeat, and I have yet heard of no officers of quality that have come off but Lt. Colonel Lauder, whom my Lord Ruthven spoke with as he came from St. Johnston this day, and gives the same account of their being wholly routed, but the confusion is such here that the particulars are hardly to be got. We have given orders at council this afternoon, to draw all the standing forces to Stirling, and have sent to the west country to raise all the fencible men, and Sir John Lanier has writ to the English forces in Northumberland to march in here, and is going to Stirling to command, for Mackay is either killed or taken by all the account we have yet got, but you shall quickly have another flying packet or an express. I am sorry for these ill news I send you to acquaint his Majesty with; and my humble opinion is, that his Majesty must first beat Dundee and secure this kingdom, or he attempt any other thing; and now Dundee will be master of all the other side of Forth where there are so great numbers of disaffected to join him, so the king must make haste to assist us to reduce him, for I fear we shall not be able to defend this side of Forth long, and the king will know what new men are after a ruffle given. We do not know what to do with the prisoners, there are so many of them in the Castle and Tolbooth here, and desire the king's command in it if they may not be sent some to Berwick, and some there to the Tower, in a man-of-war we hear is just now coming up to Leith. I intend to adjourn the parliament to-morrow or next day, every body desiring it to October. In this confusion and disorder we are in here, and having so many other things to despatch, all I can further say is, that I beg you may haste down the king's commands in this unhappy juncture, to your Lordship's most humble servant,

HAMILTON.

SIR JOHN DALRYMPLE TO LORD MELVILLE.

Edinburgh, July 28, 1689.

MY LORD,

This day brings us sorry, sad, and surprising news. We have good hope that your son is safe; he is wounded in the shoulder, but was mounted after all was broke; there hath been treachery in the leading them to that place, and the seige of Blair, and my Lord Murray's raising his men hath all been concerted, and yet I do admire that so good a party, so good officers and soldiers not surprised, but having well fought it, could have been oppressed with twice so many new men; we have no perfect accounts, but there is great loss of officers. I fear poor honest G. Major Mackay his brother is killed, and Colonel Ramsay and Colonel Hastings, and my Lord Kenmuir, I fear poor Belhaven is gone; Annandale's troops, wanting officers, made the first disturbance. The Lord is punishing the spirit of contention that reigns amongst us, by these who were no people. Argyle has about 3000 men on the other side, but new men, and though he be within a day's journey of Lochaber, yet he never knew that Dundee was marched. Dundee had not above 100 horses; the Athole men are more cruel than the enemy's army, so I fear few will either get off or get quarter, except some of the horse which ran first, and the foot officers, their servants are all come away with their horses; this makes a great consternation here; we have ordered all the forces we have to Stirling, and have ordered all the fencible men to be rendezvouzed, but I wish you may order us troops from England, for the countrymen will not do any service, and they will now become intolerable; some people already appear not so concerned as the stroke requires. I think the other side of Tay is lost, and Fife is in very ill tune,—the Lord help us, and send you good news of your son. My dear Lord, adieu.

For my LORD MELVILLE,
Lord Secretary of State for Scotland, at London.

MAJOR-GENERAL MACKAY TO THE DUKE OF HAMILTON.

Stirling, the 29th July 1689.

MAY IT PLEASE YOUR GRACE,

I am sorry I have not better account to give your Grace of our last expedition, but satisfied in my own mind that I have undertaken nothing but upon such grounds as more capable commanders might readily be deceived in. For I take God to witness, (who knows the secrets of hearts) that I do not make such an idol of vain-glory and reputation, as to oblige me to enterprise the least thing which my judgment might represent to be contrary to their Majesties' service and the present government, upon that account. But considering that my forces were superior in number to the enemy's, as I could very well know, being the space of two hours in order of battle, within a musket shot to them, (not judging it fit to attack them, being ranged upon a hill above a plane, where I drew up troops) and judging my men far beyond theirs in the use of their arms and fermity in occasion, I thought I might safely, according to the rule of common prudence, engage them, though it pleased * * * * but it seems that God (in this as well as in all acts of the universe) will let us see the vanity of human confidence. In short, there was no regiment or troop with me, but behaved like the vilest cowards in nature, except Hastings' and my Lord Leven's, whom I most praise at such a degree as I cannot but blame others, of whom I expected more, &c. &c.

H. MACKAY.

MAJOR-GENERAL MACKAY TO LORD MELVILLE.

Stirling, the 29th July 1689.

MY LORD,

As none is more grieved that any thing prejudicial to their Majesties' service should fall to my share, so none shall use more diligence to repair the losses so far as may depend of me, than myself. My Lord, your son hath behaved himself with all his officers and soldiers extraordinary well, as did also Colonel Hastings with his. I have given a large account of matters to my Lord Commissioner, which I desired might be sent your Lordship. I am extremely in pain that my wife shall have the news of my death, before this enclosed can be at her. None of those who fled to Dunkeld and St. Johnston could say anything of me, for they were gone near an hour before I carried off your son's men and Hastings' by another way than the fled went, to be free of the people of Athole, whose disaffection I discovered of a long time to the prejudice of the service. This day late I came with that little body of the debris of those two regiments, to Stirling, without halt or rest for two days and two nights, to prevent the enemy's diligence to cut off my passage, and am now so overtaken with sleep that I can say no more, but that I am unchangeably, my Lord, your Lordship's most humble and obedient servant,

H. MACKAY.

APPENDIX. 151

A SHORT RELATION AS FAR AS I CAN REMEMBER, OF WHAT PASSED, BEFORE, IN, AND AFTER THE LATE DEFEAT IN ATHOLE, OF A PART OF THEIR MAJESTIES' FORCES UNDER MY COMMAND.

Strathboggie, the 17th August 1689.

After near three months' chicane with a very small parcel of forces against a numerous enemy, and at last having obliged them to disperse, and separate, and having left the north well secured, I returned to Edinburgh to hasten the necessary preparations for the design I had formed to go to Lochaber and secure a strong garrison in the heart of the Highlands, as in my judgment the most feasible and readiest way to subdue those Highland rebels. I met, however, with such delays before the number of 800 horse for the transporting for a fortnight's subsistence of meal only, that the enemy, who, questionless was advertised of our design, had time to gather together his forces depending of several Highland chiefs, and to march to Athole to secure that country (capable to put 12 or 1500 men under arms) for their party, which I had certainly prevented if the horse and provisions had not been too slowly furnished; of this I accuse none, for I believe it was want of use more than any other thing else which occasioned it.

Coming to St. Johnston, there was a letter shewn me, from my Lord Murray, wishing the person to whom it was sent might shew me that a speedy march was altogether necessary to prevent the junction of his men with Dundee, which he should not be able to hinder if the said Dundee should prevent my coming to that country. Upon which advertisement, having six good battalions of foot by me, and about 100 horse, having sent orders to four troops more of horse and two of dragoons to follow in all diligence, I marched to Dunkeld, where I was informed that my Lord Murray had retired from before the castle of Blair, my Lord Marquis of Athole's house: upon which I presently judged that Dundee was marching into the country, which thoughts were confirmed by a letter from the said Lord Murray, who wrote that according to my desire he had secured a pass by which I should pass conveniently with baggage and horse with 80 men, but since they were but countrymen and volunteers, he was not sure they should stay there long: whereupon I sent Lieutenant-Colonel Lauder with 200 chosen fusileers of the whole army, to keep the said pass till I should come up. About ten of the clock I arrived at the said pass, and having met with my Lord Murray, he told me that the most part of his men were gone from him to save their cattle from the Highlanders; with all that he thought he should get them kept from joining Dundee so long as he should stay upon their head but that by no means they would join me. I told him, if better could not be, he should do as he said, till they should see the issue of the matter, so, having passed the said pass, before I got up the regiment of Hastings' and the Earl of Annandale's troop which I left behind the baggage, lest the enemy or the Atholemen, which I trusted as little, might send a party to attack them behind, I discovered the Highlanders approaching and gaining the heights, and pretty near before I could get my men to the ground which I judged by their motion they would be at. So changing my march and facing with every battalion as it stood by a *quart de conversion* to the right, having viewed the ground where I judged apropos to range them, I made every regiment march straight before its face up a steep brea, above which there was a plain capable to contain more troops than I had, and above that plain the matter of a musket-shot, a rising of a hill above which and betwixt it and a great hill at his back Dundee had place enough to range his men. I could not have ranged mine but upon one line, both because I would not be outwinged nor obliged to draw so near, the enemy having the advantage of the hill above us, by which he should force us to attack him against the height or be incommodated with his too near fire. The enemy seeing me ranged sooner than he thought (having, as I believe, designed to come down upon the same ground before I could get possession of it, in which case he should have forced me over a river with his fire which could not be without manifest hazard of great disorder) he halted upon the height the space of more than two hours, wherein nothing passed but some light skirmishing. At last toward sunsetting they began to descend, and having made a ragged fire threw away their snaphans, and ran down the hill with drawn broadswords and targes; the battalion of Hastings, which was ranged upon the right hand, because the rest were drawn up in order before it had passed the defile, that of my regiment, my Lord Leven's and Kenmore with the half of Ramsay's battalion, made pretty good fire, the other half of Ramsay's with Balfour's whole battalion, and Lauder's detachment of 200 men, gave ground, or rather fled without any firing. When the enemy came down I had my eyes much upon their horse, which I judged scarcely so strong as our two troops, and having remarked that they seemed to attack about the middle of the line, when I perceived the most part of our fire spent, I called out the said two troops which I had behind the line by an interval, of a design to cause one of them flank the approaching Highlanders to the left and the other to the right, which had been of such effect had they resolution to obey their orders, and would have so encouraged the foot that in all appearance the Highlanders would soon have run for it: but the said horse not advancing, notwithstanding I brought them up myself, and that the Lord Belhaven who commanded them did behave very honestly, after a little confused firing they renversed upon the Lord Kenmuir's right wing, and so began the first breach so near as I could remark. Dundee with his horse wheeling to our right came upon the battalion of my regiment, by whose fire according to their own confession, both Dundee, Pitkur, one Ramsay and others were killed at the first onset, but in a very short time all did run except a part of the Earl of Leven's regiments, which by the diligence and fermity of the said Earl with his Lieutenant-Colonel, Major, and others, and a part of Colonel Hasting's regiment, which, after they had lost ground, the Colonel with his Lieutenant-Colonel and other officers brought up again, and kept the field of battle.

When all had scoured off which stood about me, so that I found myself abandoned in the midst of the enemies, I pierced through them, being well horsed, and seeing some redcoats in the field, I went to them, and sent presently after the runaways, desiring the officers to do their utmost endeavour to get as many rallied as possibly they could: but after near an hour's expectation, till it began to be dark, and seeing the enemy preparing of all sides to attack me, having in all but about 400 men, which we could not possibly bring in any order, and receiving notice that none of the officers could persuade their men to stand, much less to return back, having advertised the men to march off softly, we retired in the best order we could over the little river, and so retired by such ways as I judged should be the securest, and would evit the rencounter of the Atholemen, who, as I was informed of officers and soldiers afterwards, killed more men, and made more prisoners, three times over, than Dundee's men, for we judged that the enemy lost more men in the flight than we did in this occasion. I could learn of no commanding officer that misbehaved, though I confess that my Lord Leven, Colonel Hastings, and their officers have distinguished themselves in this occasion above all others. The brigadier Balfour, my brother, and others were killed after their men abandoned them. Lieutenant-colonel Lauder was abandoned by his party, and laboured without success to rally them; colonel Ramsay, the same; but two miles from the field of battle, he gathered about two hundred men, with which he joined me, when I came off. I marched then with about six or seven hundred men through the highland ways, till I came to castle Drummond, where I had a garrison; and Monday, from thence to Stirling; Tuesday, I despatched order to the Lord Colchester's regiment with all the troops of new levied horse and dragoons thereabouts, to the number of 400, and with them on Wednesday took my way to St. Johnston, both to hinder the junction of the shires of Perth and Angus with the enemies, and to keep them in the hills. At St. Johnston we surprised a party of a couple of hundred men, whereof 150 were killed; thither I sent for the three battalions that were left of the Hollands regiments, with Sir John Lanier's and Hayford's regiments, ordering Sir John when he should come up to halt at St. Johnston till he heard from me; while upon the enemy's motion to the Breas of Angus, I marched with the horse and dragoons I had by me to Forfar, to hinder that shire from rising in favour of the enemy, and upon their further motion over the hills to Aberdeenshire, I went to the town of that name, and from thence approached the enemy nearer; but judging by the nature of his post fit to receive such as would come in to him both from the high and low countries, I sent for Hayford and Livingstone's dragoons, having for dispatch taken no infantry with me, to oblige them to leave that post, which regiments joined me the last of them this day. I am of opinion, and my intelligence doth confirm it, that they shall soon weary of it, if they get no soudain succour from Ireland. To-morrow I intend to march in sight, if the enemy do not draw to the hills. This is a short summary of what past as to the late affair, but certainly the enemy is in a worse state now than before his victory, for he durst never set his nose in the low country, because I was over all to oppose him.

H. MACKAY.

FROM MAJOR-GENERAL MACKAY TO LORD MELVILLE.

Blair Castle, the 30th August 1689.

MY LORD,

Since my last to your Lordship from Strathboggie, the enemy finding he could advance nothing in the north, I being continually in his way, and betwixt him and all communication with the low country, he turned southward by the same way he went north, and I followed him as close as I could, considering I would not engage myself in any bad ground with horse and dragoons, only leaving Sir Thomas Livingstone with his own regiment which I had called from Inverness, three troops of Cardross' dragoons, and six troops of the new levies in Aberdeen and Banffshire. On coming to this place I found the castle empty and intier, which might be the effect of a threatening message I sent up the country as soon as I arrived at St. Johnstone, that if the castle of Blair were burnt, I would not leave a house standing betwixt it and Dunkeld. I had some of the country gentlemen by me to have the benefit of his Majesty's gracious indemnity, but I told them, since they could not otherwise secure the peace sufficiently, they must bring in all their arms, insuring them as then of the protection of the government, but that I could not judge it secure enough to receive them upon their bare swearing of the oath of allegiance. To-morrow I expect the answer of some of them, and shall be obliged to deal rigorously with such as shall refuse to come in upon those terms, for they have shewn so much enmity to the government already, that we cannot be sure of them otherwise; meantime the Highlanders are separate, and each returned to his own home, from whence I fancy they will not gather in haste so completely, except they have encouragement from Ireland, and I am of opinion if they let pass the limited time prescribed by his Majesty for their submission, that it ought not to be given them any more, but to rouse them out of the nation as the bane thereof, particularly the Lochabrians.

If the frigates which had order to sail about this north, to join Rooke, had order to receive directions from me, they had notably contributed to force them to obedience, for Maclean, Macdonald, and Clanranald, who are of the considerablest of them are Islanders, and soon subdued with three or four frigates, and some land forces aboard of them, which would certainly so dishearten the rest, that they would quickly give it over. I am now about the garrisoning of some places in the nearest highlands, it being impossible without starving of the forces, to think to place any forces at Inverlochy, for this year, the season being so far advanced, that we cannot expect much more fair weather, and no possibility to be supplied with victuals but by sea, which is very uncertain, except it were there before us. I make no question but it may be an easy matter, to make this kingdom peaceable, if things go well in Ireland and at sea, as I hope they shall, by the blessing of God. My Lord, if the king sends down subaltern officers to Colonel Livingstone's dragoons, he shall lose thereby several good and serviceable officers which I have been obliged to cause place for the necessity of the present service, there being after the discovery of their treasonable design, but four subalterns in all, with the colonel and major, for all officers in the regiment. I wrote for some commissions also for my own regiment, of which I sent a list; in time of war, and at this distance, it ought to be much left to the commander-in-chief to place officers, if he be known to be a man who principally doth regard the interest of the king's service, in choosing of officers; for the small number allowed us in the three regiments upon such strong companies, hath no question contributed to their disorder in the late occasion. One Lieutenant Arnault, of Balfour's regiment, hath behaved himself very honestly, and is a careful officer, who had his colonel's promise to be recommended to the first vacant company of his regiment, which hath fallen out to be the colonel's own, he deserves it very well, and your Lordship will have no discredit in recommending him. I am extremely weary of this sort of war, and it is certainly more fit for a man of fewer years, and more accustomed with the manner of the country, than for me; so that nothing but my zeal for their Majesties' service, and the interest of the Protestant religion, could make it supportable to me; so that if that be so far secured this year as to confine the rebels so within their own hills as that they cannot trouble the government, or that they happen to submit to it, I hope his Majesty will have the goodness to permit me to take my winter quarters in Holland, if it please God I live so long. For I can assure your Lordship, that I have wrestled not only with a great weakness of body for the most part of the time I have been in this kingdom, but also with great fatigues, inconveniences, and difficulties, particularly to get the forces to subsist, by reason of the slow and irregular methods of the government in those things to which they have been so little accustomed, together with the scarcity of money, without which the most knowing will but slowly advance matters, except we should make war as the Highlanders, by giving liberty to commit all sorts of disorder and violence, in which case we could keep an army as good as theirs of the same sort of people, but I would never be the commander of such an army. Our new levies have not proved generally very good, especially the foot regiments, I mean the levies ordered by the convention of estates; for my Lord, your son's regiment was shattered at the late bad rencounter, though, I thank God for it, the king's service hath lost nothing except the loss of some few honest men, whose time was come. I am always, my Lord, your Lordship's most humble and obedient servant,

H. MACKAY.

FROM THE SAME TO THE SAME.

Edinburgh, the 21st December 1689.

MY LORD,

Your Lordship's of the 12th I had two posts ago, but have received nothing as yet from my Lord Portland or by Colonel Cunningham. It hath been my opinion, that, in the beginning of such a signal charge, considering that all such as did go along with it could not be supposed to have been acted by truly christian and self-denied principles, but that many of them had too great a regard to the particular advantages which they proposed to themselves thereby. I say, my Lord, it was my opinion that the people should have been in some measure humoured, though thereby some persons in esteem by his Majesty might for a time be deprived of the outward marks of his royal favour, for the words of Solomon's counsellors are not in vain recorded, who said to his son, if thou be a servant to this people for this one day, then will they be thy servants for ever. If my endeavours or direction, or person or interest, can contribute anything to his Majesty's service and the promotion of this cause, your Lordship needs no ways to question it, hoping that God, (who hath been the author of so signal a deliverance, at the point of time when the ruin of the Protestant interest was projected and far advanced in the councils of men) will return, (after he hath let us see how little we have to trust to our own prudence or force) to be (in all such as he in his providence hath called or shall call, to have any direction in the advancement of this cause), for a spirit of judgment to them that sit in judgment, and for strength to them that turn the battle from the gate.

I confess, that when I consider that proverb, whereof our Saviour made use against the false calumnies of the Jews as to his miracles, that a kingdom divided against itself cannot stand, I think I might have some grounds of apprehension of the fall of Scotland in some notable disaster, for there is nothing but divisions and factions in Parliament, in Council, in the Church and in the Country. But when I make reflection that it is the undoubted truth of God for which we stand up, and which I question not but our King and some of those whom he doth employ, (whether in the cabinet or in the field) do sincerely mind, and prefer incomparably above all temporal considerations (which in comparison are but a vanity), I cannot but have some lively hope, that he will not leave unperfected a deliverance, which his providence hath thus far advanced, and for the accomplishment whereof, there are, without doubt, many faithful prayers daily put up to heaven in all Protestant churches of the world. Considering withal, that it is not for our sins and crimes against God, (though numerous and conscious to every one of us), that we are hated of our enemies, but for our adherence to his saving truth. I hope he shall do it for his own great name's sake which is invoked upon (and by) us, and for his truth, which, by their great advantages over us, would be spoken against and blasphemed by the enemies thereof. Therefore, though I am of opinion that the means to prevent trouble and unreasonable divisions ought to be diligently and carefully used, I labour to support always my hope by the contemplation of God's almighty power, and over all present providence and direction, overruling all the actions of his creatures good and bad, so that all things must tend to the end which he hath proposed to himself concerning them, in his eternal, unchangeable, righteous and holy counsel; and as he wanteth not innumerable means inconceivable to us, to redress that which we in our finite judgment think is unredressable, so is he bound to no means. Therefore, my Lord, let every faithful servant of God, called to any public administration, make use of such reflections for his support in difficulties, but not for an occasion of tempting providence by neglecting the means; for I must take the liberty to say, that the interest of the service, and the means of restoring peace in Scotland, hath been too long neglected, and that for my own part, I had lost my patience so far, that I often wished I had never been employed in it, but I consider that the heart of the king (who hath made choice of me for service) is in the hand of the Lord, from whose providence I also wait for a favourable success thereto, notwithstanding of all those difficulties and clouds overshadowing this comfortable blink of the deliverance of the Protestant churches of Europe, which he can quickly dissipate after he hath tried our faith, and retired our confidence from the arm of flesh to fix it in him. The tenor of your Lordship's letter, (which seemed as well to regret as to apprehend the present state of affairs dangerous at that rate, that the Protestant interest may be judged to lie again at stake) hath given occasion to this discourse, and assure yourself, my Lord, that if the prospect of all the advantages which the world can propose, should come in the balance, it would weigh in my estimation, no more than the wind in comparison of the Protestant interest, for which, with God's strength, I shall cheerfully sacrifice all that can be dear to me on earth, which is all at present from, my Lord, your Lordship's most humble servant,

H. MACKAY.

APPENDIX.

FROM THE SAME TO THE SAME.

Edinburgh, the 31st December 1689.

My Lord,

I find by his Majesty's late order for modelling and reducing the Scots forces, that little regard is had to what I have reiteratively written upon that subject, which I cannot question but hath been laid open before his Majesty; therefore I must conclude, that there is more credit given to some other men's relation of matters belonging to my profession, and depending of the character which I bear here, of commanding in chief their Majesties' forces, than to mine. For this, I would not be in the least offended, if I did not see that those informations do not only level at me as incapable to judge of the most convenient places for garrisons, or what sort of forces are most fit to be lodged in the different places of the kingdom, but also are against the service; for whoever hath informed, that well-affected Highlanders, being formed in regular bodies, are not the fittest for the Highlands, and to be employed in the houses next adjacent to the Highland rebels, have informed very ill. We know the contrary by experience of late, that when we place south-countrymen and strangers in those Highland countries, among the hills, they dare not stir a foot from their garrison, by reason they cannot trust to the guidance of their countrymen who are about all our garrisons, and enemies in their heart to our King's service, and this interest in general. About Indernesse, we have the Mackenzies and the Frasers, of the behaviour whereof I have sent your Lordship lately a letter, and do send you hereby one received to-day. If they have given over their design, 'tis by reason of a supply of horse and dragoons lately sent thither, which body, (I mean of horse and dragoons) if the King will break, (as I hope he shall not) I am apprehensive he shall not be long master of the north, and will cost him more than the keeping of them for a few months more can stand him, to recover it. The Laird of Grant's regiment in the north, about Indernesse, have made lately out of houses where they are partly posted, some successful enterprizes upon their neighbouring rebels, because they know the convenience of the ground, which our other forces placed in Blair of Athol, Finlanrig, Braymar, and other places, are not capable to do, because they are strangers in the country, and cannot trust to the inhabitants ; so that, my Lord, whoever meddles to give the King advice for changing the regiments from one place to another of the kingdom, without consulting him who commands his forces here, do take a little too much upon them, and haply by the consequence more than they could well justify. This, in my opinion, is one of the things most regarding the commander's judgment, being in the country, and supposed to have had the necessary informations whereupon to ground his measures in the disposition of the forces. My Lord, as to houses which are not necessary to be garrisoned, I know none, except the want of forces to supply them render them necessary to be abandoned; for the houses of Brahan and Castle Leod, belonging to the Lords Seaforth and Tarbat, when they were garrisoned, it was judged very necessary, as it is yet, for all that some men may say to the contrary, not so much to offend the enemy, as to cover the well-affected in Ross-shire from the depredations, not only of the open rebels, but also from the ill-affected Mackenzies and Frasers, who rob them under the colour of the said rebels. You find, by the enclosed, as well as the other I sent a while ago, that they were for certain in arms ; for Sir James Leslie (no more than I) hath no other quarrel against them but upon public account. My Lord, I have many reasons to be weary of this command, and to wish, with all my heart, some other might be pitched upon to supply it ; for such as are fed with the fancy of great ambition and expectations, and haply have not experienced so many different faces of that which men call fortune as I have, and are younger to recover a lost reputation, may undergo such difficulties more cheerfully, without examining them so narrowly. But, my Lord, I am not lodged there, and therefore, when I have not wherewithal, I can advance and humanly secure the interest of the service, I had rather quit all expectations, though they were more apparently advantageous than ever I did form them in my mind, than appear upon the stage to my confusion. It was my lot always to serve his Majesty with more difficulties than any other of my charge, at which I would never repine, God knows, in this quarrel, if my concern were alone interested thereby; for I wish this interest did go well, and were once well secured, though I were to-morrow reduced to a piece of bread; and I wish also, with all my heart, that all who pretend zeal for it were of the same mind, for then we should not see the King so embarrassed in his affairs at this time, as I have apprehended of a long time he should be, and now find it to my regret. My Lord, I could say much more upon the subject, but 'tis late, and the post waiting, so that I can add no more, than that I am, my Lord, your Lordship's most humble and obedient servant,

H. MACKAY.

FROM THE SAME TO THE SAME.

December 1689.

MY LORD,

If I did not judge it absolutely my duty, (however it may happen to be taken) so long as I am here, to represent persons and matters, as I can judge most advantageous for their Majesties' service, and the re-establishment of the peace and quiet of the kingdom, I had long since given over to write, because I seldom or never get the satisfaction to know whether any I propose be had in any regard, or the contrary. I remember to have written several times of the Scots horse, that they would never be fit for service if they were not regimented; I hear now from other hands that they are to be so, but I do not know if any regard be taken of the Master of Forbes, who, I am sure, hath done more for their Majesties' service this year, than many that make greater pretensions, and though he be such a person, as I am persuaded doth not serve this cause upon principles of self-interest, when there are nevertheless some charges to be distributed, which might help to accommodate a family, which (though of a considerable following) is not of the richest, and so entirely engaged in their Majesties' interest, I am of opinion that it would be of a good example such were not neglected. I can bear him witness (who have had occasion to remark men's temper in this kingdom) that from one end of Scotland to the other, none hath been more through stick and cordial in this cause, nor made better figure (keeping all the country about him, which abounded with ill-affected people for this government, in awe) than he, and hath been of very good use to me when I had but few or no forces to oppose a great multitude of rebels. I understand from the Earl Leven that your Lordship hath spoke for Edinglassie; one thing I would have your Lordship to advert unto, that, if the representations of such as shall command at any time their Majesties' forces in this kingdom, be altogether neglected, particularly in time of war and civil troubles, his credit is presently out, and can act no further than just command what regular forces he hath, in the beginning of this last summer, had not done the business, if my credit with some families had not got them to join with me; and though I am hopeful that whosoever shall command hereafter, shall not have so much need of such shifts, nevertheless, since the affairs of the world are so evidently subject to strange revolutions, there is no doubt but such as do well ought to be encouraged, to be a good example to others. I know your Lordship hath much to do, and if I knew to whom to address so fitly what touches the service here as to your Lordship, I would not have given you so much trouble, but I forgot to desire the king's explication upon that point; and now since I am in expectation that his Majesty will give me some months of this season, wherein I can do but little service here, to look after my family, and labour to leave it in some better order then I left it last, upon such a short warning as I had from his Majesty, I do not think it worth the pains to change methods, or look after another correspondent at court. There is one Van Hill, captain in the Earl of Leven's regiment, a very good officer, who hath served long among horse. If the troops be designed for regiments, he would be a very fit major for one of them, for certainly they'll need, in each regiment at least, a major that served abroad and among horse; this is of the nature of all my other recommendations, that is, men in whom I have no interest but that of the service; for since I came to Scotland I do not remember that I recommended a relation of mine but Major Mackay, who was put by, though he had the grant of it before from the king; but any wrong which may happen to be done to me or my relations, over whom I shall have any power, shall never lessen the number of their Majesties' faithful servants; for I do thank God for it, that neither the passion of ambition, or desire to be accommodated with abundance of temporal convenience, doth ever disquiet my mind. I expect daily orders concerning the Danes, for if they be shipped out of England to Ireland, the ships must go thither. I am, my Lord, your Lordship's most humble and obedient servant,

H. Mackay.

FROM THE SAME TO THE SAME.

Edinburgh, the 13th January —90.

My Lord,

Finding the bearer hereof, Captain Hill, of the Earl of Leven's regiment, an officer who can be very useful to me for the ensuing campaign, (being a person understanding pretty well both foot and horse, particularly the latter, and to the boot, a sober, diligent, and careful man) I pray your Lordship to recommend him to the King from me, for the charge of adjutant-general of his forces in Scotland, having hitherto had great want of a capable person for that charge, both as to the regular distribution of orders, mustering of the forces, and bringing of our small cavalry upon some foot of service. I beg then that his Majesty for the interest of his service, (which necessarily, in spite of me, will be neglected if I have not the ordinary helps) may be pleased to grant Captain Hill a commission for the said charge. And further, to allow me two aides-de-camp for the ensuing campaign, for in these particulars I ought not to be considered as a major-general under superior commanders, but as commander-in-chief of so many forces, and in an occasion much doth depend upon the having a set of good men for the speedy and regular distribution of the orders, and is greatly the reason that I cannot be so sure of the state of the forces when separate as otherwise, being obliged to make use of the officers of one regiment to muster another for want of such officers, upon whose report I could make state. If his Majesty be pleased to grant the foresaid commission to Captain Hill, he may be employed to see dispatched such supply of arms, ammunition and other necessaries, as he shall resolve to let me have for the carrying on, and with divine assistance, ending of this war, according to a memorial which I shall send up to that effect. I pray your Lordship to forward this solicitation, as also the dispatch of the necessary supplies whereof we cannot be furnished here; for though no man breathing shall, with God's assistance, more cheerfully encounter all sorts of difficulties for this cause and their Majesties' service than I shall do, yet where they can be remedied, I ought not to be overcharged. I shall give his Majesty by the post, account of the particulars; my earnest desire is that we might make a considerable progress in the reduction of the rebellion in this kingdom before the opening of the campaign in Ireland; and in order to our early camping (notwithstanding we are clothing for the third time since our coming to Scotland) I have given orders for making surtouts for all the regiments paid out of England, as also, tents, in case the ingredients can be had here. If it please God they do well, his Majesty can always consider their losses and expences, but till then I shall not solicit for them were they at never so much. This is all at present from, &c.

H. MACKAY.

APPENDIX.

INSTRUCTIONS FROM MAJOR-GENERAL MACKAY

For Major Ferguson, appointed to command in chief the Detachment of Six Hundred men, which are to be shipped at Greenock, and to go about to the Isles and west of Lochaber; and for Captain Pottinger, commanding their Majesties' ship the Dartmouth, with the rest of the squad under his command.

1. The said major and captain shall do all things communicatively, and digest their resolutions betwixt themselves before they communicate them to others.

2. They are expressly charged, that no divisions be among them upon the matter of their undertakings, which may prove prejudicial to the service, but that they resolve and do every thing unanimously and with one accord, the captain submitting to the judgment of the major as to landings and undertakings against the enemy by land, if occasion should offer visibly favourable thereto, and the major submitting to the captain's judgment as to sea affairs.

3. The main design of this detachment being to make a diversion, alarm the rebels' coasts, cut their communication with the islanders now in rebellion against their Majesties' authority, and to take away or burn all their boats and birlins whether in the isles or along the coasts of the rebels on the firm land; the major is to undertake nothing as to landing, but upon visible and apparent advantages and human assurance of success.

4. If the major should see palpably, that with a reinforce of three or four hundred men more, he might master the Island of Mull, he shall presently give notice thereof to the Laird of Arckinlas, sheriff-depute of Argyleshire, who is to have order from the Earl to assist him with that number of the most resolute and best armed men of the shire, and such as will willingly and cheerfully be employed in that service, and against that enemy, and that with all possible diligence, that the occasion may not be lost by delays.

5. That their first enterprize be against all the enemy's boats, to the

end they be rendered incapable to succour with men or provisions one another, and so be reduced to extremities, and haply to submit.

6. That upon giving up all their arms as well swords as guns, delivering over all places of strength, and swearing allegiance to their Majesties King William and Queen Mary, the major foresaid is hereby authorised to give protection to the inhabitants of the isles but not to their chiefs, but by casting themselves on the king's mercy, and delivering their persons prisoners to the said major, who in that case is required to treat them civilly.

7. He shall take nothing from such persons and countries as shall submit upon the foresaid conditions, but a necessary supply of provisions to his men and ships, and that moderately; and upon the contrary, shall use with all the rigour of military execution, such as shall continue obstinate in their rebellion, with this proviso, that women and children be not touched or wronged in their persons.

8. The said major commanding in chief shall have special care his men be kept under exact discipline both as soldiers and christians, to hinder cursing and swearing and all other unchristian and disorderly customs, and to chastise in their purse and persons, such as persist in them after intimation.

Being upon the coast, he shall write to the Laird of Macleod, signifying that he hath order to succour and protect his country in case he be molested by those of his neighbours in rebellion, and that the government and I are well satisfied with his behaviour hitherto, knowing that so long as our assistance was so far distant, we could not expect his open declaring for their Majesties' government; but now as it is our resolution not to abandon him, that he shall declare himself freely for us and against our enemies, and so join forces.

APPENDIX.

MAJOR-GENERAL MACKAY TO LORD MELVILLE.

Edinburgh, the 6th February 1690.

MY LORD,

I had your letter of the 1st February, I question not but you have your hands very full of affairs, and I am persuaded that his Majesty is so extremely thronged with affairs of all sorts, that it is no matter of admiration that he can not so quickly dispatch orders, as those who are entrusted with any direction in the carrying on of his service would gladly have, seeing what prejudices delays may occasion thereto; and truly my Lord, as no man (be it said without vanity) serves this interest with less regard to his own, than I do, so none is more grieved, when I see any wrong steps made therein. The reason is palpable, for having no other object to direct my thoughts I have them always fixed there, nevertheless to little purpose, if I have no better concurrence than hitherto. I have laid before the king fully my judgment as to what ought to be undertaken early this spring; and if the little assistance which I desired were timely sent, with the three small frigates which his Majesty promised, and order to the privy council for what further concurrence the state of affairs here at present may be capable of, I question not but with God's assistance, to be able to give a good account of the Highland rebellion before the end of April, the weather proving any thing favourable. I expect, therefore, my Lord, that I may be advertised timely what supply I can expect from London of the things I wrote for, to the end if it were possible the defects might be supplied here, which nevertheless I can make but little state upon, all things considered; besides my zeal for their Majesties' service, and the interest of our holy religion; my longing to be out of this country, (where I can never expect to be grateful to men, because I neither do, nor never shall espouse any faction which I despair to see extinguished therein) shall be a sufficient argument to me, to promote (so far as in me lies) what may contribute to the peaceable establishment of their Majesties' happy authority in this kingdom.

I know I have my enemies, but they may well perhaps (as understanding the trade better than I) censure my conduct, but I would nevertheless advise them to consider that the king is a prince that will hear men's reasons, and that I want not mine, of which those that would condemn me without hearing, haply do not know the weight, but I defy the malice of all the earth to find a designed wrong step, (as to what his Majesty hath intrusted me with) in my conduct.

I have sent my Lord your son to muster the forces besouth Aberdeen, who hath brought me an exact account of their state. My Lord, I do not use to flatter any, and therefore take it for none that I tell you, I am very well satisfied with his conduct as to any thing I employ him in the advancement of his Majesty's service; the truth is, though our forces are none of the best, my greatest want is of officers capable to command a separate body, though I believe such of them as have served, be good resolute men; but the chief direction is not every officer's talent, though in this so large and separate winter-quarter, I could give but very imperfect directions from so far, so that necessarily it must needs have rested mostly upon the particular commander's discretion, excepting some general instructions from time to time, according to the notion I had of the enemy and the country.

I wish the King would declare the Scots regiment which he designs for Ireland, that they may be brought south if any of them be in the north. I have never doubted but your Lordship did communicate my letters to the king, for they always touch less or more his service, whereof he ought to be always the judge. I am, my Lord, your Lordship's most humble and obedient servant,

H. MACKAY.

APPENDIX. 171

MAJOR-GENERAL MACKAY TO THE PRIVY COUNCIL.

From the Camp at Collnakeill, 28th June 1690.

MAY IT PLEASE YOUR GRACE AND LORDSHIPS,

Having of a long time judged that the only way to reduce the present standing rebellion, was to establish a garrison at Inderlochy, all the government knows with what earnestness and obstacles I laboured to get things disposed thereto; and nevertheless now we have no more than two months of fair weather to expect, so that if upon any occasion I were obliged to delay my march, I might at the same time give over the design for this year. I find myself so straitened with the want of provisions, that I must venture forward before I have the assurance of any of our victuallers being about, which is somewhat contrary to the maxim of war; but I trust in the providence of God, and I find that the wind was always good both from the east and west coasts; and I hope that the provost of Glasgow, according to his wonted forwardness in this cause, hath a while ago despatched his ship with the 1000 bolls. I had meal along with me for a fortnight at Inderlochy, had not the council excused such shires as sent out pioneers from furnishing of baggage horses, notwithstanding that the whole number of pioneers got, makes but 200. But leaving off complaints, I come to inform your Grace and Lordships, that notwithstanding, I found myself more numerous than any thing the enemy could oppose to me betwixt Athol and Badenoch. I chose rather to take my march by Braymar, Strath Don, and Strathdown (who were all in rebellion) into Strathspey, where I gave rendezvous to Livingstone with all the forces in the north almost, except Strathnaver's regiment, with some men from Balnagown at Inderness, whither I ordered also some of my Lord Strathnaver's best men, two troops of horse in the shire of Murray, and five troops of horse and dragoons under the Master of Forbes. The reason that I altered my resolutions of forming a body benorth Ness are, that I may have a formidable body of forces together, in case their Majesties' service required my sudden moving toward the south, without expecting a further junction, that I may be in a condition to enter into Lochaber by more ways than one; if I should beyond my expectation meet with difficulties by the pass of Glenroy, which is the best that leads to that country, at least to make a stronger detachment above it, which is practicable with foot, than enemies' forces can be, and that I am much of the opinion that the temporizing party in the north will not move till they see the event of this expedition, seeing so many forces in a body for their Majesties' service, and ready to fall upon any that should oppose it.

I have ordered 300 of Balnagown's men, (a person well affected and most ready for this interest and service, and who ought, as such to be considered of the government) to fortify Inderness garrison, whither I dispatched two troops of horse; I expect also 300 of my Lord Strathnaver's men in the said garrison, and I wish my Lord himself were there, to command all, whose quality, interest, and zeal for this service, may contribute much to the security of that country in absence of the forces.

I entreat earnestly that your Grace and Lordships do not recal me before I have sufficient time to fix the garrison at Inderlochy, but that a way may be found to give me often notice of the state of affairs in the south, whereby I may judge rightly of the measures which are to be taken for the service in general; resting confident that nothing shall be neglected whereof my judgment shall be found capable, for the advancement of an interest to which I have self-deniedly vowed my pains without any by regards.

I wish also your Grace and Lordships take into your consideration the losses that necessarily the Laird of Grant's country would sustain by this junction of the forces, and to dispatch the said Laird to his country, who can easily keep some of his disaffected neighbours in awe, particularly Strathdown, Glenlivet, and Strath Don, though I am of opinion that my march, with the message I sent them, may make them see the issue before

APPENDIX.

they trouble their neighbours much. The Master of Forbes is always at great charges and pains for the service, and hath of the countrymen placed garrisons over all the shire of Aberdeen where it is needful. I recommend him then earnestly to the consideration of the government, and that a letter of thanks and approbation of his measures, with assurance of reimbursement and reparation of his expences and losses for the service, be written to him; for such forward persons ought not to labour under discouragements. I resolve to march to-morrow with 6000 men to Badenoch, from whence I have but three day's march to Inderlochy; I hope my victuals will serve me thither, and some few days over, and that God, the principal author of this happy change for all sincere Protestants, will conduct every thing that conduces to the security and advancement of this service.

I have added to the three Highland companies in pay, 300 men of my Lord Reay's country, which my nephew, Major Mackay, hath armed for this expedition, and do expect, with the help of those 600 brisk Highlanders, to be provided of fleshes in Lochaber. I caused pay every thing that was taken for the army in Strathspey, because of their losses otherwise. This is all at present from, may it please your Grace and Lordships, your Grace and Lordships' most humble and most obedient servant,

H. MACKAY.

FROM THE SAME TO THE SAME.

Inderlochy, 7th July 1690.

MAY IT PLEASE YOUR GRACE AND LORDSHIPS,

My Lord Commissioner's letter of the 28th June, with a postscript of the 30th, put a stop to the thoughts I had, to make a detachment capable to subdue the Isles of Mull and Skye, during my abode here, being willing to expect the event of the maritime engagement which was then expected to oppose the attempts of the ill-affected, if, as God forbid it should fall out cross for us, in as formidable a posture as I can; and that the rather, because I am certain that, without more succours for them, as we can well apprehend, they must, within three or four months, beg the peace. Surely their obstinacy deserves a severe treatment, for, hitherto, though this be the fifth day I am in this country, none of them hath made any cordial application as yet; but, though I am not ignorant how such fantasques, whose country is now in my remembrance, should be used, I will rather refer it to the government; because all that I can do to a dispersed lurking enemy, the governor of Inderlochy can do it much more effectually within three months, that is, to burn their houses, and destroy their corns. This government may be of great use, if it be speedily supplied with necessaries, otherwise it will turn to nothing, whatever be done to the rest of the forces, it must, at least, and ought to be paid some months by advance, and the governor supplied with some fund of money, whereby he may be always stored; certainly both officers and soldiers which are left here ought to be encouraged, by providing liberally for them, for the country is not very tempting. I would willingly take my way out of this country, by the head of Lochness, to garrison Glengary's house, if your Grace and Lordship's order for my speedy repairing southward doth not determine otherwise, which would be more to force him to obedience and submission than for communication, which I judge more effectual and ready from the western parts of the kingdom, so long as those rebels are not brought under entire subjection, as I have no commission from the King or your Grace and Lordships to treat with those obstinate rebels; and, knowing that my Lord Argyle, who is solely engaged in their Majesties' service and interest, is more concerned in such treaties than I am well informed, I willingly waive it, referring the matter to such as know better his Majesty's intentions, and his Lordship's concern to do the rest; resting satisfied to put things in that posture, with God's assistance, that this enemy shall not trouble us much, whatever may fall out more in any other part of the kingdom.

Buchan, with Dunfermline, and such other low country gentlemen as were with them, are gone by the way of Badenoch, whether further I cannot tell, but not one man of this country with them. I suspect they will labour to form a party in Aberdeenshire, but I question if they find a readiness to join them so long as I am above them; however, I am resolved to leave this garrison in a posture of defence, to which the speedy arrival of the planks, cannon, and other materials, would contribute much. Your Grace and Lordships would seriously mind the speedy supplying of this important post, from the west, of such necessaries as I sent you a list of, given up by Colonel Hill, otherwise all the pains and expences men have been at may prove fruitless, which, necessarily, would be of ill consequence. I shall forbear to use this obstinate enemy according to my judgment, and the ordinary practice of war, because, as I touched above, the government, if disposed thereto, can always get it done by the garrison, while I labour to make them the arbiters of their enemy's lot, which, as it always hath been, so shall it hereafter be in Scotland, the only design of, may it please your Grace and Lordships, your Grace and Lordships' most humble and obedient servant,

H. MACKAY.

The wrights, whose stay hath put me some days behind, are at last arrived.

MAJOR-GENERAL MACKAY TO THE DUKE OF HAMILTON.

Inderlochy, 10th July 1690.

MAY IT PLEASE YOUR GRACE,

My two last letters were to your Grace and council, to the end they may lay to heart the speedy supplying of this garrison, and now I send one of the commissioners, who shall have particular directions from Colonel Hill of things to be furnished. I pray your Grace, therefore, that it may be resolved, without any interrupting business, and the garrison sufficiently provided of money and provisions, with all diligence, otherwise there will be great grounds to accuse the government, of an inexcusable negligence in matters of greatest importance for the peace and quiet of the kingdom. I have written to Arckinlas to intimate to my Lord Argyle's chamberlains in Kintire, to send butter, cheese, and what other provisions they can furnish to the garrison upon the bearer's precept, which I oblige myself shall be paid by the general receivers, upon sight; but, though such things may happen to take effect, they must not be trusted to; if the garrison be supplied with money, it will not want provisions; it must not be paid by precepts as your other forces, but with ready cash, otherwise it shall go to wreck. One would admire how far our works are advanced in three or four days, so that any time next week in case the service required it, I shall be ready to march and leave this fort not only pallisaded round, but most of the works at their full height, and that, notwithstanding our men have nothing but meal and water, with now and then a little aquavitæ to the workmen. Of all the pioneers I got about 150, which I sent home out of Strathspey. Many of our baggage-men desert us with their horses, most whereof fall into the hands of the enemy. If the meal from Glasgow and other parts come not, the garrison will be very speedily reduced to great necessity, because of the 2000 bolls arrived, the army consumes much, have nothing else to eat, for the parties I had out, met with no cattle within twenty miles.

The regiment of Angus makes great difficulty to remain here in garrison, which proceeds more of their officer and minister than of the soldiers. It were very unreasonable to leave any of the stranger forces in such a remote garrison, since if the kingdom happen to turn peaceable, they may and doubtless shall be speedily disposed of elsewhere. Your Grace then would write to Lieutenant-Colonel Foulerton to signify that the confidence the government hath in those men is the reason they were designed for that garrison at first, till Lochaber should be subdued, which is hoped shall not be long, and then if they be not pleased with their post, that they shall be relieved by others, which may easily be done by the shire of Argyle ; withal if it might be thought fit to send them to Ireland they may be transported as readily and more complete from Inverlochy as from the west ; however 'tis very incommode to have men in the service who must needs choose their post. I confess I am no admirer of a devotion which doth not teach men their relative duty according to their vocation. I leave here also betwixt 4 and 500 men of Grant's regiment with some Highlanders. I cannot resolve to give the second command to the Laird of Weem, so long as Foulerton shall be here, though I know he might be very serviceable to the garrison, both as to his intelligence and credit, and that there is not the least absurdity in the thing, it being very practicable in all countries ; but many men pretend to know that understand very little. I hope things are peaceable in the south, since I get so few expresses, though they may be easily conveyed through Argyleshire over Dunstaffenage. I am much of the opinion they will have some respect for this body in the midst of their friend's country, which certainly this garrison, if carefully provided, will separate from their party, at least so as not to trouble so much the rest of the kingdom hereafter. I shall be obliged to return shortly, though it were but to leave some provisions for the garrison ; for neither the meal of Glasgow or Sutherland is come as yet, nor yet a barque which I ordered out of Caithness with 400 bolls, nor have we any notice of the two ships with the planks, cannon, and ammunition. Colonel Hill assures me that there must be double the number of planks which was provided, therefore more would be immediately secured at Glasgow though they should cost more, and in case they be not found there, sent from Leith as formerly : this should be done speedily, because the winter draws near apace. I wish the cannon and ammunition were come, lest some enemy's ships might come to incommode the garrison, before it be well covered towards the sea, which will take time. I find the palisades which I sent of great security for the fort, for here it would not be possible to get any, there being no proper wood within distance, and the country not like to submit till the winter force

2 A

them. There is a talk among our enemies that something will be undertaken by the Earl of Arran, Marquis of Athole, and others, before I return. I do not believe it, nevertheless if any such thing should occur, and that any considerable numbers from that hand should make head towards me, a motion would be made from that hand towards Perth to threaten both Athole and Breadalbane's country, and your Grace would labour to give me speedy account of the state of affairs, and as often as possible. If I can learn of no opposition on my return, I have thoughts of leaving the Earl of Argyle's regiment, in the shire of that name, with which, and what he can join to it of the shire, together with the help of the frigates whose provision draws to an end, he can easily subdue Mull this campaign yet; but if I hear of any alarms southerly, I will march with all the forces except the garrison, that being of greatest consequence. I make no question but there is account sent the king of our progress hitherto against the enemy, otherwise I had laboured to have done it from here. I recommend earnestly to your Grace the care of this post, which I look upon as the most important of the kingdom at present, and that which will at length make such as would sell their credit and service at such a dear rate to the King, of no greater use, nor more necessary to him, than a Lothian or Fife laird; therefore let it be by no means neglected, though other things should be postponed, but let the person which Hill employs be speedily dispatched back again with the necessary supplies. The rest of the planks may be had before the first, if they happen to come safely to be wrought. The queen would be advertised also how matters go. I hope in God before this time that there shall be good news both out of Ireland and of the fleet, whereof I shall long to be partaker. I am, may it please your Grace, your Grace's most humble and obedient servant,

H. MACKAY.

APPENDIX.

FROM THE SAME TO THE SAME.

Mouline, betwixt Blair and Dunkeld, the 24th July 1690, at 11 o'clock A. M.

MAY IT PLEASE YOUR GRACE,

Yesterday morning, I gave your Grace and the council account of the approach of the army from the head of Lochgarry, but the letter was intercepted by one Kinloch, who followed Buchan at Dunkeld, as I am informed by the people of that town. I left Colonel Hill with his garrison well secured, and so provided, that, speedy measures being taken for his further supply, as the nature of that post seems absolutely to require, he shall not readily have occasion to apprehend any thing which can menace him from the enemy. I got six half coulverains from Captain Pottinger, and six small pieces from the ships of burden for him, and left him well enough provided of ammunition till he get more by the ships from Leith; his stock of meal I suppose about 1800 bolls. I left him also sixty fat cows, eight barrels of herring, with a good quantity of the aquavitæ, and £500 sterling in money, which, considering the work which he shall have to make with the number of men, cannot last very long; besides, that post must be provided for a twelvemonth during the fair weather. This I recommend to the government's serious consideration, that being a post of that importance, and so difficult to re-possess, if lost by neglect, that no time should be lost to have it supplied with all necessaries, both for lodging and subsisting, particularly of money to pay the garrison, and buy bargains of provisions, which would save ships' freights after a while; but meal must absolutely be sent, those being wares not to be had for money there; but other provisions, I suppose, he may be served of, provided money fail not; that garrison ought to be kept in good humour, and capable to serve well. They want, and ought presently to be supplied of surtouts, breeches, stockings, and shoes.

Your Grace's letter of the 10th I got, but after I was away from Inverlochy, and advanced as far as Badenoch; the tenor whereof, if I had not been accustomed much with that sort of language, and known something more than haply your Grace can judge of the state of the enemy, would alarm me. God doth, in his goodness, work for us, otherwise such a timorous spirit as doth act this government would be capable to expose us to the scorn of our enemies, and hinder all progress of the forces. Now, since your Grace doth reproach me to have, contrary to your judgment, hazarded the loss of the rest of the kingdom for the conquest of Inverlochy, (which I, as well as your Grace, would judge a foolish exchange) being come this length with the army, I desire your Grace may propose in council, whether there be any pressing present service for me in these southern parts, or that otherwise they may be put for ten or twelve days in quarters of refreshment, because the foot hath suffered much by the continued rains and work; and where your Grace and the council judge they should best refresh, and at the same time keep the ill-affected most in awe. These directions would be sent me with all speed, being resolved to camp some days at Perth, till your orders with the council's come to my hand. The commissaries would be sent to see the forces want not provisions, having brought nothing from the fort but what the soldiers could conveniently carry, and have been eight days by the way, whereof I rested one in Badenoch to put a garrison at Ruthven, with directions to Captain Mackay, with his Highland company of my Lord Reay's men a hundred strong, to secure himself withal, which is all at present from, may it please your Grace, your Grace's most humble and most obedient servant,

H. Mackay.

FROM THE SAME TO THE SAME.

Perth, the 26th July 1690.

May it please your Grace,

I have received your Grace and Lordships' of the 25th, giving account of your calling of some west-countrymen to Stirling and

Falkirk, which I judge needless, now the army is come back again from the Highland expedition; withal they occupy the quarters which I designed for the forces; for now I suppose, our greatest care must be towards England, if any trouble should occur there during the King's absence; and Stirling, with the adjacent towns and villages within ten or twelve miles, would be fit posts to look to both south and north. I judge most of the horse and dragoons which were not in the Highlands ought to be sent north. To keep those low countries in awe, I had left some of the horse which I had with me; but because I knew not how I should find matters here, being so hastily writ for, and that they wanted recruits, I took them all south, except Belhaven and Stewart's troops, which lie at Elgin in Murray; and there is no foot now in the north beside the garrison of Fort-William in Lochaber, and Ruthven in Badenoch, but Strathnaver's regiment at Inverness, whereof two companies are lodged at the houses of Urquhart and Erchlas. I judge foot in that country, during the good weather, not so useful as some horse and dragoons, therefore I resolve to send Jackson north with the three troops which he has at Stirling, and the troop of horse which is said to be Elphinston's, and then I believe we shall be pretty well secured to that side; while we shall have * * * seven troops of horse, with Livingstone's regiment of dragoons, a troop of Cardross' and the horse guards, with the three Dutch regiments, Sir James Leslie's and the Earl of Leven's, all very good forces, to be ready to march where the service shall most require it. And, in case of a considerable landing any where southerly, whether in England or Scotland, the said body could march towards it, while the western shires' men might be disposed for the security of Forth and the government: besides those, Cunningham's regiment will be in pretty good condition of service. I have here also nine companies of the Earl of Argyle's regiment, with as many of Angus'. These forces upon the Scots repartition will certainly turn to nothing without speedy supply of money; and I admire to understand no measures have been taken all this while to furnish them.

The money for the garrison of Fort-William must be sent the governor, and not comprehended in the precepts of the regiments to whom they belonged; and speedy care would be taken for to get that post supplied of all necessaries during the fine weather, and the Laird of Grant to agree with the commissaries for deals and other wood to be ordered by him speedily to Ruthven; together with a number of wrights for the accommodation of that house for a garrison of a hundred foot and twenty dragoons, which will be of great service to keep the country below in peace, whereof Grant is one to be benefited thereby; meanwhile, by the order I left, the garrison is secured against enemy attempts. This is all at present from, may it please your Grace and Lordships, your Grace and Lordships' most humble and most obedient servant,

H. MACKAY.

MAJOR-GENERAL MACKAY TO THE PRIVY COUNCIL.

Perth, the 28th July 1690.

MAY IT PLEASE YOUR GRACE AND LORDSHIPS,
Having examined the state of the forces, I find the sickness which began to affect them at Inverlochy or Fort-William doth increase, viz. the bloody flux, so that if we expect more service of them for this running season, there is a necessity to lay them for a little time in quarters of refreshment, which I have accordingly ordered so near that in a day most of them can be together. They are disposed as follows: my regiment at Stirling, Ramsay at Lithgow, Leslie at Falkirk, Angus and Kenmore at Borrowstoness and adjacents, Livingstone at Kilseith; the six troops of horse in the villages about Stirling; Argyle and Lauder at Perth, and Glencairn somewhere thereabout, as the commanding officer of that part of the forces which marches now to Stirling shall inform himself, that it may be accommodate; because now that I have got some biscuit from Dundee, I take Livingstone's dragoons, four troops of horse and six hun-

dred commanded foot, to look after those people that are infesting the country. I have sent orders to Jackson to march northward with his three troops of dragoons which are about Stirling, because that the rebels having got some horse together, they may, with the help of the broken Highlanders, be uneasy for the party we have there, and whatsoever may fall out in the south, the north ought to be so well cared for, that the enemies may have no footing in the low country. It were fit that such of our party as are north-countrymen, and have interest to raise men, were sent thither, among whom chiefly my Lord Strathnaver, and the Laird of Grant; for it is not the question of protestants divided in court, party, and club, but of protestants and papists, now when our enemies' main or only expectations are from France, so that whosoever is not zealous in such a cause, with all the self-deniedness which our religion requires, can hardly expect the advantages which it promises, only to such as seek first the kingdom of heaven, and for the rest depend upon God's providence to have it added to them.

I have often pressed that Fort-William be cared for timely, and that the forces be furnished with money to put in case to do the service, for surely the king's money ought not to be spared to lose his service, for in cash upon occasion it cannot help much, but in well composed forces there is a prospect at least humanly of security whatever may fall out.

I could wish there were present order given for 11 or 1200 surtouts for the garrison of Fort-William, the men being ill clothed for the approaching cold wet season; plaiden waist-coats would do well also; for shoes and stockings there hath been a memorandum given to a certain commissary depute called Campbell, who is ordained to attend the said fort: shirts would not be forgot also. The said mounting can be found of their retention money, and cost nothing but the credit making to the government.

Your Grace and Lordships would consider that it is an insupportable burden for me to have the care of all those things, for 'tis impossible for me to exercise my thoughts effectually how to dispose the forces to the most advantage to the service, if I be obliged to give directions for and solicit all things that may be found requisite for the particular detail and economy of them; therefore to make the service go well on, it ought to be made as easy for any who happen to have the chief command of the forces as possible, otherwise he shall necessarily neglect the chief part and end thereof, which is to contrive how to make use of them to the most advancement of the service. Your Grace and Lordships therefore, would establish the committee of war which I proposed, to inspect the letters and propositions which I have written, that no delay be made in things essential for the present service and juncture, for though I have the design and will, I thank God for it, good and sound in this matter, my spirit and body cannot support the weight of all, and necessarily many things must be neglected if I should be charged therewith, which are the present thoughts of, may it please your Grace and Lordships, your Grace and Lordships' most humble and obedient servant,

H. MACKAY.

No. II.

PEDIGREE OF THE SENIOR BRANCH OF THE SCOURY FAMILY.

Lieutenant-General Hugh Mackay of Scoury (as already stated in the body of this work) married, in 1673, Clara, third daughter of the Chevalier Arnold de Bie, of Wayestein, of an ancient Dutch family knighted in France, and at that time resident at Bommel in Guelderland, of which town he had formerly been burgomaster. The de Bies were an opulent mercantile family of great respectability in Amsterdam, where their descendants continue to live, and maintain the same high station in society. By Clara de Bie, the General had a son, Hugh, and three daughters, the eldest, Margaret, married to George, third Lord Reay, from which marriage the three last Lords of Reay have descended. Hugh was only twelve years of age at his father's death, but through the favour of King William, got a company in his father's regiment, rose to the rank of Major, and died at Cambray in 1708. He married a Swiss lady of the De Lancey family, and had two sons, Hugh and Gabriel, and several daughters, all settled in Holland. Gabriel died unmarried, Lieutenant-Colonel of the Honourable General Stewart's regiment of the Scottish brigade. Hugh was a Lieutenant-General in the service, and Colonel-commandant of what might with propriety be, and frequently was, called the Mackay regiment. He died at Breda, in 1775, and by his death, the eldest branch of the Scoury family became extinct in the male line. He married Isabella de Savornin, by whom he had two daughters, Anna Louisa, and ———. The former married Lt. General James Prevost, colonel of the 4th battalion, 60th regiment of the British service, who, together with his wife, on the death of her father, obtained his Majesty's licence, to take the name and arms of Mackay of Scoury, as appears by the London Gazette of 6th September 1775. General and Mrs. Prevost had two daughters, the elder married to Count Cornabe, of a Walloon regiment in the Austrian service, of whose issue, if any, or of General Prevost's second daughter, or of the other descendants of the great General Mackay, dispersed all over the continent, the author regrets his inability to procure any authentic information. His descendants in Britain now existing, are but few in number; viz. the Hon. Mrs. Marianne Fullarton, widow of Col. Wm. Fullarton of Fullarton, M.P., and her sister, the Hon. Miss Georgina Mackay, both daughters of George, fifth Lord Reay, grandson of the foregoing Margaret, Lady Reay, the great general's daughter. Donald, the fourth Lord, had a daughter Mary, married to Major Thomas Edgar of the 25th foot, and of this marriage there were several sons in the army or navy, whose issue, if any, cannot be traced.

No. III.

PEDIGREE OF THE BORLEY, OR JUNIOR BRANCH OF THE SCOURY FAMILY.

On the demise of Lt. General Hugh Mackay the younger, without male issue, in 1775, the representation of the Scoury family in the male line devolved on the descendants of his great grand-uncle, Donald Mackay of Borley, second son of Donald, the first of Scoury, and next brother of Colonel Hugh, the great general's father. Donald of Borley connected his family a second time in marriage, with that distinguished race of warriors and defenders of the protestant faith, the Munroes of Foulis, by uniting himself to his cousin, Christian, daughter of the Rev. Robert Munro, minister of Creech, and proprietor of Meikle Creech, brother of the Laird of Foulis. By this lady he had, besides other children, two sons, William and Angus, the latter, ancestor of William Mackay, Esq. Prince Edward's Island, and George Mackay, Esq. Stewart Hall. The eldest son William, usually designed Captain William of Borley, from having commanded a company of foot in the battle of Worcester, returned to the country after many hair-breadth scapes, settled there, and married a daughter of Corbet of Arboll, by whom he had three sons, Hugh, Donald, and John. Hugh is the same who is mentioned at page 22, as having been appointed captain of an independent company, and at page 35, commandant of Ruthven Castle, in both which situations he is said to have displayed great activity and zeal for the service. He married first, the Hon. Ann Mackay, daughter of John Lord Reay, and secondly, the only daughter of P. Dunbar of Siderra near Dornoch, by whom he had a numerous issue, now all extinct with one exception, the wife of Captain Matchet of the Suffolk militia. Captain Hugh's eldest son Patrick, after selling Siderra to the Earl of Sutherland, in 1732 accompanied General

Oglethorp on his colonizing expedition to Georgia, together with three of his brothers. Their only descendants who lived to the present times were Lieut. Gen. Hugh Mackay Gordon, who died in 1823, colonel of the 16th foot, and Lieut. Governor of Jersey, and his two brothers, Alexander and George, both majors in the army. The youngest of Captain Hugh's children, John Mackay of Tordarroch remained in the country, and left a son George, a captain in the 60th regiment, who died at New York in 1782, leaving two sons who died unmarried. Captain Hugh himself departed this life in 1723 aged 53, and his descendants having been accounted for as above, we come to his next brother Donald, a member of Council in the ill-fated colony of Darien. Returning to it from Jamaica in 1702, he harpooned for his amusement a shark of enormous size, and having unfortunately twisted the rope about his arm, was dragged overboard and devoured by the monster. The next in succession was his brother, the Rev. John Mackay, minister successively of Durness and Lairg, in his native county, a man to detail the various excellent points of whose character would far exceed our present limits. Suffice it to say, that, to herculean strength of body, he added corresponding powers of mind, which he carefully cultivated at the Universities of Edinburgh and Utrecht, and finally dedicated to the service of his Maker, in the above two parishes. In 1706 he was inducted minister of Durness, and translated in 1714 to Lairg, where he died in 1753, aged 73, respected as a scholar, and a gentleman, and revered as a faithful minister of the gospel. He married a daughter of John, and grand-daughter of James Mackay of Kirtomy, by Jane, third daughter of the Hon. Sir James Fraser of Brea, Kirtomy himself being grandson of Hugh Mackay of Strathnaver, and Lady Jane Gordon, and nephew of Donald Lord Reay. Mr. John Mackay left one son, Thomas, and three daughters, from one of whom was descended Captain William Polson, of the Virginia Rangers, a corps of which the illustrious Washington was commandant. In 1755, Captain W. Polson was killed in Braddock's bloody engagement with the French and Indians, in which also

APPENDIX.

his brother John, then an ensign in the line, was severely wounded, but recovered, rose to the rank of Major of the 92d regiment, and, in 1780, commanded, jointly with the renowned Nelson, a successful expedition from Jamaica, against Fort St. Juan, on the Spanish main. Mr. John Mackay's only surviving son, Thomas, succeeded his father as minister of Lairg, and, with a bodily constitution as delicate as his father's was robust, inherited his ardent piety, and unwearied zeal for the interests of religion among his flock. He died in 1803, aged eighty-six,—father and son having thus been ministers of the gospel ninety-seven years, of which they spent eighty-nine in the same parish, where their names will long be remembered with affection and reverence. Mr. T. Mackay married his cousin Margaret Montgomery, whose unaffected piety and domestic virtues made her a blessing to her husband, his family, and his parish. She died in 1773, leaving three sons, and two daughters. The eldest son, John, is the author of the present work. The second son, Hugh, a captain of cavalry in the service of the East India Company, and a commissary on the staff of the illustrious Wellington, was killed in the memorable battle of Assye, 23d September 1803, at the muzzle of the enemy's gun, and at the moment of victory. The Author of the History of "Twelve Years of Military Adventure," after describing the battle of Assye, mentions him in the following terms: "Among the slain I cannot help particularizing Captain Mackay of the 4th native cavalry, commissary of cattle to the army. He had previously asked permission of the General to head his squadron in case of an action, and had been positively refused. Instead, however, of remaining with the baggage, as others similarly circumstanced did, by a noble act of disobedience, he risked his commission, and lost his life."*

The late Major-general Sir John Malcolm, G. C. B., governor of Bombay, writes to the Author as follows: "I knew your brother, Captain Mackay, well, and held his character, both as a man and an officer, in the highest respect. In 1803, he had the sole charge of the gun bullocks,

* Vol. i. p. 172.

and enjoyed in his department as much of the confidence of his commander-general Wellesley, as any officer in the army."

The great Captain, Wellington himself, in a letter to the author, writes to the same effect, " I had a great respect and regard for your brother, Captain Mackay, and perfectly recollect the occasion on which he gallantly fell in the service of his country" &c.

A brother officer, Colonel Welsh, in his Military Reminiscences, writes in the same strain, " Captain Hugh Mackay was one of the finest fellows I ever knew. Brave to a fault, yet modest, unassuming, humane, and generous. He was adored by the 4th native cavalry, to whom, though never their commander, he was a common father; proud and unbending sometimes to his superiors, but to his equals or inferiors, ever mild and conciliatory. Being a public staff officer, he was not permitted to do regimental duty, but, on the eve of the battle, he wrote to Captain Barclay, the adjutant-general, requesting the General's permission to join his corps, on the march and in action, but got a positive refusal, and was told he could not be spared from his own department, the public cattle of the army. He offered to resign, was told he could not be spared at that moment, on which he wrote privately to Captain Barclay, that whenever he should see his corps going into action, he would at all hazards join it, that he knew he should thereby forfeit his commission, but he trusted if he did, it would be with honour. He joined accordingly, heading the charge of his own regiment, and in a line with the leading squadron of the noble veteran 19th dragoons, he fell, man and horse, close to one of the enemy's guns, pierced through by several grape shots. When in the very heat of the action news was brought to the General that Captain Mackay was killed, his countenance changed, and the tear which fell upon his cheek was nature's involuntary homage to the memory of a kindred spirit."

The Rev. T. Mackay's third son William, was by profession a mariner, and one of the most scientific and skilful navigators of his time in the Indian seas. In 1795, being second officer of the ship Juno, of 450 tons, he was wrecked on the coast of Arracan. The ship sprung a leak in a storm, and being loaded with timber could not go to the bottom, but sunk hull deep into the water, leaving the masts standing. The ship's company, seventy-three in number, including the captain's wife and her maid, scrambled up the rigging to escape immediate destruction, in which situation fourteen of their number continued twenty-three days without food, and at length, through the mercy of God, reached the shore. The rest perished miserably, some of hunger, some of thirst, some raving mad, while others, to put an end to their sufferings, threw themselves overboard. W. Mackay was one of the survivors, and published a narrative of their sufferings, perhaps the most affecting that ever was given to the world. In 1801 he had an escape from shipwreck in the Red sea, whither he had been dispatched by the Bengal government with stores and provisions for General Baird's expedition to Egypt, and of this too he wrote an account little less interesting, which is subjoined to a new edition of the narrative of the Juno, published by Blackwood of Edinburgh, in 1831. Some of the finest, and most touching incidents in Lord Byron's admired description of a shipwreck in his poem of Don Juan are taken almost verbatim from the narrative of the Juno. The noble poet's biographer, Mr. Moore, speaking of the two versions, that of the real distress by W. Mackay, and that of the fictitious by Lord Byron, gives a decided preference to the former. " It will be felt, I think," says he in a foot note to his Life of Byron, (quarto edition, vol. i. p. 32) " by every reader, that this is one of the instances in which poetry must be content to yield the palm to prose. There is a pathos in the last sentences of the seaman's recital, which the artifices of metre and rhyme were sure to disturb, and which indeed, no verses, however beautiful, could half so naturally and powerfully express." W. Mackay never had a perfect recovery from the effects of his sufferings on the wreck of the Juno, and died in 1804, at Calcutta, where a monument was erected to his memory by his friends, as was done by the officers of his regiment, for his brother Hugh, on the spot where he fell at Assye. In the church yard of Lairg, there is a cenotaph commemorating the characters of the two sons, Hugh and William, and of their venerable father and grandfather, with an inscription which, referring to the two former, concludes thus, "Their bodies lie in the opposite quarter of the globe, but their monument is erected where their memory is dearest, near the remains of their pious fathers, and amidst many living whose gratitude will attest, that fraternal affection has not overcharged this record of their virtues."

> "Nor you, ye proud, impute to these the fault,
> If memory o'er their tomb no trophies raise,
> Where, through the long drawn aisle, and fretted vault,
> The pealing anthem swells the note of praise."

APPENDIX.

No. IV.

Intended for insertion as a foot-note to Hugh Macleod of Assynt, page 2, line 6.

The Macleods of Assynt branched off from the Macleods of Lewis, and were represented by the late Donald Macleod, Esq. of Geanies, the venerable Sheriff-depute of Ross and Cromarty, whose great-grandfather was the last proprietor of the Assynt estate, of the name of Macleod.

No. V.

Intended for insertion as a foot-note to Munro of Foulis, page 2, line 14.

The Munroes of Foulis are a family of high antiquity, and great respectability, in the county of Ross,—Sir Hugh Munro, Bart., the present proprietor, being the twenty-eighth individual of the family who has possessed the estate. It has produced many eminent men, not a few of whom fell in the field, in the cause of the Protestant religion and liberty, during the two last centuries.

No. VI.

COUNT SOLMS.

Many authorities, both British and Foreign have been consulted, with the view of collecting some notices respecting this nobleman; but although he seems to have been a sovereign prince and ruler of a small hereditary domain in Germany, all enquiries respecting him have been nearly fruitless.

The house of Solms is supposed to be descended from that of Nassau, and divided into several branches, to one of which, probably that of Bransfeld, the Count in question belonged.

Collier, in his Dictionary, has the following meagre notice respecting him and his hereditary dominions, under the word *Solms*.

"Solms, Lat. Solmia, a county in Germany, in Weteravia, with a little town of that name situate on a hill. It has Hesse to the east, Treves to the west, and the town of Solms stands three miles west of Marpurg. It is subject to a Count of its own, whose residence is at the Castle of Bransfeld. Count Solms came over with the Prince of Orange into England 1688, and served him, when King of England, with *very much honour* in Ireland, &c." The words, &c. which conclude the notice, must imply that Count Solms served King William "with very much honour," in Ireland and other countries; but if we are to believe the reports of the British historians, the qualifying expression, "with very much honour," can only be considered as complimentary.

Count Solms is mentioned as having been sent by the Prince of Orange to surround Whitehall with guards, and take possession of that palace after King James' return from Feversham. He appears to have executed this order with strictness.

APPENDIX.

At the seige of Limerick in 1690, we find that Count Solms, as well as the Earl of Portland, were found fault with by the younger Duke Schomberg, for having neglected to send a detachment of horse of sufficient strength to protect that convoy which General Sarsfield destroyed, and afterwards blew into the air with gunpowder: on which occasion King William's loss was considerable both in men and provisions. It does not however clearly appear where the fault really lay; but it seems that the king did not in this instance ascribe it to Count Solms, since he, on leaving Ireland in the same year, entrusted him with the command of the army; this post he retained during a very short period, General Ghinkel being appointed his successor.

But it appears to be a well established fact, that the battle of Steinkirk was lost by Count Solms' fault, for more than one British historian lay this calamity to his charge, and both King William and the parliament were highly displeased with his conduct on that occasion.

On the 23d of November 1692, Count Solms' conduct was severely animadverted upon in a debate in the House of Commons, and steps were taken, although these seem to have been ineffectual, to remove him from the command of the English infantry in future.

He was killed in the battle of Landen in the year 1693, of which we find the following brief notice in Rapin, " The confederates lost in all about 7000, and among these there was scarce an officer of note, only the Count de Solms had his leg shot off by a cannon ball, of which he died in a few hours."

No. VII.

GENERAL BARON DE GHINKEL, EARL OF ATHLONE.

The Dutch General, Godard van Ghinkel was born of noble parents in Guelderland, or according to some at Utrecht. He entered very early on his military career, and obtained the order of the elephant long before the accession of the Prince of Orange to the English throne.

It is remarkable that all the historical dictionaries and encyclopædias of this country are entirely silent as to the history of this general, since the scene in which he acted, and the high command with which he was entrusted, were such as to render him at all events an historical person, whatever might be said of his merits or his talents.

On the other hand, it is more remarkable, that a complimentary and overstrained account of his achievements is given by Mons. Nicolle in the "Biographie Universelle," which entirely ascribes to him the conquest of Ireland. Collier with more discrimination, says, that the other generals who acted along with him in the Irish campaign did, by their bravery and conduct, greatly contribute to his success. If proofs were wanting to shew that Mons. Nicolle has scarcely penetrated the surface of this part of our history, it would suffice, that he laments as an injustice done to General Ghinkel, the preference given by the States General to the Duke of Marlborough when the latter was appointed commander-in-chief in the succession war. Mons. Nicolle however admits, that in his last campaign Ghinkel accomplished nothing which would make his citizens repent of their injustice! He died at Utrecht in the year 1705.

No. VIII.

BENTINCK, EARL OF PORTLAND.

William Bentinck, (or Benthinck) Earl of Portland, was King William's minister, and his most intimate and faithful friend. He was born in Holland, and descended from a noble and ancient family of Guelderland. At first he was a page, and subsequently gentleman of the bedchamber to the Prince of Orange, whom he accompanied to England in 1670. When the Prince of Orange became Statholder, he promoted Bentinck to the command of his favourite regiment of Dutch guards. In 1675, Bentinck's self-devotion and attachment to his master was displayed in a manner to which history probably knows no parallel. The Prince was taken dangerously ill of the small-pox, and the therapeutics of that age knew no remedy to save him, but increased animal heat with the chance of contagion, which was expected to afford relief to the sufferer. Bentinck, who never had had the disease, offered to lie in the Prince's bed for this purpose. The Prince recovered, and the page caught the disease, with symptoms which were in an unusual degree severe and dangerous. This service was faithfully remembered by King William to the last hour of his life. In 1677, Bentinck was sent over to England to negotiate the Prince's marriage with the Duke of York's eldest daughter. In 1688, the Prince having resolved on his expedition into England, Bentinck was employed to secure the aid and countenance of the young Elector of Brandenburgh, and in this mission he was successful beyond the expectations of his master. During the progress of the Revolution, he often mediated between the Prince and the English nobility. In 1689, he was raised to many high and lucrative offices at court, naturalized by act of parliament, and ennobled by the style of Baron of Cirencester, Viscount Woodstock, and Earl of Portland. In 1690, he accompanied King William to Holland, and acted as his envoy at the grand congress of the Hague. In 1695, the King granted to him several Lordships in Denbighshire. This grant was vehemently opposed by the Commons, who were jealous of the Earl of Portland, partly as foreigner and partly as a court favourite, and accordingly the grant was revoked, but the Earl was soon recompensed by other grants from the crown, constituting a great portion of the present possessions of this noble family. Portland accompanied King William in his campaigns, both in Ireland and Flanders, and was the principal negociator of the peace of Ryswick, after which he became ambassador extraordinary to the court of France. It seems to have been during his absence on this mission, that Keppel, afterwards Earl of Albemarle, chiefly rose in the royal favour; but this rival so roused Portland's jealousy, that he resigned his posts in the royal household, resolving for the future to serve him only in state affairs. We cannot find fault with the Earl of Portland if he wished, by a resignation in such terms, practically and tangibly to express some such notion as this: "Offices of frivolity, idleness, and adulation I resign; for these Keppel, no doubt, is the more suitable man; but, in active and important service, I am aware that he cannot fill my place." Still the King withdrew not from him his esteem and confidence. He gave into his hands almost the entire government of Scotland, and employed him in negociating the treaty for the succession to the crown of Spain, called the *Partition treaty*. For this he was impeached by the House of Commons; and some immoderate grants of land in Ireland to him, as well as to the Earl of Albemarle, were attacked by the House. In 1701, when King William died, Portland's influence ceased, and along with it the animosity against him. The last words spoken by King William were an enquiry after Portland; his last action was the pressing of that nobleman's hand to his heart. After the King's death, he lived in retirement at Bulstrode, and spent a portion of his immense wealth for several useful and charitable purposes. In this latter period of his life, his chief amusement was gardening, for which, he in all probability, had acquired a taste in his native country. He died 23d November 1709. The biographers of the Earl of Portland speak of him as a man who did not inspire either love or hatred in a very high degree; but many circumstances in his life shew that he was a nobleman of high honour and integrity. Being once offered fifty thousand pounds sterling, for his vote in Parliament, and his influence with the King his master, he scornfully rejected that offer, and thus had an opportunity of demonstrating to the Commons, that his detestation of wealth basely acquired was at least equal to his love of riches acquired by fair and honourable means.

He left children by both his wives, and his eldest son, Henry, was in 1716, created Duke of Portland, Marquis of Titchfield &c.

No. IX.

GENERAL DE RUVIGNE.

Of the origin of the family of Ruvigne, or Rouvigne, little is known, owing probably to a circumstance mentioned by the author of Lady Russell's Life, viz. That protestant families in France, during the reign of Louis XIV. were excluded from the public records. The Marquis of Ruvigne was a person of considerable property and influence, and frequently employed as a mediator between Louis XIV. and the Hugonot party. His estate having been confiscated at the revocation of the edict of Nantz, he sought an asylum in England, and attached himself ever after to the interest of King William. His two sons were in the battle of the Boyne, the elder of whom being killed, the younger continued to serve in the English army as a Major-General, and is the individual here mentioned. Though in no respect distinguished, his services were rewarded with the Earldom of Galway, and a grant of land from the confiscated estates, a glaring instance of William's partiality to his foreign officers, and neglect of the British, particularly of General Mackay, who was Galway's immediate superior officer, and whose pre-eminent services in the Irish war, were universally acknowledged. It is supposed, and not without reason, that the extraordinary rewards bestowed on Galway, were less on account of his military services, than as a compensation for the great losses of his family in the protestant cause, and in reward of their personal attachment to King William. This is the same Earl of Galway, who afterwards made such a figure in the succession war for the crown of Spain, and died in 1729, unmarried. His father, the Marquis, was uncle to that illustrious woman, Rachel, Lady Russell, daughter of Wriothesly, Earl of Southampton.

No. X.

GENERAL TALMASH.

The Hon. Thomas Talmash, was second son of Sir Lionel Talmash of Helmingham, bart., and Elizabeth Countess of Dysart, afterwards Duchess of Lauderdale. He was a brave officer, and is said to have served in seventeen campaigns.

He entered into the revolution with great zeal, and was appointed colonel of the 2nd, or Coldstream regiment of foot-guards. When Rapin says, that Talmash supported the opinion of General Mackay and the Duke of Wirtemberg, in a council of war, when the fording of the Shannon was resolved on, that assertion is thus to be understood: Mackay finding his own preferable measure abandoned by the generals, saw that there was only left a choice between the two other measures proposed, and not approving of either of these, he still gave the preference to the fording, in which, Talmash and the Duke of Wirtemberg supported him. In the attempt made by the English and Dutch to destroy the harbour of Brest, 1694, General Talmash was wounded in the thigh, of which he died a few days after, at Plymouth, being at that time member of Parliament for Chippingham.

INDEX.

INDEX.

Angus, Earl of, killed, 130.
Annandale, Earl of, commissioned to raise a troop of independent horse, 16.
Athlone invested, 113—taken, 118.
Athole, Marquis of, peculiar advantages of his situation, 23—professes great zeal and affection for the new government, 24—falsifies his professions, *ib*.
Aughrim, battle of, 120.

Balfour of Burleigh raises men, at his own expence, to aid the Dutch patriots, 8.
Balfour, Brigadier, killed, 50.
Ballimore taken, 112.
Bargeny, Lord, his regiment ordered to be reduced, 72.
Beaufort, Duke of, commands the expedition to Candia, 5.
Belhaven, Lord, commissioned to raise an independent troop of horse, 16—dispatched with intelligence of the victory near Perth, 62.
Berwick, Marshal, his opinion of the capture of Athlone, 118.
Blair of Blair, and Pollock taken at Perth, 25.
Blantyre, Lord, his regiment ordered to be reduced, 72.
Breadalbane, Earl of, delivers himself up and takes the oaths, 70—sent to the king at Chester, by Melville and Tarbat, 85—his character, *ib*.—sends 500 of his vassals to join the Pretender, and dies, *ib*.
Buccleuch, Scott of, raises men, at his own expence, to aid the Dutch patriots, 8.
Buchan, General, lands on the Isle of Mull with forty officers, 90—proceeds to the east coast with 1200 men, *ib*.—his followers burn Edinglassie house, *ib*.—eighteen of their number hanged by Edinglassie, *ib*.—surprised by Livingstone at Cromdale, 92—joined by Invercy and his men, 96—and Cannon pursued by Mackay to Inverness and retreat to Lochaber, 98.
Burleigh, see Balfour.
Burnet, Bishop, his character of Mackay, 131.

Callender, Earl of, surrenders and takes the oaths, 70.
Cameronian regiment, their gallant defence of Dunkeld, 68—sing a hymn of praise after the battle, *ib*.
Campbell of Calder, appointed to treat with the Highland chiefs, 83.

INDEX.

Cannon, Brigadier, joins Dundee with 500 Irish, 45—marches towards Perth with 4000 men, 63—falls back to Angus and Mearns, *ib.*

Cardross, Lord, appointed to command the garrison at Finlarig, 70—appointed Colonel of a new regiment of dragoons, 72—particulars of his history, 67.

Chambers, the historian, though in the opposite interest, does justice to Mackay, 61.

Chatham, Earl of, his eulogium on the Highlanders, 89.

Churchill, Duke of Marlborough, brother Subaltern with Mackay, 5—appointed a Major-General the same day with him, 110.

Cleland, Lieutenant-Colonel, of Cameronian regiment, killed at Dunkeld, 68.

Cohorn, Dutch engineer, killed in the defence of Namur, 128.

Convention, the Scottish, declares King James forfeited, 39.

Coul, Sir Alexander Mackenzie of, professes attachment to the new government, 35.

Cunningham, Colonel, appointed to a new regiment, 72.

Douglas, Sir Robert, killed at Steinkirk, 130.

Duffus, Lord, surrenders, and takes the oaths, 70.

Dundee, Viscount, appointed to command the royal dragoons, 15—dismissed, and Sir T. Livingstone appointed in his room, *ib.*—denounced as a rebel by the convention, and flies to arms, 17—marches toward Aberdeen, pursued by Mackay, 18—joined by the Gordons, and other disaffected clans, 19—arrives at Inverness, where he finds Macdonald of Keppoch, *ib.*—intimates to the magistrates of Elgin his intention of lodging there the following night, *ib.*—changes his mind, and proceeds toward Lochaber, 20—makes a rapid march into Perth, and takes Blair and Pollock prisoners, 25—informed by Ballechin of Ramsay's retreat, descends from Lochaber in the hope of intercepting him or Mackay, 27—disappointed, he attacks Ruthven castle, takes, and burns it, 29—pursues Mackay down Strathspey, but is in his turn compelled to retrograde, and chased to Lochaber, 34—returns to the Lowlands with 2000 Highlanders and 500 Irish, 45—before quitting Lochaber, sends Blair and Pollock to the Isle of Mull, *ib.*—proceeds towards Blair castle, 46—thence making a detour towards Urrard house, 47—perceives Mackay drawing up his men on the flat below, *ib.*—killed, 50.

Dunfermline, Earl of, sent by the Jacobites to King James, 100.

Dunkeld, account of the battle of, 68.

Edinglassie, Sir G. Gordon of, assists in the detection of Livingstone's plot, 33—sent to reconnoitre the enemy, 65—appointed Major of Eglington's regiment, 72.

Eglington, Earl of, appointed Colonel of a new regiment of horse, 72.

Farquharson, see Inverey.

Ferguson, Major, and Captain Pottinger, command the reinforcements sent to Mackay, 88.

Finlarig, a garrison placed there, 70.

Forbes, Captain John, surrenders Ruthven castle to Dundee, 29—released, and proceeding to Mackay's camp, meets two spies, *ib.*

Forbes, Master of, joins Mackay with 50 horse, 33—assists in detecting Livingstone's plot, *ib.*

—informs Mackay of Cannon's strong position near Aberdeen, 64—appointed Lieutenant-Colonel of Eglington's dragoons, 72—chases Buchan from Aberdeenshire, 96.
Forbes of Culloden, short account of his family, 104.
Forbes, Duncan, Lord President, mainly instrumental in suppressing the rebellion of 1745, 105.

GALWAY and LIMERICK taken, concludes the Irish war, 124.
Ghinkel, Baron de, succeeds Solms as commander-in-chief in Ireland, 110—wavering and irresolute summons frequent councils of war, 114—feels the effects of his neglect in not establishing magazines, 119—created Earl of Athlone, 125.
Glasgow, magistrates of, their patriotic conduct, 80.
Gordon, Sir George, see Edinglassie.
Gordon, Duke of, commands Edinburgh Castle, 17—surrenders to Sir John Lanier, 39.
Grant, Laird of, joins Mackay at Forres, and receives a letter of service, 20—his patriotic and noble-minded reply on finding his country exposed to the enemy, 30.
Guthrie, Major, of Cardross' regiment, 72.

HALKET of Pitfirran, raises men at his own expence to aid the Dutch patriots, 8.
Hamilton, Ducal family, short account of, 16.
Hamilton, Duke of, President of the council, 18.
Hamilton, Duchess of, attached to the Presbyterian interest, 24.
Hamilton, Lieutenant-Colonel Gustavus, leads the advanced party across the Shannon, 117.
Hamilton, Lord George, Earl of Orkney, his regiment in the battle of Aughrim, 121.
Hastings, Colonel, distinguishes himself in command of the right wing at Killiecrankie, 51.
Hauly, Lieutenant-Colonel, next in command to Sir T. Livingstone, in the action near the Spey, 34.
Hesse Darmstadt, Prince of, on the advanced party crossing the Shannon, 118—at Aughrim, led by youthful enthusiasm, advances contrary to orders, 123—killed, 118.
Hill, Captain, appointed Adjutant-General by Mackay's recommendation, 85—dispatched by him to the King at Chester, 16.
Hill, Colonel, sent by Melville and Tarbat to treat with the Highland chiefs, 84.
Hodges, Colonel, grandfather of Colonel Gardiner, killed at Steinkirk, 130.

INVEREY, Farquharson, Laird of, escapes from the party sent to seize him, 37—burns Braemar House, 38—his house burnt in retaliation, by Mackay, 39—blocks up Abergeldie, 97.
—defeated by Major Mackay, but escapes, *ib*.
Inverlochy, Cromwell's plan of erecting a fort there, recommended by Mackay to the council, 36—carried into effect, 88.

JACKSON, appointed Lieutenant-Colonel of Cardross' Dragoons, 72.
James II. recalls the Scottish Brigade, on the occasion of Monmouth's Rebellion, 11—demands their assistance in 1688, but refused, 12.

KENMORE, Viscount, receives a letter of service to raise a regiment, 16.
Keppoch, see Macdonald.

Killiecrankie, account of the battle of, 49.

LANIER, Major-General Sir John, appointed to command at Edinburgh in Mackay's absence, 18—joins Mackay at Stirling, 59—commands at Forfar, and receives an express from Ramsay, informing him of Cannon's approach to Dunkeld, 68—unfortunately delays sending the desired instructions till he arrived at Perth, when it was too late, *ib*.—killed at Steinkirk, 130.

Leven, Earl of, receives a letter of service to raise a regiment, 16—his gallant behaviour at Killiecrankie, 51—placed at the head of the commission to re-model the army, 73.

Livingstone, Colonel Sir Thomas, sent to the north in pursuit of Dundee, 17—his design of seizing Dundee's person frustrated, *ib*.—defeats a body of the enemy near Balveny, 34—left with a strong garrison at Inverness, 36—marches to Cromdale to oppose Buchan, 91—surprises Buchan and Cannon there, 92—succeeds Mackay as commander-in-chief, 108.

Lovat, Lord, declines joining Mackay, 35.

Luxembourg, Duke of, lays siege to Namur, 128.

MACDONALD, of Keppoch, meets Dundee at Inverness, 19.

Mackay, Captain the Hon. Æneas, on his father's death is sent to the general in Holland for his education, 117—arrested by order of King James, *ib*.—released, and appointed Major of Livingstone's dragoons, *ib*.—assists in detecting Livingstone's plot, 33—disappointed of promotion through Melville and Tarbat, 76—pursues Buchan and Cannon to Cromdale 93—defeats Inverey, 97—sent to arrest Lord Seaforth, 98—appointed Lieutenant-Colonel of his uncle's regiment, 117—commands the regiment on the passage of the Shannon, 116—and at Steinkirk, 117—succeeds General Mackay as Colonel of the regiment, *ib*.—promoted to the rank of Brigadier-General, *ib*.—having been repeatedly wounded, is ordered to Bath for the recovery of his health, where he dies, *ib*.

Mackay, Angus Dow, of Strathnaver, fights a bloody battle with Donald lord of the Isles, at Dingwall, and marries his sister Elizabeth, 1.

Mackay, Donald of Strathnaver, heads his clan at Bannockburn, 1.

Mackay, Donald of Scoury, succeeds his father in that estate, 2.

Mackay, Iye Dow of Strathnaver, gets quiet possession of his family estate, 2.

Mackay, Hugh of Scoury, a colonel of foot, succeeds his father Donald, 2—taken at Balveny, released, and returns home, 3—dies, leaving four sons and a daughter, *ib*.

Mackay, Lieutenant-General Hugh, of Scoury, born about 1640, 1—appointed ensign in Dumbarton's, or the Royal Scots regiment, 4—accompanies it to France, *ib*.—visits England, and is presented at court, *ib*.—returns to France, and serves under Condé and Turenne, 5—employed by the Venetian Republic at the siege of Candia, and receives a medal in reward of his gallantry, *ib*.—promoted to a company in Dumbarton's, *ib*.—enters the Scottish Brigade, and service of the States General, *ib*.—marries Clara de Bie, 7—serves in the battle of Seneff, and siege of Grave, 7—preferred to Claverhouse, and appointed Lieutenant-Colonel of the regiment, afterwards Commandant of the brigade, 11—called to England on occasion of Monmouth's rebellion, *ib*.—appointed Major-General and a Privy Counsellor in Scotland, 12—returns to Holland, and accompanies the Prince of Orange to England, at the Revolution, *ib*.—one of six individuals excepted from pardon by King

James, *ib.*—commands the red division of the invading army, *ib.*—seized with a fever, proceeds to Scotland, and is appointed commander-in-chief, 13—issues letters of service to various individuals, 16—orders Sir T. Livingstone to the north, in pursuit of Dundee, 17—proceeds thither himself, 18—arriving at the town of Dundee, he assembles 450 horse, foot, and dragoons, and marches northwards, *ib.*—disappointed to find Grant had not preceded him, according to his instructions, 19—the magistrates of Elgin inform him of Dundee's threatened visit to their town, 20—quickens his march across the Spey in consequence, *ib.* arrives at Elgin, and is joined by Grant, to whom he gives a letter of service to raise a regiment, *ib.*—resolves to meet Dundee, but learns that he had proceeded towards Lochaber, *ib.*—remains two days in Elgin, and writes to his friends in Ross and Sutherland, to meet him at Inverness, *ib.*—arrives at Inverness, and invites Lovat, Seaforth, and other chiefs to meet him there, but disappointed, 21—joined by Strathnaver, Reay's guardians, and Balnagown, all hearty in the cause, 22—forms 100 Mackays into an independent company, and gives the command to Hugh Mackay, younger of Borley, *ib.*—orders further reinforcements from the south, and Colonel Ramsay to come with 600 men by the Highland road, *ib.*—led by Athole's professions of attachment to the new government, to consider him a friend, 23—being unapprised of Ramsay's detention, marches southward to meet him, and disconcerted at his non-appearance, 26—sends messenger after messenger with fresh instructions for his guidance, these intercepted by Ballechin, 27—marches again to meet him, *ib.*—receives a messenger to announce his retreat, and Dundee's entrance into Badenoch, *ib.*—reduced to great perplexity in consequence, 28—marches down Strathspey twenty-four hours without a halt, *ib.*—joined by Lieutenant-Colonel Livingstone with the two troops left at Dundee, which increased his perplexity, *ib.*—informed by two deserters that there were traitors in his camp, viz. Lieutenant-Colonel Livingstone, &c. *ib.*—his critical situation in consequence, 29—orders the deserters into custody, till the truth of their relation could be ascertained, *ib.*—they inform him of their communications with Blair and Pollock, *ib.*—confers on the subject with Sir T. Livingstone and Major Mackay, *ib.*—informed by Captain Forbes of his meeting with Livingstone's spies, 30—his measures of precaution in consequence, *ib.*—orders commanding officers of regiments to prepare for resuming their march, *ib.*—learns that Dundee is in motion towards him with a force four times superior *ib.*—resolves to retreat, and intimates his intention to Grant, reply of that noble-minded chief, *ib.*—of three routes to avoid Dundee, prefers that down the river side by Balveny, where he halts to refresh, 31—meets Edinglassie, who furnishes him with scouts, *ib.*—they bring him intelligence that Dundee had not yet quitted Strathspey, *ib.*—proceeds on his march to meet his expected reinforcements, *ib.*—takes post at the foot of Suy hill, to await their junction, 32—his pious reflections on the providential preservation of his small force, *ib.*—lets his men rest, and requests a supply of provisions from Lord Forbes's house, *ib.*—his reinforcements at length arriving, he faces about to meet Dundee, 33—the traitor Livingstone sends notice to Dundee of the junction of the reinforcements, *ib.*—the dragoons sent with this intelligence discovered and seized, *ib.*—arrests Lieutenant-Colonel Livingstone, and the other traitors, and sends them prisoners to Edinburgh, *ib.*—orders Sir T. Livingstone to attack 500 of the enemy near Spey, 34—reinforces colonel Ramsay at Perth, and orders him to Inverness, *ib.*—chases Dundee to Lochaber, *ib.*—repairs Ruthven castle, and gives the command to Captain Hugh Mackay, 35—proceeds to Inverness, and finds all quiet, *ib.*

places a garrison of 100 Mackays at Brahan castle, *ib.*—ditto of Rosses at Castle Leod, *ib.* —remains a fortnight at Inverness, draws up a plan for building a fort at Inverlochy, which he communicates to the Duke of Hamilton and council, 36—to secure the northern shires, leaves a strong garrison at Inverness, under the command of Sir T. Livingstone, *ib.* proceeds from Inverness towards the south, *ib.*—his instructions to the Earl of Mar having been frustrated by that nobleman's death, sends a detachment to occupy Braemar house, 37—this plan frustrated by the negligence of the commanding officer, *ib.*—proceeding on his march, overtaken by an express, communicating the disgraceful conduct of the party sent to Braemar house, 38—calm and composed notwithstanding this vexation, manifests the influence of religion on a character naturally impetuous, returns to redress the evil, and as a measure of necessary retaliation, burns Inverey house, 39—descends Dee side, and places a garrison at Abergeldie, *ib.*—returns to Edinburgh, *ib.*—and finds the castle surrendered by the Duke of Gordon, *ib.*—but no preparations for his expedition, 40—orders stores and provisions to Perth, 41—proceeds to Stirling, *ib.*—thence to Perth, the rendezvous of the expedition, *ib.*—historians of this period for the most part Jacobites, *ib.*—they exaggerate the amount of his force, *ib.*—marches with his whole force to Dunkeld, 43—early next morning advances towards Killiecrankie, 44—arrived there, detaches Lieutenant-Colonel Lauder with 200 fusileers to an eminence in front, 47—makes a speech to his men, 48—orders his nephew, Captain R. Mackay to drive the enemy from some houses in front of the line, *ib.*—dreading a night attack, felt intense anxiety to engage as the sun declined, 49—gratified at length by seeing the enemy begin the attack, *ib.*—invents the method, with little variation, still in use of attaching the bayonet, *ib.*—perceiving his men giving way, spurred on his charger through the thickest of the enemy, hoping his own men would be piqued to follow him, but in vain, 51—his pious reflections on the occasion, 52—conducts the wrecks of his army slowly across the Garry, 55—rejecting the advice of his officers to return by the direct road to Perth, strikes across the country towards Tayside, *ib.*—overtakes Ramsay with 150 fugitives, *ib.*—stops at a hut for information as to the country, and marches towards Weem castle, where he is hospitably received, 56—proceeds by Drummond castle to Stirling, where he gets the first intelligence of Dundee's death, 57—before retiring to rest, writes to the council not to be disheartened, 59—disapproves of, and reverses the measures proposed by the council, *ib.*—resolves to return towards Perth, 60—marches thither with 2000 horse and foot, *ib.*—attacks and defeats a body of Highlanders detached by Cannon, 62—sends Belhaven with the tidings to the council, *ib.*—pursues Cannon on his retreat towards the north, 64—arrives at Aberdeen, and is welcomed by the inhabitants, *ib.*—anxious for the safety of his garrison at Abergeldie, orders reinforcements to join him, *ib.*—arrives at Strathbogie, and embraces this first leisure since leaving Killiecrankie to send the council a full account of the battle, 65—returns to Perth and places a garrison in Blair castle, 69—the Atholemen having delivered up their arms, are received by him into the King's peace, *ib.*—visits Edinburgh to confer with the council, 70—thrown into perplexity by letters from Lord Melville ordering a reduction of the military establishment, 71—against this he repeatedly remonstrates, but in vain, 72—a commission appointed to reduce and remodel the army, *ib.*—feels the indignity of not being placed at the head of the military commission, 73—solicits leave of absence for the winter but refused, 76—disappointed of an interview with the king, writes

INDEX.

to Portland, 77—his letter to Portland laid by Melville before the king, *ib.*—sends his Majesty a statement of his views, *ib.*—recommends the erection of a fort at Inverlochy, 78—requests to be either supported or relieved from his command, 79—of the two routes to Inverlochy, recommends that by sea from Greenock, but disregarded, 80—his successful application to the Magistrates of Glasgow for aid, *ib.*—chagrined with the continued silence of the court, again begs to be relieved from his command, *ib.*—receives from the king a remittance of £4000 for his expedition, *ib.*—pays his respects to Lord Melville, the new commissioner, on his arrival at Edinburgh, and communicates to him his plan for subduing the Highland chiefs, 82—proposes in council the re-appointing of the former commissary of stores and provisions, *ib.*—overruled, and a creature of Melville's, unfit for the office, substituted, *ib.*—hands over to the officer the £4000 remitted to him by the king, *ib.*—judging Tarbat's plan feasible of buying off Argyle's claims on the chiefs, recommends it to Portland, and he to the king, 83—is afterwards convinced of its inefficiency, and of the selfish motives of its abettors, *ib.*—sends Adjutant-General Hill to the king, at Chester, to explain his Inverlochy plan, 85—it being approved by the king, he prepares to carry it into effect, 87—proceeds to Perth, and thence to Inverlochy with 3000 horse and foot, *ib.*—finds Major Ferguson and Captain Pottinger before him, 88—finishes works which he deems sufficient, and is recalled by the council, *ib.*—returns to Perth, leaving 1000 men in the garrison, *ib.*—his perplexities on arriving there, 94—marches northward to repel Buchan and Cannon, 97—relieves the garrison of Abergeldie, and while he respects the intrepidity of Inverey, judges it necessary to burn his house, *ib.*—pursues Buchan and Cannon to Inverness, *ib.*—resigns the chief command and succeeded by Sir T. Livingstone, 108—receives testimonies of approbation from all ranks, *ib.*—publicly entertained by the magistrates of Edinburgh, *ib.*—accompanies the king to the Hague, and joins his family, 109—resolved in council to employ him, in the approaching campaign in Flanders, as Lieutenant-general, *ib.*—this destination changed for Ireland under Duke of Leinster, *ib.*—by another change, three foreign officers placed over his head, 110—returns to England, and thence passes over to Ireland, 111—dissatisfied with the defenceless state of Mullingar, 112—disapproves of the places proposed for passing the Shannon, 114—recommends one of two others but overruled, *ib.*—it being his turn to command, boldly claims his right, 116—and effects the passage, *ib.*—gets complete possession of the town, 118—his judicious suggestions and prompt movements the chief causes of the success at Aughrim, 123—made Lieutenant-General, and appointed to command the British division of the grand army, 126—killed, 129—draws up a prayer which he recommends to his troops to offer up, 134.

Mackay, Captain Hugh, appointed Commandant of Ruthven Castle, 35—with his company of foot outruns the dragoons, 92.

Mackay, Captain the Honourable Robert, sent for education to his uncle in Holland, 117—dispatched by the General to bring back the runaways, 53—receives eight broad-sword wounds at Killiecrankie, and faints with loss of blood, *ib.*—having never recovered from his wounds, comes home to Tongue and dies, 117.

Mackenzie, Sir George of Tarbat, account of, 74.

Mackenzie, Sir Alexander of Coul, made professions of attachment, but nothing more, 55.

Mackenzie of Redcastle, ditto ditto, *ib.*

Mar, Earl of, declares his adhesion to the new government, 37—dying soon afterwards, his administrators engage in the opposite interest, *ib*—his regiment ordered to be reduced, 72.

Meloniere, la, a French Protestant general, serves in Ireland, 111.

Melville, Lord, account of, 71—joins Monmouth's invasion, *ib.*—created an Earl, 81—recommends the plan of buying off the Highland chiefs, 83—Melville and Tarbat employ the veteran Colonel Hill to treat with the chiefs, 84.

Munro, Laird of Foulis, raises troops for the service of Gustavus Adolphus, 4.

Munro, Lieutenant-General Sir George, third commissioner for re-modelling the army, 73.

Murray, Lord, professes great affection for the new government, 24—proceeds to Blair, and refused admittance by Ballechin, 40.

NAMUR, beseiged and taken by Luxembourg, 128.

Nassau, a Dutch general, employed under Mackay, 111.

ORANGE, William, first prince of, and sons, grateful for the services of the Scottish auxiliaries, 9.

Orange, William, second prince of, dies, leaving an infant son, 10.

POLWART, Lord, appointed to a troop in Cardross' regiment, 72—his services and sufferings rewarded with the earldom of Marchmont, *ib.*

Preston of Gorton raises men at his own expence, to aid the Dutch patriots, 8.

RAITH, Lord, Melville's eldest son, at the head of the treasury, 81.

Ramsay, Colonel, his march northwards countermanded, 25—permitted to recommence it, 26—alarmed by indications of hostility in Athole, returns to Perth, *ib.*—reinforced, is again ordered to Inverness, 34—one half of his regiment engaged at Killiecrankie, 50—retreats with 150 of his regiment, 55.

Reay, Donald, first Lord, raises troops for the service of Gustavus Adolphus, 4.

Reay, John, second Lord, taken at Balveny, and sent prisoner to Edinburgh, 3.

Reay, George, third Lord, marries Margaret, General Mackay's eldest daughter, 185—contributed to the suppression of three rebellions, 106.

Ruvigne, Marquis of, next in command to Mackay in Ireland, 110—created Baron Galway, 125.

SEAFORTH, Earl of, declines to join Mackay, 35—comes from the Highlands to the low country to join Buchan, 98—intimidated by Mackay's unexpected appearance, offers security for his submission, *ib.*—Mackay insists on the surrender of his person, to which he at length accedes, *ib.*—and is sent prisoner to Edinburgh, 100—follows King James to France, and dies, *ib.*

Solms, Count, commands the white division of the Prince of Orange's invading army, 13—succeeds Marshal Schomberg as Commander-in-chief in Ireland, 112—and is succeeded by de Ghinkel, *ib.*—a rash order of his at Steinkirk, cause of Mackay's death, *ib.*—killed, 195.

Southesk, Earl of, surrenders, and takes the oaths of allegiance, 70.

Strathmore, Earl of, surrenders, and takes the oaths of allegiance, *ib.*

INDEX.

Strathnaver, Lord, has a letter of service from Mackay, and joins him at Inverness with 300 men, 22.

Sutherland, Earl of, a strenuous supporter of the revolution, 106.

Stewart of Ballechin, intercepts Mackay's messengers, and sends their dispatches to Dundee, 27—takes possession of Blair Castle, 40—and refuses to surrender it to Lord Murray, ib.

TALMASH, Major-General, fifth in command in Ireland, 110—is proposed by Ghinkel for command in passing the Shannon, 116—offers to accompany Mackay, (to whom the command was accorded) as a volunteer, 116—his rashness at Aughrim censured, 123—the British part of the army dissatisfied that no mark of honour was conferred either on him or Mackay, 125.

Tettau, a Danish Major-General, sixth in command in Ireland, 110—next in command to Mackay in the passage of the Shannon, 118.

VAUBAN, a French engineer, opposed to Cohorn at Namur, 128.

Vaudemont, Marshal, his opinion of the British generals, 126.

WEEM, Laird of, sends his son with 100 men to Mackay at Killiecrankie, 57—his hospitality to Mackay and his men when retreating from Killiecrankie, ib.

William, second prince of Orange, dies, leaving an infant son, afterwards King William, 10.

William, third prince of Orange, receives Mackay into the service of the States-General, 7—opposed to Condè and Luxembourg at Seneff and Grave, 11—receives into his service disbanded English officers and men, and forms them into a corps, of which he gives the command to Mackay, ib.—prefers Mackay to Claverhouse in filling up a vacant Lieutenant-Colonelcy, ib.—invades England, with an army of 15,000 men, 13—invested with sovereign authority in England, ib.—gives a commission as Commander-in-chief to Mackay, ib.—is declared king of Scotland, 39—proceeds to Chester, on his way to Ireland, 85—rejects Melville and Tarbat's plan for subjugating the Highlands, and adopts Mackay's, 87—fights the battle of the Boyne, 95—proposes to employ Mackay as a Lieutenant-general, under his own immediate command in Flanders, 109—changes that plan, and sends him to Ireland, ib. makes an unsuccessful attempt to raise the siege of Mons, 110—dismisses Mackay at an audience of leave, without a word of explanation or apology, 111—his partiality to his foreign officers excites discontent in the army, 125—forms the grand confederacy against Louis XIV. ib.—appoints Mackay to command the British division of the confederate army, with the rank of Lieutenant-General, 126—his conversation with Marshal Vaudemont concerning the British generals, ib.—repairs to Holland, to take the command of the grand army, 128—arriving at Steinkirk, spends some hours in reconnoitering the ground, and marshalling his troops, 129—under him served Solms, Wirtemberg, Elector of Bavaria, and Mackay, ib.—sends peremptory orders to Solms, to withhold no longer the aid required by Wirtemberg, ib.—gives a quartermaster's commission to Mackay's servant, in testimony of his approbation, 130—attends Mackay's funeral, ib.—his exclamation on that occasion, ib. —his remark on the effect of Mackay's devotion, 131.

Wirtemberg, Duke of, second in command in Ireland, 110—third in command at Steinkirk, 129.

ERRATA.

Page 13, line   3 from the bottom, *for* was *read* were.
— 58, —   22, *for* wore *read* were.
— 67, —   16, *for* encreasing *read* increasing.
— 77, an asterisk awanting refering to the note.
— 78, line   16, *for* adventures *read* advantages.
— 79, —   9, *for* there *read* thither.
— *ib.* —   18, *for* stones *read* stores.
— 102, —   3 from bottom, *for* episcopalian doctrines of passive obedience and non-resistance *read* Jacobite doctrines.
— 106, —   25, *for* ; he *read* ,
— 111, —   13, *for* bigotted *read* bigoted.
— 113, —   1, *for* may *read* many.
— 118, —   21, *for* occular *read* ocular.
— 136, —   4, *for* cooly *read* coolly.

www.ingramcontent.com/pod-product-compliance
Lightning Source LLC
Chambersburg PA
CBHW082038230426
43670CB00016B/2699